C++ Footprint and Performance Optimization

R. Alexander

G. Bensley

SAMS

A Division of Macmillan USA
201 West 103rd St., Indianapolis, Indiana 46290 USA

C++ Footprint and Performance Optimization

International Standard Book Number: 0-672-31904-7

Library of Congress Catalog Card Number: 99-068917

Printed in the United States of America

First Printing: September, 2000

02   01   00   4   3   2   1

Trademarks

Warning and Disclaimer

PUBLISHER
Michael Stephens

ACQUISITIONS EDITOR
William E. Brown

DEVELOPMENT EDITORS
Tony Amico
Beverly Scherf

MANAGING EDITOR
Matt Purcell

PROJECT EDITOR
Natalie F. Harris

COPY EDITORS
Michael Dietsch
Andrew Simmons

INDEXER
Sandra Henselmeier

PROOFREADERS
Pat Kinyon
Tony Reitz
Matt Wynalda

TECHNICAL EDITOR
Greg Guntle

TEAM COORDINATOR
Pamalee Nelson

MEDIA DEVELOPER
Dan Scherf

INTERIOR DESIGNERS
Gary Adair
Anne Jones

COVER DESIGNER
Anne Jones

PRODUCTION
Darin Crone

Overview

Contents

About the Authors

As the authors of the book you are about to read, we would like to introduce ourselves. With more than 10 years of professional IT experience between us, we have worked on vastly different projects for different companies. One of us is currently involved in designing time-critical embedded software, the other is working on Internet and satellite-transmission software for digital video communications.

In our spare time we have been working on a project which involved developing advanced techniques for optimizing C/C++ code for speed and size. We found that while working on professional software, the same kinds of problems and pitfalls kept arising, whether during development of embedded software or even desktop applications. It seemed to us that a deeper understanding of these problems could not only aid in writing better software, but also be of great assistance during fault solving. That is why we decided that the result of our project should be a tutorial in which we share our findings of practical problems and the solutions we used, as well as our theories on optimizing software.

The book you are holding now is in fact one that we, and many of our colleagues, have been looking for since we started in the IT business.

R. Alexander
G. Bensley

Dedication

To Olivera, Tjitske, and Leanne, who somehow found the restraint to not kill us.

Acknowledgments

We would like to thank the people at Sams for recognizing the value of this project and helping us develop it into the book you are now holding. Special thanks go to those on the home front who had to endure our absence and more than their fair share of duties around the house.

Tell Us What You Think!

As the reader of this book, *you* are our most important critic and commentator. We value your opinion and want to know what we're doing right, what we could do better, what areas you'd like to see us publish in, and any other words of wisdom you're willing to pass our way.

As a Publisher for Sams, I welcome your comments. You can fax, email, or write me directly to let me know what you did or didn't like about this book—as well as what we can do to make our books stronger.

Please note that I cannot help you with technical problems related to the topic of this book, and that due to the high volume of mail I receive, I might not be able to reply to every message.

When you write, please be sure to include this book's title and author as well as your name and phone or fax number. I will carefully review your comments and share them with the author and editors who worked on the book.

Fax:	317-581-4770
Email:	footprint@macmillanusa.com
Mail:	Michael Stephens
	Sams
	201 West 103rd Street
	Indianapolis, IN 46290 USA

Introduction: Why Optimize?

Nowadays, software is virtually everywhere. Though you might initially think only of PCs and industrial computer systems when talking about software, applications are much more widespread. Consider washing machines, electric razors, thermostats, microwave ovens, cars, TVs, monitors and so on. Obviously these examples span many different kinds of architectures and use a variety of microprocessors. Different optimization techniques for performance and footprint size are needed here.

Even an examination of those writing today's software reveals much diversity. There is the generation of software implementers who were schooled specifically in writing software—that is, doing requirements analysis, design, and implementation. There are also those who taught themselves to write software, starting perhaps as hobbyists. And more and more we see people from different disciplines switching to software writing. This means that it is no longer a fair assumption that all programmers have, in essence, a technical background.

C/C++ programming courses and books give an excellent introduction to the world of C/C++ programming. Basically accessible for all ages and disciplines, they make it possible for anyone to write a working C/C++ program. However, standard techniques have many pitfalls and inefficiencies to avoid when actively developing software—be it commercially or as a hobby. Without completely understanding the consequences of programming decisions on a technical level, implementers unwillingly compromise the speed and size of the software they write.

The basis for an efficient program is laid long before any actual code is written, when the requirements and design are made and the hardware target is chosen. And even when the software is eventually written, a simple matter of syntax might be all that separates those who produce optimal executable code from those who do not. If you know what to write, you can easily optimize your code to run many times more efficiently. Efficiency can be increased even further with specific programming techniques, differing in level of skill required from the programmer.

Aim of This Book

As the title suggests, the aim of this book is to help the reader optimize performance and footprint of software. Regardless of whether the reader is a software architect, an implementer, or even a project leader, this book serves as a tutorial to help the reader acquire or enhance the following essential skills:

- Analyzing where and when in the development process problems tend to arise
- Recognizing pitfalls of standard design and programming techniques
- Improving C/C++ programming skills
- Gaining detailed technical insight into programming techniques
- Learning useful solutions and when to use them

These skills form the basis for creating efficient software. This book guides even beginning programmers into using the advanced techniques offered here for writing better software. More experienced programmers can get going right away with the advanced topics and will also find this book to be a helpful repository of all the do's and don'ts they have to continually keep ahead of. The many hints, insights, and examples given on the development process will also be of use to project leaders and architects.

Who This Book Is For

This book starts with several chapters on optimization theory and then introduces technical subject matter and examples with increasing complexity. This means that beginning programmers can use this book as a tutorial to guide them into optimizing techniques, and more experienced programmers can go through to the more complex subjects at a faster pace. Readers not directly involved with actual program implementation, such as project leaders or architects, can still benefit from familiarizing themselves with the concepts discussed in the first part of the book and several "pitfall" and "tips" sections of later chapters. The many examples of problems and solutions actually encountered in the field, which are used throughout this book, will be useful to anyone with software-related interests.

The Structure of This Book

This book is divided into three distinct parts.

- Part I, "Everything But the Code" (Chapters 1–3)—This first book part discusses optimization theory of the aspects of software development that precede actual implementation. It offers advice and practical examples with solutions in areas such as choosing between programming languages, examining target hardware, looking at device interaction, setting up correct system requirements, designing new systems, and optimizing systems that already suffer from performance problems.

- Part II, "Getting Our Hands Dirty" (Chapters 4–13)—This second book part discusses implementation problem areas by looking at examples of problems often encountered in the field. It shows where and why problems are likely to occur and offers ready-to-use solutions for efficient function calling, memory management, IO, and setting up and handling data structures.

- Part III, "Tips and Pitfalls" (Chapters 14 and 15)—This third book part gives an overview of sneaky problems and traps you can encounter when using C/C++.

For the code samples used throughout this book, go to the Web site at http://www.samspublishing.com and search for this book's ISBN, 0672319047.

Everything But the Code

This first part discusses optimization theory of the aspects of software development that precede actual implementation. It offers advice and practical examples with solutions in areas such as choosing between programming languages, examining target hardware, looking at device interaction, setting up correct system requirements, designing new systems, and optimizing systems that already suffer from performance problems.

Part I consists of the following chapters:

Optimizing: What Is It All About?

IN THIS CHAPTER

This chapter provides an extensive introduction to optimization. It explains the definitions and jargon used and clarifies why it is so important to know when and how to optimize software. Often the term *optimization* is associated with performance enhancements only; however, the amount of memory and other resources an application claims is important to minimize also. Both performance and footprint optimizations are discussed in this chapter.

Performance

The first part of this chapter discusses optimization from the performance viewpoint. Here not only software and hardware characteristics are discussed, but also how performance is perceived by users of a system.

What Is Performance?

What does performance actually mean in relation to software? The simple answer is that performance is an expression of the amount of work that is done during a certain period of time. The more work a program does per unit of time, the better its performance. Put differently, the performance of a program is measured by the number of input (data) units it manages to transform into output (data) units in a given time. This translates directly into the number of algorithmic steps that need to be taken to complete this transformation. For example, an algorithm that executes 10 program statements to store a name in a database performs poorly compared to one that stores the same name in five statements. Similarly, a database setup that requires 20 steps to be taken before it knows where new data is to be inserted has a higher impact on program performance than a database setup that does the same in 10 steps. But there are more things to consider than purely technical implications, which is what this section will highlight.

Of the software that is written today, a very large part is set up to be used by one or more users interactively. Think of word processors, project management tools, and paint programs. The users of these kinds of programs generally sit behind their computers and work with a single program until they have completed a certain task—for example, planned the activities of a subordinate, drawn a diagram, or written a ransom note. So let's examine how such a user defines performance; after all, in most cases he will be the one we do the optimizations for. Basically, there are only three situations in which a user actually thinks in terms of performance at all:

- When a task takes less time than anticipated by the user.
- When a task takes more time than anticipated by the user.
- When the size or complexity of the task is apparent to the user.

Examining these situations can provide further guidelines for defining performance. Here follow three examples that illustrate the bullet points:

A task can take less time than anticipated by the user when, for example, this user has been working with the same program on the same computer for years and her boss finally decides to upgrade to next-generation machines. The user is still running the same program, but because the hardware can execute it faster, performance seems to be better. Also, the user has become accustomed to a certain kind of behavior. In the new situation her expectations are exceeded, she no longer has to twiddle her thumbs when saving a large file or performing a complex calculation.

A task can take more time than anticipated by the user when, for example, this user works with a program that handles a large base of sorted names. On startup, the program takes about 15 seconds to load and sort its data, without giving status updates. Even if its algorithms are highly optimized, the user views this unanticipated "delay" as poor software performance.

The size and complexity of a task can be apparent to the user when, for example, the user works with a program that searches through megabytes of text files to find the occurrences of a certain string. This action takes only seconds and, because of her technical background, the user knows what is involved with this action. Her perception of the performance of the search program is therefore favorable.

These examples demonstrate that performance is more than a simple measure of time and processing. Performance from the view point of a user is more of a feeling she has about the program than the actual workload per second it manages to process. This feeling is influenced by a number of factors that lead to the following statements:

- Unexpected and unexplained waiting times have a negative effect on the perceived performance.
- Performance is a combination of hardware and software.
- Performance depends on what the user is accustomed to.
- Performance depends on user's knowledge of what the program is doing.
- Repetition of a technically efficient action will still affect perceived performance no matter how knowledgeable the user is.

Why Optimize?

Although optimization is a logical choice for those who write time-critical or real-time programs, it has more widespread uses. All types of software can in fact benefit from optimization. This section shows four reasons why:

- As programs leave the development environment and are put to use in the field, the amounts of data they need to handle will grow steadily. This eventually slows the program down, perhaps even to the point of it being unusable.

- Carefully designed and implemented programs are easier to extend in the future. Consider the benefits of adding functionality to an existing program without concern about degrading its performance due to problems in the existing code.

- Working with a fast program is more comfortable for users. In fact, speed is typically not an issue until it slows users down.

- Time is money.

A tempting question that you are bound to ask sooner or later is, Why not just buy faster hardware? If your software does not seem able to cut it anymore, why not simply upgrade to a faster processor or use more or faster memory? Processing speed tends to double every 18 months, so algorithms that might have posed a problem six months or a year before might now be doable. But there are a number of reasons why optimizing software will always be needed.

A faulty design or implementation decision in an algorithm can easily slow it down 10–100 times—when sorting or storing data, for example. Waiting for hardware that is *only* twice as fast is not a solution.

Programs, and the data they handle, tend to grow larger and larger during those same 18 months, and users tend to run more and more applications simultaneously. This means the speed requirements for the program might increase as fast as, and sometimes even faster than, the hardware speed increases.

When programmers do not acquire the skills to optimize programs, they will find themselves needing to upgrade to new hardware over and over again.

With software that is part of a mass-market system (for example, embedded software in TVs, VCRs, set-top boxes, and so on), every cent of cost will weigh heavily. Investments in software occur only once, whereas investments in hardware are incurred with every unit produced.

While processors continue to become faster and cheaper, their designs change also. This means that more investments need to be made to upgrade other parts of the systems.

The lower the system requirements for a certain program are, the larger the market it can reach.

Buying new hardware to solve software problems is just a temporary workaround that hides rather than solves problems.

One thing to keep in mind when talking about performance problems is that they are generally not so much the trademarks of entire programs as they are problems with specific parts of a program. The following sections of this chapter focus on those programming areas that are particularly prone to causing performance problems.

Performance of Physical Devices

When a program uses one or more physical devices, performance issues can arise in those parts of the program where interaction with these devices takes place. Physical devices are slower than normal memory because they often contain moving parts and need special protocols for access. Also, different kinds of devices operate at different speeds. Important performance decisions include determining which kind of device to use for what purpose and when and where in the program to access the devices. Chapter 12, "Optimizing IO," explains this in greater detail.

Examples of (relatively) slow physical devices include hard disks, smartcard readers, printers, scanners, disk stations, CD-ROM players, DVD players, and modems.

Here are some considerations when using physical devices:

1. It stands to reason that the more frequently a set of data is used, the closer you will want to place it to the program. Data that is referred to constantly should therefore, if possible, be kept in internal memory. When the data set is not too large and remains constant, it could even be part of the executable file itself. When the data set is subject to change, however, or should be shared between programs, it would be wiser to store it on a local hard disk and load it into memory at runtime. It would be unwise to store it on a network drive; unless you specifically intend for the data to be accessed by different work stations or to be backed up remotely, the use of a network drive would just add unwanted overhead. The choice of device should clearly be closely related to the intended use of the data that it will store.

2. During the design phase of a program, look closely at *how* and *when* the data is accessed. By making a temporary copy of (a block of) data, it is possible to increase the speed of accessing it. For example, consider the following scenario in which it is necessary for a program to access data being used by a physical device. This creates no problem when both the program and the device are merely reading the data and not changing it. However, when the data is being changed, some kind of locking mechanism must be used. Of course, this takes time, as the program and device have to wait for each other. This type of problem can be identified at design time, and possibly avoided. For example, with a temporary copy of the data solely for use by the device, the program could continue to make changes to the data, whereas the physical device is used merely for output purposes (taking, if you will, a snapshot of the data). This way the program and the device will not trip over each other. When the device has finished, the memory containing the copy of the data can be reused. If the amount of data involved is too large either to allow efficient copying or to be allocated in memory twice, the suggested technique could still be applied, but to smaller subsets of the data.

3. It is usually a good idea to compress data before sending it when communicating with relatively fast devices over a slower connection (two computers connected via serial cable or modem, for example). When choosing the compression algorithm, be sure that the time that is won by sending less information over the connection is more than the time that is needed by the slowest end of the connection to perform the compression or decompression.

Performance of System Resources

Not only physical devices but also the system resources themselves can cause noticeable slowdown (EPROM, ROM, RAM, and so on). This does not necessarily indicate an incorrect choice of hardware but it does mean that care needs to be taken first during the design phase and later during the implementation phase of a project. For example, consider moving parts of ROM to RAM when using ROM slows down the program. Although this type of copy action eats up the necessary CPU clock cycles, it will be done only once and every single access to the memory in question will benefit from a faster response. Clearly, only the intensely used parts of the ROM should be considered for this kind of treatment—and only when there is enough memory to spare. Having said that, there need not be a fragmentation impact on whatever memory management scheme was chosen, as this piece of memory will most likely be used during the entire lifetime of the program. Refer to Chapter 9, "Efficient Memory Management," for more detail.

A similar enhancement can be made for RAM access versus CPU registers, although its application is somewhat more limited. Most compilers allow you to make suggestions about placing variables directly into the registers of the CPU. The advantage of this is that register access is even faster than RAM access. For RAM access, the CPU has to send a request for data on the internal bus to the memory address mappers, which in turn have to interpret the request to find the appropriate memory address and send the contained value as a response (some operating systems also use indirection schemes in memory access). Registers are part of the CPU chip itself and can therefore be accessed directly.

There is a downside of course. CPU registers can have different sizes but will rarely exceed 64 bits. Also, the number of registers per CPU is limited and a fair share will be occupied almost continuously. That is why in practice registers will be used for variables that are accessed often over short period of time (loop counters and so on). Refer to Chapter 6, "The Standard C/C++ Variables," for more detailed information on variable use.

Another aspect to take into account is the operating system (OS) because accessing system resources is often done through operating system calls. Keep in mind that operating systems implement these calls as generically as possible to be able to run every kind of program with reasonable results. A software designer, however, has more information on the typical resource usage of his program. This knowledge can be used to write more efficient interaction. For example, when the OS uses a relatively slow memory management scheme, certain design considerations can be made to compensate. A program might benefit from a design in which allocated memory is reused internally instead of released back to the system. Chapter 9 deals specifically with these kinds of issues.

Finally, consider examiningthe architecture documentation of the CPU(s) being used. The following practical example shows what kind of optimizations can be found. To use the Intel MMX instructions, the coprocessor needs to be set to MMX mode. This switch costs time. Then, when normal calculations need to continue, the coprocessor needs to be switched back again, causing more lost time. So to avoid unnecessary switches, instructions need to be grouped by mode as much as possible in a design that uses these two modes. Refer to Chapter 4, "Tools and Languages," for information on tools to use to determine which parts of a program cause slowdown.

Performance of Subsystems

An old proverb says a chain is only as strong as its weakest link. This holds true also for software, particularly when it comes to performance issues. Performance problems are likely to occur from using a badly designed third-party library, or indeed one that was optimized for a different kind of use. So before using subsystems, it is advisable to run some performance tests—if only to find out what to expect in practice. It might be possible to design around identified problems. But be prepared to rewrite a subsystem or look for replacements. Generally this would be considered the preferred option. Otherwise future enhancements to the program will continue to suffer from an initial bad choice. Avoid creating workarounds if there is even the remotest possibility of having to replace a subsystem at some point down the line anyway. Time constraints could force a development team to use two similar subsystems simply because the old one is too slow and it would take too much time to incorporate the new one in every part of the program. Clearly this is an unfortunate waste of time and resources.

The way in which a subsystem is incorporated into a program affects the performance of the link between the two. Simply calling the interface of the subsystem directly from the program causes the smallest amount of overhead and is therefore the fastest. It does mean that at least one side of the link will need its interface adapted to fit the other. When for some reason both sides cannot be altered—for example, because the third-party sources are unavailable—it is necessary to insert some kind of glue or wrapper layer between the two. This means that communication calls will be redirected. This means extra overhead.

However, this same kind of go-between glue layer can also be used to test the functionality and performance of a single part of a system. In this case the glue layer, now called a stub, does nothing or simply returns fixed values. It does not call another object to pass anything on. It simulates the objects being interacted with. The performance of the object being tested is no longer influenced by other parts of the system. Refer to Chapter 2, "Creating a New System," for more details on prototyping.

Performance of Communications

Performance problems are inevitable where communications take place. Think, for example, of communications between separate computers or different processes on the same computer. The following problems are likely to occur:

- The sender and receiver operate at different speeds (for example, different hardware configurations or scheduling priorities).
- The link between the sender and the receiver is slow (for example, a serial cable or modem between two fast computers).
- The sender or receiver is slowed down because it is handling a high number of connections (for example, an ISP).
- The sender or receiver has to wait for its peer to arrive in the correct program state (for example, a connection has to be set up or data has to be gathered before being sent).
- The link between sender and receiver is error-prone (for example, a lot of data needs to be retransmitted).

Where possible, programs should avoid halting activity by waiting on communications (busy-wait constructions) or using polling strategies that periodically check on connections to see whether they need to be serviced. Instead, communication routines should be called on an interrupt basis or via callback functions. This way, a program can go about its business until it is signaled to activate communication routines.

The elegance of using callback functions lies in the fact that callback functions are part of the program that wants to be notified of a certain event taking place. Thus these functions can have complete access to the data and the rest of the functionality of the program. The callback function body contains those instructions that need to be carried out when the event comes about, but the function is in fact called by the object generating the event. By passing a reference to a callback function to an object, you give the event-generating object a means to contact the program.

So switching from polling or busy-wait strategies to interrupt and callback strategies offers the following advantages:

- Programs will be smaller, as fewer states need to be incorporated.

- Programs will be faster, as execution does not need to be halted at strategic places to check for interesting events taking place.

- Responsiveness to events will be faster, as there is no longer a need to wait for the program to arrive in a state in which it is able to recognize events.

The use of callback functions is discussed further in Chapter 13, "Optimizing Your Code Further."

Application Look and Feel

Application look and feel, otherwise known as *graphical user interface (GUI)*, is important because the users' perceptions of performance are important, as discussed earlier in this chapter. A specific performance optimization task is thus to view the program from the perspective of the user. Although this is logical, it is probably not surprising that in practice this step is mostly overlooked. One reason for this is that developers and testers work with prototypes for a long time and get used to GUI inconsistencies. It is generally assumed that any look-and-feel problems will be weeded out during later phases of development as, per definition, prototypes are unfinished. The unintuitive aspects of the user interface lack, at that point, the priority to be fixed. Although developers and testers might become accustomed to the interface and overlook its problems, it is most unlikely that the user/client will be equally tolerant. Consequently, working on prototypes and beta versions is not a particularly useful way to weed out GUI problems.

It is a good assumption that users and programmers have completely different perspectives of a program for the following reasons:

- The user sees only the user interface; to her this *is* the program.

- Most of the time the user is unaware of exactly what the program is doing internally and has at best only an abstract concept of its overall work.

- The programmer focuses much more on the source code, making that as good as it can be.

- The programmer sometimes views the GUI as a necessary evil. An interface that quickly makes all the functionality of the program accessible will then be stuck on top of the program.

- Perhaps the most important reason of all is that the user and the programmer have different backgrounds, experiences, and goals with respect to the program. Ideas about what is logical will therefore differ.

The following sections provide more detail on how to identify, prevent, and overcome GUI problems and annoyances.

Unexplained Waiting Times

When programmers forget to add some kind of progress indicators at places in the program where large batches of work are being done, the program will in effect seem to be halting at random to the user. He selects a command from the program's menu and suddenly his computer seems to be stuck for a few seconds. This will be regarded as very frustrating because the user is not aware of what is happening. The programmer in turn probably did not even notice this "look and feel" problem because he *knows* what the program is doing and therefore *expects* the slowdown.

Simply adding some text in a status bar explaining what is happening, or spawning a little window with a moving slider indicating elapsed time, will greatly enhance the appreciation the end user has for the program.

Illogical Set Up of the User Interface

Another great way to irritate users is to place user interface controls somewhere where they are not expected. This might seem unlikely but there are, in fact, countless examples to be found in even today's most popular software packages. Finding the menu path File, Tools, Change Password is a practical example of this. But it does not even have to be that obvious.

While designing user interfaces, take into account the experiences of the user. For example, when writing a program for a specific OS, it is a good idea to stay as close as possible to its standard interface. So harmonize with the OS, even if it appears less logical than you'd like, such as Print being a submenu of Edit rather than File. Whether or not the intended users are familiar with the standard interface of the OS, it is wise to take advantage of the available experience, even if its setup could be improved.

Another type of experience that might be used can be found in situations where some kind of automation is done. Whenever users are *forced* to switch from some kind of manual system—for example, on paper—to a computerized system, they will already need to adapt pretty heavily. Designing a user interface that looks like, and follows the same logical steps as, their old system will benefit them greatly. This also holds true when upgrading or switching computer systems.

Problematic Interface Access

The perception a user has of the performance of a program is mostly determined by the speed at which (new) information appears on her screen. Though it is possible that some kind of delay is excepted when calling up stored data, it is unlikely that any kind of delay will be excepted when accessing menu screens. Menus and submenus should therefore appear instantaneous. When a menu contains stored data, at the very least the menu should be drawn immediately (be it a box, a pop-up, or so on) after which the stored data can be added as it becomes available.

Not Sufficiently Aiding the Learning Curve

Here is where a lot of "look and feel" problems can be solved. A good example of a user-friendly program is one that can follow learning curve of the user. A first-time user will, for example, benefit enormously from having access to an integrated help service. This could be a help menu with the ability to search for key words and phrases or perhaps even the ability to automatically generate pop-up windows with information on what the user is doing and how he is likely to want to proceed. This first-time user is also likely to use the mouse to access the user interface. After using the program a while though, this extra help is no longer needed, and pop-ups and nested menus get in the way of fast access. The user is now more prone to use hotkeys to quickly access functionality, and he will want to turn off any automatically generated help and unnecessary notifications.

When Do Performance Problems Arise?

This section deals with performance problems that can arise during use (or abuse) of existing programs. Performance problems of new systems are the subject of Chapter 2.

This chapter has shown that performance depends heavily on user perception and that certain areas in systems are particularly sensitive to performance loss. Many performance problems found in the field, however, arise because insufficient attention is paid to future use of the programs during the design and implementation phases. Often a program is closely tailored to fit the current intended use, causing it to run into performance problems almost as soon as the slightest alteration is made to the way it is used—more often than not this is because developers work under strict time constraints.

Consider a simplified example of a program that uses a database of names. Although it might work fine for its initial use of approximately 1,000 names, does that provide any certainty for its behavior if another customer decides to use it for a base of 100,000 names? It all depends on how efficient the sorting and storage and retrieval algorithms were initially implemented.

The following sections highlight different performance problems that can arise during the lifetime of a program.

Extending Program Functionality

Performance problems often arise when the functionality of a program needs to be extended. The market demands continuous updates of commercially successful software with newer and improved versions. In fact, many users consider programs without regular updates to be dead and, therefore, a bad investment.

The most common upgrades or extensions include the following:

- New and better user interfaces including "professional" editions
- Added capabilities or options
- Support for more simultaneous users
- Support for new platforms
- Upgrades to reflect changes in the nature of the data
- Added filters to increase interaction with other programs
- Support for devices
- Network and Internet capabilities

However, keep in mind that it is neither wise nor beneficial to keep enhancing software with things it was not originally designed for. What you end up with is a very unstable and unmaintainable product. The initial design (the framework of the initial functionality) should be geared toward supporting future enhancements. This also means that the technical documentation should be clearly written and up to date, perhaps even split up in function groupings that follow the design. This is a must if future enhancements are made by people other than the original developers. To add functionality properly, the programmer making the enhancements should be able to easily identify where his enhancement should go and how it should connect to the existing framework.

Code Reuse

Problems generated by reuse of existing code are closely related to those mentioned in the previous paragraph. Reuse of tested code can still cause grief even with successful identification of how to integrate new functionality in an existing, well-designed framework. Think, for example, of a program that contains a sorting routine that cleverly sorts a number of names before they are printed in a window. A programmer adding new functionality might decide to use this routine to sort records of address information to save some precious time. Although the sorting routine might have been more than adequate for its initial use, it can have severe shortcomings with respect to performing its new task. It is therefore prudent to investigate consequences of using existing code, not in the least by defining new test cases. And again, good documentation plays an important role here. Refer to Chapter 3, "Modifying an Existing System," for more details.

Test Cases and Target Systems

On the whole, programmers are most comfortable when they are designing and writing software, so they generally resist both documenting and testing. So it is not unusual that testing is sometimes reduced to merely checking whether new code will run. The question then is whether the test cases and test data used really represent any and all situations that can be found in the field. Does the programmer even know what kind of data sets will be used in the field and whether it is possible to sufficiently simulate field situations in the development environment? The first step in solving such problems is having a good set of requirements which the programmers can use. If that proves insufficient, it might be necessary to use example data sets, or test cases, from the client for whom the program is being written. Or you might need to move the test setup to the client itself to be able to integrate properly in a "real" field environment. Another common mistake is to develop on machines that are faster or more advanced than those used by the client, meaning that the test and development teams do not get a correct impression of the delays the users will suffer.

Side Effects of Long-Term Use

It is possible that programs slow down when they are used over a longer period of time. Some common problems that can be hidden quite well when programs only run for short periods of time include

- Disk fragmentation due to usage of files
- Spawned processes that never terminate
- Allocated data that does not get freed (memory leaks)
- Memory fragmentation
- Files that are opened but never closed
- Interrupts that are never cleared
- Log files that grow too large
- Semaphores that are claimed but never freed (locking problems)
- Queues and arrays that exceed their maximum size
- Buffers that wrap around when full
- Counters that wrap to negative numbers
- Tasks that are not handled often enough because their priority is set too low

These cases will, of course, take effect in the field and users will complain about performance degradation. These kinds of problems are usually difficult to trace back to their source in the development environment.

It is possible to do manual checks by

- Stepping through the code with the debugger to see what really happens (more about this in Chapter 4)

- Printing tracing numbers and pointers and checking their values

- Checking programs with profilers (refer to Chapter 4), taking care to note the relations between parts of the program (should function x really take twice as long as function y?, and so on)

Flexibility Versus Performance

Although the design should take into account all kinds of future extensions and updates, there is of course a limit to what one can do and predict during the initial design. Sadly, there often simply is not enough time to design a very high degree of flexibility, not to mention implementing it. So a choice to be made is the tradeoff between being flexible for future enhancements or achieving better performance in the present. And no guidelines can really be given here as every situation (every client and every software package) is different. However, keep in mind that a client is unlikely to appreciate a very slow program that is exceptionally well equipped to be extended in the future. Similarly, it is unwise to release a program that in testing has already shown to meet performance requirements only under the most optimal conditions. Developers need to decide where to put the performance/footprint accent, using their knowledge of the target systems and the processes involved.

Footprint

This second part of the chapter looks at optimization from the footprint viewpoint, where several techniques to reduce footprint size are discussed together with footprint problems that can arise if preventive actions are omitted.

What Is Footprint?

Strictly speaking, footprint is a spatial measurement term. The footprint of a desktop computer, for example, is about 40×40 centimeters (about 16×16 inches); that is the desk space it occupies. When talking about software, however, footprint can best be described as the amount of memory an object (a program, data structure, or task, for example) needs to function properly. This memory can be strictly internal ROM or RAM, but it is also possible that footprint requirements necessitate the use of external memory, for example, for temporary data storage. Refer to Chapter 2 for more information.

Where executable programs are concerned, different kinds of footprint sizes can be identified, as explained in the following sections.

Storage Requirements

This is the amount of memory needed when the program is inactive, the footprint of the storage, and the memory required to store the executable file and the data files it needs/has acquired. From the perspective of the user, the storage requirement is simply the amount of space needed to store the program. During development, however, the story can be rather more complicated. When development is not done on the machines that are the eventual targets for running the program, storage calculations become a lot more involved. Refer to "How to Measure Footprint Size" for more information.

Runtime Memory Requirements

This is the amount of memory needed while the program is being executed. This footprint can differ from the storage footprint for several reasons. For example, the program might not need all the executable code at once, the program will probably use working memory for temporary data storage, and so on. Moreover, the memory used during startup and execution will rarely equal that of the stored files, especially larger programs, which are those made up of more than just a single executable file. Although most often more memory is needed during execution, as one might expect, it is equally possible that a program in fact uses less memory. Practical examples of how and why runtime requirements can differ from storage requirements are given in sections that follow.

Compression

Often parts of a program and its data can be stored in compressed form. When a program uses large data files, it is unlikely that this data will be stored exactly as it is used in internal memory. It can be compressed using known or proprietary compression algorithms or even stored using a structure that is more optimal for storage purposes. Also the executable code itself might be compressed. When the program consists of several modules, the main program might load and decompress other modules as they are needed.

JPEG graphical images and MP3 sound files are examples of well-known data compression techniques. Here, clearly, footprint size reduction is chosen over performance—data compression ratios of up to 90% can be achieved. Note that these techniques do allow data loss. This can be incurred in such a way that it is not, or barely, noticeable to human eyes or ears. However, this is of course not something we would want to do to executable code. The nature of the data being compressed plays an important role in the choice of compression technique.

Whichever form of compression is used, however, the fact remains that the runtime memory requirements will most likely differ significantly from the storage requirements. Perhaps even extra memory is needed to perform the compression and decompression.

It should not be overlooked that compression and decompression take time, which means that starting a program might take longer. This highlights again the relationship between performance and footprint.

Data Structures

The structure that is used to hold and access the data might differ between storage time and runtime. Whereas data mostly needs to be small during storage, it might be far more important during runtime that it can be accessed quickly. Data that is small during storage is usually compressed and therefore moves slowly, whereas data that moves quickly during runtime is most likely not compressed, which means the data takes up a lot of space. Each storage method uses an entirely different structure.

The structure that is chosen for fast access might include redundant information in extra index files, generated before the data is accessed. For example, think of hashing tables, doubly linked lists, or sets of intermediate search results (refer to Chapters 10, "Blocks of Data," and 11, "Storage Structures"). Again it should be noted that generating this overhead will cost time. Important decisions include how much data to consider describing in these index files, when to generate these index files, and what level of redundancy should be provided by these index files (at some point generating more redundancy will no longer make the data access faster).

Overlay Techniques

Not all the executable code might be needed at the same time. Dividing a program into functional modules allows the use of overlay techniques. For example, consider a graphics editor. It contains a module of scanning routines that is used when the user wants to scan a picture. After the user closes the window containing the scanner interface, the scanner module is replaced by a module containing special effects routines. The modules do not necessarily have to be exactly the same size; just having one in memory at all times will decrease the runtime memory requirements. The more distinctly you can identify functional modules during the design phase, the better the overlay principle will work. The footprint size actually won depends on the choices the developers make. It is important to identify program states that can never occur at the same time and switch them intelligently. If it is impossible to use special effects during scanning, these two functions are a good choice for being interchanged.

You can, of course, try to overlay groups that might in some cases be needed simultaneously— or closely after each other—but then you get a much more statistical picture of footprint size. When there is a fixed maximum to the footprint size that can be used, the worst-case combination of overlaid modules should be able to fit into it.

Switching overlaid modules costs time and so has an impact on overall program performance.

Working Memory

A program being executed *will* need working memory regardless of whatever architectural choices are made about storage, compression, and overlaying. The use of working memory is very diverse. The following list shows the most common uses:

- Storing variables (pointers, counters, arrays, strings, and so on)
- Stack space
- Storing intermediate data
- Storing placeholders for data (structures, linked lists, binary trees)
- Storing handles and pointers to operating system resources
- Storing user input (history buffers and undo and redo functionality)

Cache

In certain situations, it might enhance performance to set aside some memory to act as a buffer or cache. Think, for example, of the interaction with hardware devices as described in the section "Performance of Physical Devices." Refer also to Chapter 5, "Measuring Time and Complexity," for more detail on cache use and cache misses.

Memory Fragmentation

Another subject for consideration is the fragmentation of memory. It might not exactly fit our definition of runtime memory requirements, but it certainly does affect the amount of working memory needed. While a program runs, it will continuously allocate and free pieces of memory to house objects (class instances, variables, buffers, and so on). Because the lifetimes of these objects are not all the same and often are unpredictable, fragmentation of large blocks of memory into smaller pieces will occur. It stands to reason that the longer a program runs, the more serious the fragmentation becomes. Programs designed to run longer than a few hours at a time (and that use memory fairly dynamically) could even benefit from some kind of defragmentation routines, which are usually quite expensive performance-wise. Chapter 9 discusses memory fragmentation in more detail.

The following sections give advice on how to measure and control memory requirements.

Why Is Monitoring Footprint Important?

The reasons for keeping footprint size small can be compared to driving a through a busy town. A large luxury car might look impressive, but practically speaking it is more difficult to maneuver through small and busy streets than a small car. The same holds true for finding parking spaces and squeezing into small alleys. Where software is concerned, it is also the small and practical programs (with little overhead in interface and functionality) that are the most enjoyable to work with. Large programs that pose a heavy burden on system resources will generally only be used when the user intends to work on something for a longer period of time or has a specific goal in mind that can only be achieved with that specific program. Consider the differences between a small text editor and a desktop publishing package. To edit a few lines of a text file, it would be impractical to use a desktop publishing package—much like using a helicopter to cross a street.

The main considerations for keeping footprint sizes in check are the impact on available resources and the impact on performance, as discussed here in more detail.

Impact on Available Resources

The obvious reason for keeping storage and runtime footprints as small as possible is the cost involved. For example, the larger a piece of embedded software is, the more memory is needed in a product that incorporates it. The incurred cost is directly related to runtime execution size. But not only embedded systems need this consideration. Plainly stated, the larger the footprint of a program is, the smaller is its possible market share. Not every user has a state-of-the-art machine with the largest available hard disk. A program with lower system requirements accommodates more users.

Also, a program's usability is affected by the size of the runtime footprint. If a program uses a lot of internal memory, it might force the operating system to start swapping memory to the hard disk and back. Remember also that programs virtually *never* have the sole use of the system. When there is little free internal memory left, an increasingly large part of the memory that is temporarily not needed is swapped out onto the hard disk. The chance that a certain operation will require data that is not found in memory increases. The result is a hard disk that makes a lot of noise and programs that halt and stutter, causing overall slowdown and annoyance.

Impact on Performance

Another reason to keep footprints small is the time loss (performance problems) incurred while handling programs. Because we have already mentioned many examples in this chapter, this section therefore discusses only performance issues relating to the handling of larger file sizes. Think, for example, of the following:

- Making backups of programs
- Loading programs into memory before execution (+ network traffic)
- Exchanging data and program components between processes
- Slow database access due to large data sizes

How to Measure Footprint Size

Measuring footprint size is an activity that differs strongly between projects. An exact definition, or even a set of definitions, is highly project dependent, as are the accuracy with which to specify the needed storage footprint (megabytes, kilobytes, or even in bytes or bits), how early in the project to make footprint estimations, and so on.

This section highlights issues concerned with estimating footprint sizes.

Measuring Storage Requirements

In most cases it's sufficient to simply add up the program file sizes, but there can be more to measuring the storage space requirement of a program. Think, for example, about the use of cross compilers. A lot more work needs to be done with a program developed on hardware not entirely identical to the target machine—the machine which will eventually run the program in a commercial setup. To fairly estimate the requirements for the target machine, some preliminary tests might be necessary to determine any differences of machine code or executable size on the two machines. This way, it will be easier to predict the size of the final program. For example, the processor of the target machine can use twice as many bytes to describe its instructions as the machine used for development. The target machine in turn could have a much better file management system that uses only half the overhead for block allocation. To make a better initial estimate of the target footprint, it is wise to make a good document or spreadsheet describing these kinds of differences at the beginning of the project. This is also useful during development to quickly recalculate target footprint size as the design of the program changes or its user requirements readjust.

Measuring Runtime Requirements

Added to the problems associated with using different development and target systems, the dynamic aspects of programs further complicates measurement of runtime requirements. This section discusses these aspects and offers advice on measuring them.

It is necessary to calculate the actual uncompressed runtime code size. This is the largest size of all possible module combinations; the design should clearly state which combinations of modules could be found in memory when overlaying is used.

Moreover, the dynamic memory usage of a program can be monitored. Basically this means running the program through realistic worst-case test scenarios and looking at what the program does with the internal memory. Although tests are performed with tools, it might also be necessary to write some kind of indirection layer that will catch the calls the program makes to the operating system. By having the program call a special glue layer when asking for (or returning) memory, this layer can aid by recording sizes required and released. It could even store information about memory location, making it possible to look at fragmentation patterns.

Spy software could also be used to look at the behavior of the program stack, heap size, or usage of other scarce operating resources (IRQs, DMA channels, serial and parallel ports, and buses).

When Do Footprint Problems Arise?

Runtime footprint problems can be inadvertently introduced during any phase of development, but they are unlikely to be discovered before either rigorous testing or field use of programs. The following sections explain how footprint problems could remain undetected for so long.

Design

Apart from bugs in programs, memory leakage, and fragmentation, it is also possible that conscious design decisions actually cause unnecessary or unexpected footprint problems. As we have seen before, part of the runtime footprint is used during the execution of the program for storing (intermediate) data. How the program handles this intermediate data determines its behavior when the data set grows. It is fairly likely that a routine used for transforming a certain set of data will, at some point, cause the original data and the transformed data to be in memory at the same time. An example of this is the aforementioned decompression routine. Designed very badly, this decompression routine might keep all the compressed data in memory while it allocates yet more memory to store all the decompressed data. This will not pose a problem for small files; in fact it is a very fast way of working due to the low level of instruction overhead. Consequently, this routine will seem to work fine during a test phase that uses only small files. However, as the program is called on to decompress ever larger files in the field, the problem becomes apparent. A better designed program would first take into account the amount of memory available and then determine the appropriate amount of input data to load.

Of course this example is rather extreme, but it does illustrate what kind of oversight can be made during the design phase and the unexpected impact memory management schemes can have.

Efficient memory management is described in detail in Chapter 9.

Implementation

The design of a program gives its overall description; it is usually made with a high level of abstraction as far as individually identified components are concerned. Especially when dealing with large projects, a lot of the implementation details will be left up to the implementer. The design of a component could, for example, describe it as "knowing" where to find its peer components. The implementer of that component has to choose the specific means of implementing this relationship. He could choose a linked list of data blocks, an array, or even a tree. When choosing the linked list, he still would have to decide whether to make it doubly linked and allow some kind of sorting.

Though these choices do not seem relevant or even interesting from the design point of view, they can nevertheless have an unexpected effect on footprint size. Take, for example, a programmer who has heard that using macros and inline functions can increase performance by reducing function-call overhead. In essence his assumption is correct, but in using these techniques indiscriminately, he has failed to comprehend the downside of what he is doing. The macros and inline functions, some of which he has even managed to use in nested constructions, are expanded during compile time and cause his program to become unexpectedly large. The programmer in this example would have done better by using macros and inline functions only in those parts of the program which are performance bottlenecks, lacking a more elegant solution.

There are tools, called profilers, to help locate performance bottlenecks (see Chapter 4). The use of macros and inline functions is further discussed in Chapter 9.

Compilation

The compiler options used during compile time greatly influence the generated footprint. In fact, most compilers even have specific options for optimizing the generated code for either footprint size or performance. There are hidden dangers in the use of these options however. Refer to Chapter 4 for more detailed information.

Summary

The definition of *performance* is subject to the perception of the person giving the definition. Users will have a different view of a program than developers, and project managers in turn might have yet another view. Even views of individual users vary due to differences of experiences and expectations. One reason that performance issues (and even bugs, unintuitive interfaces, and so on) come into existence at all is because of these different views.

The ideal program, as seen by the user, has the following characteristics:

- It needs little user interaction.
- It has an intuitive user interface.
- It has a short learning curve.
- It is highly flexible.
- It contains, and is accompanied by, extensive but easily readable user documentation.
- It has no waiting times during user interaction; any slow actions be performed off line and so on.
- It has readily available information for users at any given time.

The ideal program, as seen by the developer, contains the following attributes:

- It is geared toward future developments—added functionality, handling larger bases of data.

- It is easily maintainable.
- It has a good and intuitive design.
- It is accompanied by well-written technical documentation.
- It can be passed on to any developer.

Unsurprisingly, we have yet to encounter such a program, or indeed one that comes even close to satisfying most of the requirements stated earlier in this chapter. Some of the requirements seem to even openly defy each other. That is why concessions need to be made, based on the actual use of the program.

One can wonder why to optimize algorithms and functions when hardware seems to become faster and faster all the time. This chapter has reviewed several considerations about the benefits of optimization as opposed to hardware upgrades. Although hardware predictably improves every 18 months, generally the effect is a mere workaround for doubling speed at best. This does not effectively counter the increased requirements and demands of software. To actually solve these issues requires serious investigation. The following chapter explains how system design plays a further part for creating an effective environment.

Creating a New System

IN THIS CHAPTER

This chapter takes the reader step-by-step from the design stage of a new project through to the start of the implementation stage, noting at every step where optimization opportunities can be found. As such it is also a helpful checklist for consultation whenever the learned techniques are put into practice.

System Requirements

Performance and footprint issues obviously play a large role in both the implementation phase and the design phase of a software project. However, this is not where the whole process starts. The requirements phase is the first factor. The following sections discuss why and how the requirements impact performance and footprint.

Setting Performance Targets

The requirements specification should describe in clear and measurable terms what is expected from the final product. It is in essence the blueprint of what the design and implementation results need to achieve. So in addition to containing all that needs to be tested in the final product, a good and representative requirement specification can also be used as a basis for making initial cost calculations. Consequently, the requirements are where to factor in expectations concerning the speed of a program and the hardware necessary for execution.

The requirements are determined with help from the client—often through a series of interactive sessions. When a replacement system is to be built, it is necessary to get a feel for the existing system being used and the problems it suffers from. You should examine the old system and how and when it interacts with those using it. This helps in ascertaining which parts of the system really need to be lean and fast and which parts are less time-critical.

For example, consider a company whose services cause it to have a large client database. It could be important for such a company to have a database setup that allows fast storage and retrieval of client information because it needs to be used during phone conversations with clients. Because all the data processing is done after hours, it's far less important how quickly this system processes data.

However, it's not enough to merely examine the old system and identify its problem areas. The requirements for the old system are bound to be very different from those to be satisfied by the new one. People have higher expectations of a new system when an old system is automated (or an automated system is updated or replaced) because more time and money is invested. In practice, it happens all too often that the lack of hard performance requirements causes a shift in design focus. So specific targets need to be set. With only functional requirements to guide them, designers tend to focus on elegant solutions for items, such as framework setup or reusability of components. But all that amounts to nothing if the final product is just too slow.

And the same holds true where footprints are concerned. A program might be flexible and expandable, but if it does not fit on the target hardware in the first place, nobody will ever consider expanding it. So it's important to get a feel for how much space is actually necessary. It's even better to know how much space will be needed in future. If you can, you should tell the client exactly how much extra hard drive space he needs for every 1,000 new users.

The following sections focus on unexpected requirements areas that impact performance and footprint expectations.

Stability and Availability

Stability and availability are very important requirements not only for software, but also for entire systems (software plus hardware) because they impact the reliability of the system.

A system is unreliable when it crashes every few hours, produces unpredictable results (in accuracy or even response speed), or when its level of reliability depends on the amount of time it has been active (uptime). A client expects the system to be reliable around the clock. It is certainly undesirable for the design team to have to make clear that certain situations can cause actual data loss because of a hardware or software problem. This means the requirements must specify the goal level of stability and availability. The reason here is twofold: first, to make sure proper assessments and adjustments can be made during design and implementation to insure a sufficiently high reliability level; second, to make the client aware of the necessary tradeoffs. Stability and availability come at a certain cost. They influence performance and footprint size, development time, hardware costs, and so on. This cost curve is not linear either. It may be relatively easy to build a system with an 80% level of reliability. Costs are higher for the next 15%, but the following 4% might cost as much as the whole system together, and the final 1% may be unmentionably high. The client needs to decide how much the last few percentages are actually worth investing in.

The following sections examine the impact of stability and availability requirements on performance and footprint.

Impact of Stability and Availability on Performance

Characteristics of the data stream a system should be able to handle continuously are an important part of its requirements. Although a system can be equipped with buffers to capture and store certain bursts of information, the implication is that there must be, at some point before the buffers overflow, some extra time to catch up and clear the buffers. Few application areas are generous toward any data loss, so it's important to know what kind of data rate a program can handle continuously. The specific task the system is designed to carry out determines how this data rate is actually specified (the rate of input data to handle, the number of database addresses to store or process per minute, and so on). Consultations with the client should determine this data rate. Alpha and beta versions of the system should be put through stress tests. During these tests, you find out how taxing it is for the system to comply with the requirements. The system is clearly on the verge of maxing out if a simple extra task, such as moving the mouse pointer or manipulating parts of the user interface, causes difficulties. The continuous data stream it can handle is thus lower than the one it is being fed.

Enabling the use of buffers to protect against sudden or unexpected bursts of data can be specified within the requirements document, but as a maximum or "burst" data rate. It is important to note also the length of time the system is able to keep up with this maximum rate (before its performance declines or becomes unreliable) and how much time the system needs (at the normal data rate) to recover and be ready for a following burst.

A closely related issue is the responsiveness of a system. What happens when input suddenly starts pouring in after a long period of drought? Does the system respond in due time or does it experience difficulties? It seems more than logical that this should normally not be a problem, but even a household PC in everyday use can experience this. Background processes (such as screensavers, registry updates, virus checkers) ensure that the PC does not respond instantaneously after a period of low interaction. The hardware also plays an important role in responsiveness, such as green PC options, power savers, the suspend mode, and so on. When a system has to guarantee a certain response time, these options most likely need to be kept in check or maybe even turned off. It might also be possible to set specific parts of the system in some kind of standby mode and keep the input channel monitoring active. This highlights the next area of consideration; the communication channels. If a system communicates with its environment via a modem connection, for example, it might be necessary to keep a continuous connection rather than to allow the modem to log off, after which a costly reconnect would be needed before more data can be down- or uploaded. The analysis and design phases of a project should determine how best to proceed—that is, which operating mode to allow for each part of the system.

Impact of Stability and Availability on Footprint

The data burst example given earlier demonstrates clearly the tradeoff between stability and availability on one hand and the footprint on the other. The longer the system should be able to handle higher data rates, the larger its buffers need to be.

Another area to consider is the space needed for stored data. To guarantee a high level of reliability, it may be prudent to duplicate key sets of data. Think, for example, of the DOS/Windows OS where the FAT (containing information on where and how files are stored) is kept in duplicate. Also, the storage medium itself can dictate a necessary cautious approach. You might have to take into account the number of times a medium can be written to and the average number of corrupted memory units that occur during usage. For instance, corrupted sectors on hard disks must be considered beforehand. Extra space may be needed to allow extensive error correction (Hamming codes) and so on.

For more details on optimizing input and output of data, see Chapter 12, "Optimizing IO."

Concurrency

When you set up the requirements for a software project or a system, it's important to take into account the environment in which it needs to function. Part of the requirements include assessments of usage of resources not only by the system, but also by tools and tasks likely to be used simultaneously. It's wise to determine answers to these questions:

- Are there more applications running on the system simultaneously?

If so, identify them and find out about their resource usage. For example, a calculator program using large parts of system resources is not going to be very functional as it is most likely to be used as a second or third application to aid in subsets of a larger task. Also, certain resources have to be claimed and shared: serial and parallel ports, interrupts, DMA channels, input devices (such as a keyboard or mouse) and so on.

- Will a number of users be working with the system simultaneously?

A scenario like this is of course possible with a multi-user OS, like UNIX, but has an impact on the resources available for each user. It might even influence implementation decisions as used strategies (client/server strategies, COM, CORBA), locking mechanisms, and private copies of data for processing.

Investigating the resulting availability of storage and computing power will result in a requirement of the constrained context in which the program should be able to run.

Choosing the Target System

Based on the information from the previous sections, it should be apparent what is expected from the program or system. It should also be clear that decisions have to be made which will affect the overall cost of the project. Higher reliability means more expensive hardware and longer development and implementation times. Often, you even have to choose between using hardware and using software to solve a problem. The obvious pros here are the speed of hardware solutions and the flexibility of software solutions; the obvious cons are the extra cost and inflexibility of hardware development. But there are more-involved considerations; when the software is able to do a lot of error recovery, for example, the hardware can be less fault-tolerant. The cost of being fault tolerant will sometimes be higher in software, other times in hardware, so comparisons really need to be made on a case-by-case basis. There are natural limits to the available choices, of course. For example, software will never be tolerant enough to compensate for a broken power supply.

After you determine which (if any) parts of the project have to be done in with (dedicated) hardware, take a closer look at the software to use: What kind of OS is needed? The level of reliability decided on may very well influence the choice of OS. Will a cheaper or standard OS suffice, or is a proven, industrial OS warranted? Before this question can be answered, it's necessary to look at performance, footprint, and price tradeoffs:

- What kind of impact does the OS have on available CPU cycles? (Consider this for different activities, such as memory allocation, file storage, and so on.)

- What is the footprint of the OS? (Sometimes different versions of an OS can be chosen, each with its own subset of functionality and footprint size.)

- How much overhead does the OS create? (How much memory or performance is lost when spawning a task, opening a file, creating a file on disk, and so on.)

- What is the minimal guaranteed response time? (And to what extent is this influenced by background tasks like updating registry information, doing page swapping, and so on.)

- Is it a real-time OS? (And is one really needed? See requirements.)

The hardware and software choices affect performance and footprint. This is something which will be reflected again in the design. The following sections address this.

System Design Issues

After the requirements for a program or system are successfully identified, it is time to get busy with the design—that is, the complete package of documentation that an implementer needs to create the final product. In some technical literature, a separate analysis phase is identified. However, this book presents analyzing the program and its surroundings as fully integrated with finding the requirements and making the design. As such, it would be unnatural to try to treat analysis separately.

The next section examines performance and footprint issues to be dealt with during the design phase. The first part discusses the static framework of a program, and the second part discusses the dynamic objects of a program.

Application Framework (Static)

The previous section highlighted key areas where performance and footprint requirements could be found. Of course, these also have implications where the design is concerned. This section highlights the key areas for the design of the program itself:

- Design Focus

  Is it better to optimize a program for performance or for footprint? Designing a (fast) program where memory is not a scarce resource completely differs from trying to squeeze functionality into a small runtime space (such as, in-place algorithms versus memory-hungry input-to-output conversion algorithms). Consider optimizing just certain parts of a program for footprint size to save some memory. Using that saved memory in other parts of the program allows these to be even better optimized for performance.

- Functional Modeling

  Is it best to build one large program containing all functionality or to split the program into smaller tools? By running the tools separately (maybe even from a single continuous menu), it is possible to save considerably on runtime memory.

- Look and Feel

  How is the program operated? Where are delays expected? What kind of feedback does the user expect? When and where do you use double functionality (mouse, and hotkeys, and so on)? Consider having slow operations take place in the background while the main application (separate thread) stays responsive to the user.

- Subsystems

  What kind of subsystems can you identify? How do they communicate? Do they call each other's functions? Do they transfer data or share the same data?

- Flexibility

  How flexible do you want to be (and need to be) for future changes? Do you build a wildly generic framework or concentrate only on the functionality required by the current customer? Are you actually prepared to sacrifice performance to be more flexible?

- Data Flow

  How does the data flow through the designed components? Are there time dependencies? Have you considered where scheduled and where event-driven mechanisms are appropriate?

- Portability

  Do you want to be flexible enough to allow the software to be easily rebuilt to run on other hardware systems (porting the software)? If so, the set up of the software cannot be made hardware dependent. All hardware interactions will need to be done through a generic mechanism. Any hardware-specific elements will need to be put in separate modules which will be replaced during a port.

- Reusability

  Do you expect to use (parts) of your program in some future contexts? Any parts to be reused should then be identified and put together in functional groups. This is true also for the relevant documentation.

- Intelligence Placement

  Do you want intelligent submodules or do you want to keep all the decision-making power in the main module? The differences are that either the submodules become quite large or the main module does, and portability and reusability are therefore influenced.

The same intelligence choices need to be made concerning client/server applications. Who does most of the work, the client or the server?

Object Lifetime (Dynamic)

Generally, programs are made up of several functional objects of which a number of instances can be found in memory during runtime (classes, threads, libraries, and so on). Objects which are not part of the static framework of a program are generally created and destroyed as needed. This section examines typical life cycles of software objects.

Intermediate Objects

Intermediate objects are used to store intermediate results and information during processing. They are typically used within a certain part of a program only, often localized inside a single function, and have a very short life span. They do not outlive the program, and they do not outlive the function or module they are used in. An example of intermediate objects is the variables declared inside a class or function, as shown in Listing 2.1:

LISTING 2.1   Intermediate Objects

```
~
class PaintCanvas;
~
PaintCanvasManager::DoWop()
{
    int a;                           // intermediate
    ~
    PaintCanvas  firstCanvas;          // intermediate
    ~
    int intMed = nrOfProcessedCanvasses;    // intermediate
    if(~~
    {
        nrOfProcessedCanvasses = IntMed;
    }
    ~
}
```

Persistent Objects

Because persistent objects stay alive after the program terminates, they are still when the program restarts. These objects are used to retain information about a previous run. Examples of this are files in which program data is stored and keys which are set in the registry of the OS

(Windows uses this). Such objects will even outlive a computer reboot. Other persistent objects may be resident in memory, like the clipboard to which you can copy pieces of text or pictures from for instance, a word processor. Dedicated hardware may even have special memory reserved for storing persistent objects, disks, EEPROM, FLASH, and so on. The advantage of keeping objects such as these in memory is the speed with which they can be recalled when they are needed again. This can even increase restart time of the program or the dedicated hardware on which the system runs.

Decisions to make in memory management (as part of the program or system) can include deleting certain objects or moving them to disk to (temporarily) free some runtime memory.

Temporary Objects

Temporary objects fall somewhere between intermediate and persistent objects. Their lifetime is generally longer than that of intermediate objects, meaning they outlive functions and program modules; however, they do not often outlive the program itself. An example of a temporary object is the Undo Buffer. Found in most word processors, the Undo function can recall a previous version of text. The buffer content changes constantly during program execution, but the buffer itself is accessible as long as the program is active.

Temporary autosave files fall into this category also; however, their properties are closer to persistent storage than the previous example.

Spawned Objects

Spawned objects are donated to—and used by—a scope beyond their creation. Their lifetime is managed and controlled by the object or program they are donated to. Think, for example, of an object returned by a function or program module:

```
char * Donator::Creator()
{
~
    char * spawn = new char [stlen(initstring) + 1];
    ~
    return spawn;

}
~
~


void Receiver::User()
{
~
    char * spawned = donateClass->Creator();
```

```
      ~
    delete [] spawned;
}
```

The spawned object in this example is a string allocated by the `Donator` class and donated to the `Receiver` class. The donator proceeds as if the object never existed. The `Receiver` class is now the sole owner of the object and is in charge of its lifetime. Any memory leakage caused by the spawned object is in effect a `Receiver` problem.

After a receiver indicates it has correctly received a donated spawned, it is necessary to destroy all administration of the object. The communication interface is very important here because if for some reason the object is copied in the transferal, this will have an impact on performance as well as footprint. Refer to Chapter 8, "Functions."

Having examined the different storage types, you can conclude that the design should specify what kinds of objects are being dealt with, which in turn indicates how they should be stored. Short-lived, frequently used objects should be stored in memory, with perhaps more persistent copies of data for crash recovery purposes, and so on.

The Development Process

Development begins with requirements and design, culminating in implementation after the finalization the requirements and design phases. Choose a development process that takes performance and footprint issues into account from the very beginning. The following sections discuss how performance and footprint fit in the overall development process.

Prototyping

Build prototypes to show the client a more concrete idea of what the final product will look like. Keep in mind, however, that a prototype does not have to be a fully functional test version of a product. In fact, the purpose of prototyping is to offer the clients and developers a chance to get their heads pointed in the same direction *before* investing much development effort. The prototype is, therefore, more of a simulation. It hints at the look and feel of the interface and the functionality it offers.

Often, a prototype is nothing more than a user interface that has stubbed functionality. The stubs deliver predefined values instead of doing actual data processing. Or the prototype might be nothing more than a set of slides or drawings. Whatever its setup, it tests the completeness of the requirements and design.

As previously discussed, requirements are determined interactively with the client. After this, the design is made from the written requirements specification. However, these steps should not be seen as directly derivable; moreover, they are the result of translations. The person writing the requirements specification translates the interaction with the client into technical and nontechnical requirements. Quite likely, some elements will be lost in the translation because of the different backgrounds and focus of the writer and the client. For example, the writer might miss exact insight in the everyday work situation of the client, and the client, in turn, might miss insight in what is technically possible. This scenario can repeat itself in the design phase, where the original requirements may have been right on the nose. They are, however, translated once more, this time by people who are probably even more technically oriented. It is not a luxury to stand still at this point in the process and ask the client whether he still agrees with the vision finally put forward in the design. The prototype is something that clients can directly comment on.

While building prototypes, it is a good idea to keep the following issues in mind.

- Make sure the client is aware that the prototype is a simulation and not the real thing.

  The downside of a good prototype (simulation) is that the client cannot easily assess how much of the work has already been done. The client may assume that the demo constitutes the final product. During the demo, make clear to the client that all results are artificial—that the user interface is just an initial setup that does not actually do anything.

- Although it is possible for a demo to be quite fast, it is wise to avoid perceived performance issues by keeping the prototype's speed consistent with that of the final product. This will deter any false expectations on the client's behalf. It is, therefore, a good idea to use initial response predictions to build artificial slowdown into the prototype. Just make the user interface wait a specified number of seconds before it produces the predefined results. Even more prudent would be to add a percentage of overhead to the worst-case predicted responses. This way, it should be possible to make each following version of the program (prototype, alpha version, beta version, and so on) increasingly responsive.

- Footprint and other target impressions need the same treatment, as was mentioned in the previous bullet. Although most prototypes are unlikely to be resource intensive, it is a good idea to pay attention to the hardware used for the demo. This is because the client may not fully understand the technical implications of prototyping and may not even think to ask if the final product needs more memory, disks, or processing speed than the system on which the prototype runs.

Scheduling Performance and Footprint Measurements

The actual implementation begins after it is clear that the requirements and design reflect what the client has in mind. During implementation, it is important to keep doing performance and footprint tests.

Often, implementation problems occur only when the final product (be it in the alpha, beta, or release stage) is tested for performance and footprint problems. Developers might discover that the program does not run as fast as expected when used in a network with 50 users, or that the product no longer fits on the hard disk initially chosen. To avoid having to reengineer the existing code, it is better to incorporate frequent performance and footprint tests in the implementation planning.

Performance and footprint trouble can be identified early on in the implementation stage by looking for the following signs:

- Performance and footprint restrictions are getting tight, even though a sizable amount of functionality still has to be added.

- Performance and footprint test results differ disproportionately from previous tests. As the program grows, you expect it to be slower and larger, but sudden jumps in size and slowdown can indicate something has gone wrong.

- Unpredictable results. If the same test with the same software version of the project generates different results, there is some kind of dynamic behavior in play—the software test results lack reproducibility. Perhaps the program is suffering from memory leaks.

Another advantage of scheduling these tests in the planning is that implementers get used to the idea of doing performance and footprint testing as part of the development cycle. During implementation, they will be more aware of its importance and be continually reminded of the perhaps less-visible requirements for these topics.

Data Processing Methods

Basically, the functionality of every computer program comes down to processing data. Whether it is a simple calculator tool or a full-blown spreadsheet with Internet stock market interactivity, data is being provided and the program processes it and returns results. When considering the performance of a program, the data processing methods are thus of utmost importance. One way to introduce enhancements in this area is to optimize the processing of the data. However, the best optimization of processing data is not having to process data at all. The following sections discuss the moments when data processing occurs. Often, a choice can be made, hopefully in such a way that data is processed during idle program times.

Processing Immediately

The most intuitive form of processing occurs when data is processed as it becomes available. You do not expect your calculator tool to accept your calculation and send you an email with the answer the next morning. Unless the processing of data is expected to take a long time, most folks basically expect processing to occur immediately.

Some situations where it's a good idea to use immediate processing include

- The data rate is low enough for the program to handle it immediately. To put it another way, there is enough idle time for the program to do immediate processing (as with for instance software embedded in a train-ticket machine).

- The data rate is high, but the process the data has to undergo is simple enough to be executed immediately without causing unacceptable slowdown of the whole program, such as decompression software—MP3 players, for example. (The process does not necessarily have to be simple in logical terms; the hardware just has to be able to execute it in a reasonable amount of time.)

- The data rate is high, and the process is complex, but there is simply no other choice than to process the data immediately. Consecutive steps need the processed data to continue. This means placing data in waiting queues and simply processing until the job is done (such as is the case when copying a large number of files with a file manager).

Processing on Request

Processing on request is basically the opposite of processing immediately. Instead of processing the data as it comes in (input), processing occurs when the data is needed (output). This means no processing occurs other than that which is absolutely necessary. It also means that processing demands can become high when the demand for data becomes high. Still, it can sometimes be useful to postpone processing. The following advantages can be identified:

- No time is lost on processing data during input; maximum performance is thus available for the input function. This is important for programs which need to respond fast to capture available data, such as sampler software for audio (audio sampling), video, or medical data (CAT scan).

- Data that is never retrieved will not be processed. No time and memory is lost on results that are never used. Consider the downloading of compressed files. It is possible to decompress during downloading, but some files may, in fact, not be needed at all.

- When the processed data occupies more space (because of derived data), storing data before processing will use up less memory or storage. Think of tools that perform some kind of decompression (such as text file versus desktop publishing formatting, MP3 versus WAV, and so on).

Depending on the specific situation, the following disadvantages can, however, come into play:

- Timing problems may occur if the demand for processed data (output) suddenly becomes high. Data may not be instantaneously available because of the high workload. An administration program that needs to churn out paychecks at the end of the month will be very busy if all the salaries still need to be calculated.

- When the input size of the data is larger than that of the processed data, space (memory or storage) is, in effect, lost (for example, keeping audio in WAV files instead of in MP3 and so on).

- A mechanism may be needed to locate and remove irrelevant input data or allow new input to overwrite certain existing data (for example, purging a database of Christmas card recipients from the names of people who declined to send you a card for the last three years).

To make a viable decision, look closely at the characteristics of the data and its usage. In essence, processing time and speed are set against available resources.

Periodic Processing

Periodic processing is likely to be used when the results of processing are not needed immediately and the program or system has an uneven workload. Perhaps there are certain times when the data rate is low (lunch, evening, early morning), the processing is cheap (power and phone costs), or the processing is less intrusive (network communications and so on). Benefits of periodic processing are

- No extra processing during input.
- Processed data is generally available (though not immediately after being input).
- The processed input data and irrelevant data can easily be discarded.

But there can also be a downside:

- When the system needs to be active longer—for example, around the clock to catch up on processing data during the night—a high demand is placed on the availability of the system.
- Maintenance (including preventive maintenance) can be difficult to schedule when the system is active longer.
- The input data cannot be demanded instantly and limits the availability of processed data.

Batch Processing

As with periodic processing, batch processing takes advantage of the uneven workload of a system. This time, however, the processing is not necessarily triggered at a prespecified time—more likely, an event triggers the processing. This characteristic makes batch processing similar to processing on request, with the difference that whole batches or sets of data are processed.

Batch processing shares the pros of periodic processing and has the added advantage to be triggered outside the specified period(s).

Summary

Performance and footprint issues can be identified and eliminated or worked around, as early as the requirement and design phases. Special care must be taken to find out the limitations of the chosen target hardware. Also, it is important to establish that the development team and the client are in full agreement regarding the specific requirements of the system and whether the software is developing along the lines of the set performance and footprint targets. Schedule performance and footprint tests as part of the development planning. Evaluate the lifetime of the objects identified during the design and the characteristics expected from the processing of the input data.

Modifying an Existing System

IN THIS CHAPTER

This chapter explains what kind of things to look out for when modifying an existing system. To ensure a good development process, it's a good idea to take the time to identify and monitor possible performance and footprint problem areas early on as well as throughout the development cycle. Although it is often desirable to restart a project from scratch, you might not always have that opportunity because of constraints on, for example, time or budget. This chapter shows how to work with preexisting development problems—for instance, software that has to operate under new or more restrictive requirements. An example of this is existing code which is reused. The functionality might be correct, while the existing code is too slow or too large for the new application. This chapter looks at what developers can and should do when such problems arise during development.

Identifying What to Modify

To identify performance and footprint problems, it is prudent to carefully review the design and requirements documentation of a system to find out about its operating parameters. Also, it is a good idea to look at external indications that something might have gone wrong during the design or implementation phases of the project. The next section focuses on telltale external symptoms encountered in the field.

Looking at the Symptoms

Hidden problems can exist within a system, even when it manages to function within its requirements. These problems can appear later—for instance, when requirements become stricter, amounts of input data increase, or the number of users goes up. The earlier you manage to identify and eliminate possible problems (preventive maintenance), the lower the cost will be.

Consider the following checklist to quickly determine the best area to focus modifications and optimizations:

- Look at how similar systems perform (with the same hardware). Likely bottlenecks can occur, for instance, in performance or the amount of available memory.
- Determine when, how, and where the system slows down:

  Slowdowns affecting an entire system usually occur from hardware problems such as too few resources (memory, disk space, and so on), not enough processing speed (CPU speed, number of coprocessors), a slow OS, or inefficient resource management systems (memory and file management).

  Slowdowns resulting from specific interactions with the system usually require a bit of investigation. You'll have to determine exactly what happens during these actions. For example, a slow or faulty network connection can completely destroy system performance.

- Notice whether problems occur (or get worse) as time passes. Lower performance after extended use of a system is likely the result of bugs or design errors rather than specific performance problems. For more information, refer to the section "Design Flaws, Faulty Algorithms, and Bugs" later in this chapter.

- Notice whether the system disproportionately slows down while it handles larger amounts of data. This sort of failing performance is usually due either to improper system design or to memory fragmentation/leakage. It is advisable to immediately do a profile to determine the cause (as discussed in Chapter 4, "Tools and Languages").

Beginning Your Optimization

A general misconception is that optimizing software is the simple act of replacing evil bits of code (too large, inefficient, or slow) with good bits of code (lean, efficient, and fast). Although this is certainly part of the optimization process, it is not all there is to it. Working under such a premise means that valuable optimization opportunities are overlooked. This is because the process of optimization really consists of these equally important steps:

- Finding candidate areas for optimization
- Analyzing the candidate areas and selecting targets for optimization
- Performing the design and implementation of the optimizations

The next sections discuss the theory behind these optimization steps, as well as the human resource considerations. Optimization of software has an impact on project cost and resource availability, particularly when existing software is still in development. This is why human resource considerations form an integral part of any optimization plan.

Finding Candidate Areas for Optimization

Candidate areas for optimization can be found using different approaches:

- Requirements tracing
- Looking at external symptoms
- Performing profiling
- Using project test tools in regression testing

Although software projects can easily become quite large, it is still advisable to have a small group perform this optimization step, as it primarily involves gathering information. It is certainly sensible to have just one person looking at each individual software module. It can be beneficial to select someone outside of the development process for this when the process of gathering information is straightforward enough, for two reasons. First, this person is more likely to be neutral, without (subconsciously) favoring any modules. Second, this person is more likely to note and reject any unusual behavior that a developer might have become accustomed to and therefore overlook. Similarly, a new member to the development team can be given this task as an opportunity to become more familiar with the system.

The result of this optimization step is a list of characteristics of the system components, such as percentage of used CPU cycles, number of memory requests, files read or written, and so on.

Analyzing the Candidate Areas and Selecting Targets for Optimization

To perform this step, it is necessary to have considerable knowledge of the software architecture. Based on the information gathered during the previous step, choices need to be made concerning

- Which parts of the software are going to be optimized? The answer to this question depends on which parts will yield the most significant improvements, and how much development time needs to be invested in performing the optimizations that are needed.
- Who on the team can lend the greatest value in optimizing a particular part of the software?
- When is optimization of a certain software part going to take place? Synchronize this with other development activities (maybe in the same module) and overall human resource planning.

Decisions of this nature require architectural and managerial backup. Consequently, a system architect usually performs this step and consults with a project leader for human resource and project planning issues. (Refer to "Analyzing Target Areas" later in this chapter for more information.)

In selecting parts for optimization, consider the influences they will have on the amount of performance or footprint improvement that can be gained:

- The initial state and performance of the software to be optimized
- The flexibility of the design in allowing (specific) changes and adaptations
- The total size of the software (such as program, module, and library) to be optimized
- Skill and experience levels of the developers
- Resource availability (developers, tools, hardware)
- Available (project) budget
- Available time

Side effects of optimizing existing code that can come into play include

- Additional time and expense
- Potential new bugs introduced from new code
- Regression tests to ensure sound functionality
- Documentation updates (design, manuals)

The architect directly oversees the optimization process when it is limited to bug fixes. However, the architect needs to devote more attention to optimizations related to design errors—a redesign might even be needed in this instance of the faulty software (modules/functions).

Note that only two or three individuals have worked on the optimization up to this point. In smaller projects, several roles might even be handled by a single person, thereby using even fewer resources. It is therefore fair to say that impact on the normal development process has probably been minimal.

Analyzing candidate areas for optimization is discussed in more detail later in this chapter in the section "Analyzing Target Areas."

Performing the Design and Implementation of the (Selected) Optimizations

The previous paragraphs show that the actual implementation of optimized code (replacing the evil parts with the good parts) constitutes roughly of one third of the work and time invested in finding problem areas and devising solutions. This does not mean, however, that the implementation is trivial. For example, the parts to be optimized might very well be found in the fundamental layers of the software, on top of which the rest of the system was built. This is the case, for instance, with layers that closely interact with the hardware, the OS, or third-party libraries. Note that tinkering around here can affect the stability of the entire system. It is a good idea to put an expert on these kinds of jobs, preferably the original developer of the software (unless, of course, it was sheer incompetence that resulted in the performance problems).

This step ends with conducting regression tests to ensure that all existing functionality is unaffected.

Analyzing Target Areas

The next two sections go deeper into the mechanics of the second step of the optimization process: analyzing the candidate areas and selecting targets for optimization.

3

MODIFYING AN EXISTING SYSTEM

Design Flaws, Faulty Algorithms, and Bugs

When the information of step 1 is available (profiler data, problem analysis, and so on), it is prudent to have another look at the design. In essence, compare the timing information found in step 1 with that estimated at design time. Questions to consider include, Which parts of the system were expected to be slow? and How slow were they expected to be? It now becomes even more clear how important quantifiable requirements and design estimations are (refer to Chapter 2, "Creating a New System"). Time previously spent on those two topics is now paying off.

The following sections examine some common situations which can be found when comparing the results of step 1 with the requirements and design.

Unpredictably Excessive Processing Time

When parts of the system exceed the amount of time initially anticipated, quite likely a coding problem—introduced in the implementation phase—is at the heart of this behavior. This could simply be a bug or perhaps even a problem with the chosen algorithm.

Some typical examples of the kinds of bugs found in the field are

- Loops that do not terminate in time
- Functions that are called too often
- Counters that wrap around
- Incorrect placement (or the omission) of such program statements as ";", "}", "break", "if", "else", and so on
- Semaphores and other kinds of (critical section) locks that do not match or circle around into a deadlock
- Variables that are incorrectly initialized before use or that are not updated when they need to be
- Input data that is not checked on corruption, or valid values
- Input data is not available, causing the program to wait or use buffered data (or perhaps even uninitialized memory)
- Debug code that is accidentally being executed (#ifdefs missing or placed incorrectly, debug options in the compiler which are turned on unintentionally)

Some typical examples of algorithm problems found in the field are

- Inefficient calculations (calculating sine/cosine and so on instead of using precalculation tables)
- Inefficient functions for searching, replacing, and sorting data

- Resource managers that perform poorly (memory managers, file interaction classes, and so on)

- Caching mechanisms that do not work properly or are not optimally tuned

- Interrupts that are never generated or that are serviced at moments when they are not useful (due to being blocked before)

- Blocks of data that are marked as *deleted* but which are never actually deleted, making searches and insertions in data structures slower

- Inefficient conversions of data formats

- Inefficient storage methods (writing a text character by character rather than in blocks at a time)

For most bugs, just turn directly to the code and begin repairing. This is true also for some algorithm problems; however, most will likely need some kind of redesign. In such cases, those parts of the system were not originally well designed, so more damage than good can come from quickly hacking a patch or workaround. Sometimes, more time is needed for parts of the system that might have seemed trivial at the start.

Predictable Processing Time

More drastic measures might be necessary to optimize performance and footprint when processing times are approximately what is expected but are still too slow. Although it is possible to make existing algorithms somewhat more efficient, the source of the problem usually is in the design. It's necessary to redesign the entire process, not merely the algorithms. To do so, go back to reacquaint yourself with the original problem domain that your system is supposed to solve.

These performance problems are present at a very high abstraction level (the design), and thus introduced not by the implementer(s) but by the architect(s). This means that optimizations will be very time consuming and most likely will result in fairly extensive code changes or additions. These design flaws can generally be traced back to poor, or constantly changing, requirement specifications. In fact, without complete requirements, developers can create software that completely misses its mark. Consider the following scenario. A pen manufacturing company might give developers incomplete requirements for their database. So they create a beautiful and elegant database that is lighting fast at finding specific product entries. However, this manufacturer produces only twenty distinctly different products. He accesses the database through client entries, of which there are thousands. This example shows that without clear requirements that reflect what is expected of the system, the design and implementation might miss the correct focus.

The architect designs the system based on impressions from reading the requirements (and from any interaction with the actual clients or end users). The implementers further interpret the requirements as they write the code. Any considerations overlooked at the beginning of this process will likely be lost.

Unpredictably Reduced Processing Time

You might keep in mind that reduced processing time can be a red herring. Remember that you are optimizing existing code because it suffers from footprint or performance problems. Investigate all unexpected behavior, including parts of the system that are unexpectedly fast or use less memory than anticipated. These characteristics are likely indications of problems. For example, data might be processed incompletely or incorrectly. This might even be the cause of performance problems in other parts of the system. One thing is certain: any existing code problems will crop up sooner or later to make your life miserable (if you want to know exactly when, just ask Murphy). Preventive maintenance is essential.

Looking at the Data Model

Chapter 2 provides an overview of typical life cycles for different types of software objects. This section examines the different characteristics of the program data that can be managed by these objects. How and where this data is stored has an impact on both footprint and performance, as does the choice of when to store, process, and transmit the data.

Many performance and footprint issues are directly related to data access. Performance of most systems will drop drastically when data is needed but cannot be accessed immediately. Likewise, footprint size will become problematic when you try to store too much data close at hand. Intelligent data models are therefore very important in creating an efficient program or system (refer to Chapter 11, "Storage Structures," for technical details and examples). When profiling information indicates that data access seems to be a bottleneck, take another look at the data models used. Note that the (plural) term *data models* is used here purposely. Systems generally use vastly different types of data (program configuration data, user data, stored input, and so on). Often, it will be unwise to use the same data model for different types of data, even though this might save on development time. Identifying the separate types of data is important.

Distinguish different data types by these key characteristics:

- The frequency with which the data is accessed
- The specific program modules that access the data
- The block size of the data
- The number of blocks expected to be stored simultaneously at any given time

- The time of creation or receipt of the data
- The specific program modules that create or receive the data
- The typical lifetime of the data in the system

When the different data types are identified, consider how to store and access each type. This is where data models come in.

Storage Considerations

It is important to determine per data type, whether you are dealing with many small blocks, a few large blocks, or perhaps combinations of both. Sometimes it is advisable to group data (blocks) together into larger blocks. This way, it can be stored and retrieved more efficiently, especially when grouping is done in such a way to group data that is likely to be needed simultaneously. However, sometimes it is advisable to split up larger blocks of data for exactly the same reason. Handling data in blocks which are too large can prove equally inefficient. For example, performance can drop suddenly when the OS needs to start swapping memory to and from storage to find a large enough continuous address space. However, consider keeping the data completely in cache when it is accessed often. Refer to Chapter 5, "Measuring Time and Complexity."

Processing Considerations

You might want to split up or shift the moments at which you process the data. It might be possible to divide the processing step into several substeps. This way, you can store the intermediate processing results to save storage and optimize idle CPU time (effectively evening out the CPU workload). You might even consider shifting the whole processing of data to an earlier or later part of the program.

Transaction Considerations

After obtaining profiler information, consider these questions so that you have a more complete picture of the situation (refer to Chapter 4): How and when does the data come into the system? How and when do you transmit or display the processed data?

When the data arrives in bursts, a different data model is needed from when it trickles in at a low rate. The extent to which data arrival can be predicted also plays a role. Sometimes it is possible to use idle time when data comes in. When input arrives via keyboard, for example, it is unlikely to be taxing for any kind of system.

The answers to these questions provide different details for the data models than those the profiler can give. This is because the profiler cannot account for expectations and predictability. After you map out these data interactions, concentrate on leveling out the CPU load. Even a small amount of leveling will be beneficial. This also holds true for memory usage. Spreading out memory usage over time affects not only runtime footprint but also performance. An added advantage here is that the memory which is freed up during this action can be used for instance to increase cache and buffers to boost performance.

Performing the Optimizations

The section "Analyzing Target Areas" helped you determine which software parts of a plagued system to optimize and whom to select for doing the optimizations. This section examines actual implementation issues of performing those optimizations. As such, it is a detailed addition to step 3 in our optimization process, Performing the Design and Implementation of the (selected) Optimizations. This section still has a theoretical focus. It marks the end of the first part of this book. The second part of the book focuses more on programming examples of implementation issues.

After you select a portion of a program to optimize, and before you actually change program code, it is necessary to decide whether to rewrite the existing functionality or to replace it. As mentioned in the previous section, this decision is best made by the architect, perhaps even in conjunction with the project leader.

Replacing Existing Functionality

When you decide to replace parts of a program that either perform poorly or are too large, you basically have two options:

- The replacement part is an existing piece of software.
- The replacement part is designed and implemented from scratch.

It is of course possible to mix these two options, combining existing code and new code. This section describes both cases in their pure forms. Mixed combinations will generally have mixed characteristics.

Using Existing Software

It may be possible for you to find a fully functional replacement part, either in-house (perhaps as part of another project) or from a third-party company. For example, with a slow memory manager, consider replacing it with an existing memory manager that is better equipped to handle the specific dynamic characteristics of your system. Similarly, when you have problems with the data your system needs to handle, consider buying a database management system (DBMS) from a company that specializes in building DBMSs. Of course, there are pros and cons to consider when choosing to use existing software.

Pros of using existing software include

- It does not need to be designed or implemented.
- It has already been tested and might even have proven itself in the field.
- The complete development cost of the software does not have to be assigned to the project budget, only the acquisition costs.
- Problems with the existing software do not have to be solved within the project. (This can also be a liability, as shown in the next list.)

The preceding list shows that using existing software means less development time and more certainty regarding the quality of the software. However, we have yet to look at the cons.

Cons of using existing software include

- Unless your contract with the provider of the software specifically states so, you have no control over updates to the existing software. This means that when a bug is found in the purchased module(s), you can only report it and hope it will be fixed before you have to deliver your system to your client.
- The existing software will have to be integrated into your system. This can mean that changes to interfaces, and even glue layers, are needed. Every extra indirection incurred when using third-party functionality uses up some the performance you are trying to win.
- The existing software was almost certainly written based on different requirements than those specified for the part you are replacing. This can mean a certain mismatch or difference of focus where parts of the functionality are concerned.
- There is always the danger that development on that software will be discontinued some time in the future when the provider of the software is a third party. This can be a disaster when you expect to need support on the software or updated versions.

When the sources of the software become available to the project, this can soften many of the cons. Also, for some static parts of the system, future support might be unnecessary. Simply taking the offered functionality "as is" might do. Often, however, you might not even have the luxury to make a decision. When your requirements are too specific to find third-party solutions, or when existing solutions are too costly to acquire or incorporate, it's necessary to just do the work in the project itself.

Designing and Implementing from Scratch

Consider the following pros and cons when building the replacement part from scratch.

Pros of writing new software for replacement include

- Using the results from the previous solution, you have more information to compare and measure against so that in early stages it's apparent if the new solution is on the right track.

- Because you write everything yourself, you can tweak and tune the new design and implementation to fit your purposes perfectly.

- Wherever the new design calls for changes to interfaces, no glue will be needed. You can adjust both sides of all interfaces.

- Future changes to your system (requirements changes, functional updates, and so on) can be handled internally in the project. When new versions need to be made, it is unnecessary to request third parties to make changes to certain parts of your system.

- No copyright issues need to be settled. This means you do not have to charge your client for using third-party components.

The preceding list shows that the main advantage of building in-house replacement parts is the control you have over the different facets of development.

Although the cons of rewriting system parts are fairly straightforward, they are included here for completeness.

Cons of writing replacement software from scratch include

- Designing and implementing new software will take time.

- New software will mean more testing and perhaps even new bugs. Again, this will take up development time.

- You do not know with a great amount of certainty how much performance or footprint size you will actually win with this new code. You can make estimations, but you are dealing with a part of the program that has previously produced problems with predictability.

This list shows that rewriting software parts negatively affects development time without giving any real assurances about results. Comparing the four lists on replacing software parts, it's logical to replace with existing software when

- A replacement of sufficient—and known—quality can be found. When specific performance or footprint data is missing, some time needs to be spent on evaluating the software.

- Your targets for maintainability of the replacement software can be met.

- There is not enough time or resources to rewrite the software internally in the project.

In all other cases, it makes more sense to do optimizations within the project.

Tuning Existing Software

This section focuses on the parts that need to be fine-tuned to gain increased performance and footprint results. Because these problems are not caused by design flaws as such, but rather faulty algorithms and bugs, the implementers will probably be doing the work in this step on their own.

Some typical examples of performance and footprint tuning problems found are

- Coding bugs
- Inefficient algorithms and processing methods (too few stop clauses for loops and switches, inappropriate allocation time and place for variable memory, and so on)
- Inappropriate use of inline functions (for more detailed information on efficient use of inline functions, see Chapter 8, "Functions")
- Inappropriate use of macros (for more detailed information an efficient use of macros, see Chapter 8)
- Incorrect use of compiler settings, or using compiler settings that are not optimal for the specific module characteristics (for more detailed information on compiler settings, see Chapter 4)

The debugger and the profiler are invaluable tools when tuning software, and they are discussed in detail in Chapter 4. Not only do these tools assist the developer in finding bugs by allowing program actions to be monitored as they are executed, but they also give more insight into which parts of the program use excessive amounts of CPU cycles. So it is easier for you to find problematic lines of code. After you create a list of implementation problems, spend some time "playing" with the system. Make small changes to the different parts of the code to assess the benefits or side effects that might occur. Frequently, this is the first time the implementer takes a good look at the code purely from a performance/footprint viewpoint and the implications of interdependency of different parts of the code. Moreover, this is the time to note the interaction between hardware, software, and tools. Taking this "play" time should provide the addition of more quantifiable information, such as shown here:

- Time needed to solve a specific problem
- Dangers of side effects while solving a specific problem
- Benefits to be gained by solving a specific problem
- Impact of solving a specific problem for different parts of the system

The focus here is on the specific implementation areas, rather than overall system design. However, note that the final item listed provides a brief look at the overall picture. This is necessary because it eliminates useless benefits to lesser or unused portions of your system, or those which are less time-critical than others. Now your choice should be fairly straightforward—which problems to solve and in what order? You should be able to maximize the visible benefits within the allotted time. One final remark on tuning software: *After changing the code, repeat any and all tests!* It has been stated before, but it simply cannot be stated too often. Practical experience teaches that, often, only tests that seem directly related to the changes that have been made are performed.

Summary

The process of optimization consists of three equally important parts:

- Finding candidate areas for optimization
- Analyzing the candidate areas and coming to conclusions
- Performing the design and implementation of the (selected) optimizations

After candidate areas have been discovered and selected for maintenance, a mix is to be chosen of replacing and fine-tuning existing code.

With code replacement, an additional choice must be made between redesigning or finding an existing replacement part. Existing replacement parts should be used when

- A replacement of sufficient and known quality can be found.
- Your targets for maintainability of the replacement software can be met.
- There is not enough time or resources to rewrite the software internally in the project.

This chapter concludes Part I. The following part, "Getting Your Hands Dirty," discusses implementation-specific problem areas by investigating programming examples of problems found in the field. Insight and ready-to-use solutions are given for subjects such as function calls, memory management, IO, handling data structures, and the correct use of programming tools.

Getting Our Hands Dirty

PART

II

This second part discusses implementation problem areas by looking at examples of problems often encountered in the field. It shows where and why problems are likely to occur and offers ready-to-use solutions for efficient function calling, memory management, IO, and setting up and handling data structures.

Part II consists of the following chapters:

Tools and Languages

IN THIS CHAPTER

This chapter introduces valuable optimization tools and gives insight into the importance of the choice of programming language. A helpful guide to choosing the right language, and even mixing languages, is provided.

Tools You Cannot Do Without

The following sections provide a short introduction to several kinds of tools, give an overview of their interrelation, and highlight their use. Not intended to be a tutorial, they provide some basic information needed in later parts of the book. For more information on specific tools, refer to the manuals provided with those tools. On the UNIX operating system, these man pages can be accessed via the man command by typing man *toolname*.

Users of Microsoft's Developer Studio can access many tools via its main menu; however, some tools are supplied only with the Professional or Enterprise Edition—or early editions—of the Developer Studio.

Whether the tools are used via an integrated GUI environment or not, they all serve the same basic purpose. As such, this chapter can be of interest regardless of the preferred system of use.

The Compiler

The compiler is a tool that transforms a program written in a high-level programming language into an executable binary file. Examples of high-level programming languages are Pascal, C, C++, Java, Modula 2, Perl, Smalltalk, and Fortran. To make an executable, the compiler makes use of several other tools: the preprocessor, the assembler, and the linker. Although these tools are often hidden behind the user interface of the compiler itself, it can be quite useful to know more about them, perhaps even to use them separately.

Listing 4.1 shows an example of compiler input. This is a C program that prints the text Hello, Mom! onscreen.

LISTING 4.1   Listing Hello.c

```
#include <stdio.h>

int main(int argc, char *argv[])
{
    printf("Hello, Mom!\n");

}
```

This chapter uses the GNU C Compiler (gcc) as the example compiler. It is available for free under the GNU General Public License as published by the Free Software Foundation. There also is a C++ version of this compiler (often embedded in the same executable) which can be called with the g++ command. In all this chapter's examples, the C compiler can be substituted by the C++ compiler.

The command gcc hello.c -o hello will translate the source file hello.c into an executable file called hello. This means the whole process—from preprocessor to compiler to assembler to linker—has been carried out, resulting in an executable program. It is possible, however, to suppress some phases of this process or to use them individually. By using different compiler options, you can exert a high degree of control over the compilation process. Some useful examples are

```
gcc -c hello.c
```

This command will preprocess, compile, and assemble the input file, but not link it. The result is an object file (or several object files when more than one input file is specified) which can serve as the input for the linker. The linker is described later in this chapter in the section "The Linker." Object files generally have the extension .o. The object file generated by this example will be called hello.o.

```
gcc -c hello.s
```

When the compiler receives an Assembly file as input, it will translate this as easily into an object file. There is no functional difference between object files generated from different source languages, so a hello.o generated from a hello.s will be handled the same by the linker as a hello.o generated from a hello.c.

```
gcc -S hello.c
```

This option suppresses the compilation process even earlier, resulting not in an object file but in an Assembly file: hello.s (this file could be used as input in the previous example).

Listing 4.2 provides the assembly output generated by the compiler for an Intel 80x86 processor, using the hello.c example as input. Depending on the compiler used, output may differ somewhat.

LISTING 4.2   The Assembly Version of hello.c

```
        .file    "hello.c"
        .version "01.01"
gcc2_compiled.:
        .section  .rodata
.LC0:
        .string  "Hello, Mom!\n"
.text
        .align 16
.globl main
```

LISTING 4.2 Continued

```
        .type      main,@function
main:
        pushl %ebp
        movl %esp,%ebp
        pushl $.LC0
        call printf
        addl $4,%esp
.L1:
        movl %ebp,%esp
        popl %ebp
        ret
.Lfe1:
        .size      main,.Lfe1-main
        .ident     "GCC: (GNU) egcs-2.91.66 19990314  (egcs-1.1.2 release)"
```

This Assembly code can be turned into an object file by invoking the assembler separately. This way, it is possible to fine-tune the Assembly code generated by the compiler. The assembler is described in section "The Assembler," later in this chapter.

```
gcc -E hello.c
```

This command will only preprocess the input file. Because the output generated by the preprocessor is rather lengthy and involved, it is therefore discussed separately in the section, "The Preprocessor," which can be found later in this chapter.

Figure 4.1 shows the process by which an executable is obtained.

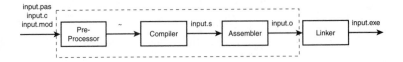

FIGURE 4.1
The compilation process.

Note that no output file has been specified for the precompiler. When the precompiler is used separately from the compiler, it sends its output to screen. This output can, of course, be redirected to a file (gcc -E hello.c >> outputfilename.txt).

A final remark concerning compilers: Most compilers will simply take any intermediate file you throw at them and translate it into an executable. For instance, gcc hello.o -o hello will just link the provided object file and generate an executable, and gcc hello.s -o hello will assemble and link the provided Assembly file into an executable.

The Preprocessor

As you discovered in the previous section, the -E option of the compiler command allows us to use the precompiler separately. Doing its name proud, the preprocessor takes care of several processes before the compiler starts its big task. The following sections describe the main tasks performed by the preprocessor.

Include File Substitution

The #include statements are substituted by the content of the file they specify. The include line from the example

```
#include <stdio.h>
```

will be replaced with the contents of the file stdio.h. Within this file, further includes will be found which in turn will be substituted. This is the reason care should be taken not to define circular includes. If stdio.h were to include myinclude.h and myinclude.h were to again include stdio.h, the preprocessor would be told to substitute indefinitely. Most preprocessors can deal with these kinds of problems and will simply generate an error. It is wise, however, to always use conditional statements when handling includes (see the section "Conditional Substitution," later in this chapter).

The <> characters tell the preprocessor to look for the specified file in a predefined directory. Using double quote characters ("") tells the preprocessor to look in the current directory:

```
#include "myinclude."
```

In practice, you will find that you use double quotes when including the header files you have written yourself and <> for system header files.

Macro Substitution

Macro substitution works in a way which is very similar to include file substitution. When you use a macro, you define a symbolic name (called the macro) for what is in effect a string. The preprocessor hunts down all the macros and replaces them with the strings they represent. This can save the programmer the trouble of typing the string hundreds of times. An often-used macro is the following:

```
#define MAX(A,B) ((A) > (B) ? (A) : (B))
```

Anywhere in the code where you use the macro MAX(variable1, variable2), this code will be substituted by the preprocessor. The compiler will find the following string:

```
((variable1) > (variable2) ? (variable1) : (variable2))
```

Note that this macro happens to look like a function call. The downside to this approach (using a macro instead of a real function) is that the code is found everywhere in the program where the macro is used. The upside is that there is no function call overhead. The use of macros during optimization will be discussed in detail in Chapter 8, "Functions."

Conditional Substitution

The preprocessor can also be used to conditionally substitute pieces of code. This means the preprocessor determines which pieces of code the compiler will get to see (and translate). An example of this with which you are probably familiar is the following conditional statement:

```
#ifndef __HEADERFILENAME__
#define __HEADERFILENAME__
~
#endif
```

This piece of code tells the preprocessor that only if the symbol __HEADERFILENAME__ is not yet defined, it can continue. The next statement the preprocessor encounters is one defining the very same symbol. This means that if the preprocessor encounters the file containing this piece of code again, it will skip the rest of the text until it has passed the #endif statement. When this piece of code can be found in the file myinclude.h, including this file twice will not cause the code represented by the ~ character to be substituted more than once.

Another often-used example of conditional substitution is generating different versions of executables from the same source file:

```
~
a += a + 1;

#ifdef DEBUG
printf("The value of a = %d", a);
#endif

b += a;
~
```

Compiling this piece of code can generate a debug version which will print the value of a onscreen (when #define DEBUG is found somewhere by the preprocessor) or a normal version which does not print a; when DEBUG is defined nowhere in the program. Be sure, however, that the definition of DEBUG is encountered by the preprocessor before any conditional DEBUG statements are encountered.

Symbolic Substitution

Symbolic substitution is basically a simplified macro; again a symbolic name is replaced by a string or a value:

```
#define DEBUG 1
#define FILENAME "input.c"
```

When the preprocessor is used separately, it becomes possible to determine whether compiler errors are generated from within the code or from somewhere in the include file hierarchy. You can study the preprocessor output to determine whether or not the macros are expanded the way they are expected to be.

The Assembler

An assembler is a tool that translates human-understandable mnemonics into microprocessor instructions (executable code). Mnemonics are in fact nothing more than symbolic text representations of those microprocessor instructions. For instance, the mnemonic ADD A,20 (which adds 20 to the value of register A of the microprocessor) will be translated by the assembler into the following numbers: 198 and 20. It should not surprise you to see that microprocessor instructions (or machine instructions) are numbers; the computer memory holds nothing but numbers. This example shows that mnemonics are highly machine dependent, as every mnemonic instruction represents a microprocessor instruction for a very specific microprocessor (the example is taken from Z80 mnemonics). An Assembly program written for a 68000 microprocessor cannot simply be assembled to run on an 80386. The program is not portable and has to be completely rewritten. Another quality of this close proximity to the actual hardware is that Assembly is very useful for optimizing programming routines for speed/footprint.

Listing 4.3 shows a small piece of a mnemonic listing for a 68000 microprocessor:

LISTING 4.3   An 68000 Assembly File

```
       move.l    (a0), d0
loop:  jsr       subroutine
       sub       #1, d0
       cmpi      #400, d0
       bne       loop
       move.l    (a1), d0
```

This example will be fairly easy to read for someone familiar with 68000 mnemonics. However, Assembly listings (programs) tend to become lengthy and involved. Often, the goal of a piece of code does not become apparent until a large part has been studied, because a single higher programming language instruction will be represented by many Assembly instructions. Development time is therefore high and looking for bugs in Assembly listings is quite a challenge. Also, working with Assembly requires the programmer to have a high level of system-specific technical knowledge.

4

**TOOLS AND
LANGUAGES**

In the early days of computer programming (even until the late 1980s), the use of Assembly languages was quite common. High-level languages, such as Pascal or C, were not that common, and their predecessors were slow (in both compiling and executing). The generated code was far from optimal. Nowadays, compilers can often do a far better job of optimizing Assembly than most developers could, so Assembly is only used where software and hardware interact closely. Think of parts of operating systems, such as device drivers, process schedulers, exception handlers and interrupt routines. In practice, when you find Assembly, it is most often embedded within sources of a higher programming language. Listing 4.4 shows the use of Assembly in a C++ listing:

LISTING 4.4   A Listing Mixing 68000 and C/C++

```
void f()
{
    printf("value of a = %d", a);
}

#asm
    label:      jsr         pushregs
                add.l       #1, d0
                rts
#endasm
```

It might surprise you to see that languages can be mixed and matched like this. If so, it will surprise you even more that C and C++ can even be mixed to take advantage of their independent merits; there's more about this in the section "Mixing Languages." Note that mixing Assembly with a higher-level language makes the source less portable because the Assembly will still only work on one specific microprocessor.

In the section "The Compiler," you saw how to make an executable from an Assembly file. It is, however, also possible to generate an object file from an Assembly file. This is done by calling the assembler with the -o option:

```
as hello.s -o hello.o
```

The generated object file can serve as input for the linker, which is the subject of the next section.

The Linker

Using the linker is the final phase in the process of generating an executable program. The linker takes the libraries and object files that are part of the project and links them together.

Often, the linker will also add system libraries and object files to make a valid executable. This might not always seem obvious, but an example will make that clear; because stdio.h is included in the hello.c program, it can use the printf command. This command, however, is not part of some ROM library, so the code implementing the function has to come from somewhere else. This is why the linker will have to add a system library to the executable.

To use the linker separately, use the command

```
ld hello.o -o hello <system options + libraries>
```

The previous sections show how to transform the hello.c program into an executable with a single command and how to break this command up into separate steps. Listing 4.5 is a short example of using the separate steps together to complete the whole process:

LISTING 4.5   Separate Steps to Create an Executable

```
gcc -S hello.c
as hello.s -o hello.o
ld hello.o -o hello <system options + libraries>
```

As expected, the result of this example is the same as that of the command:

```
gcc hello.c -o hello
```

The Make Utility

The Make utility is very closely related to the chain of processes that creates an executable from a higher-level source file. As the previous sections show, you can use a single command to create the executable of the example program hello.c. But this program is simple; it does not use multiple modules or have complex project interdependencies. As programs grow, they are often split into functional modules, use third-party libraries, and so on. Compiling such a program (project) can be made complicated by the interdependencies between modules (and even between source files!). The Make utility aids in checking up on dependencies and recompiling all objects that are affected by a change in one or more source files, making it possible to rebuild the entire software tree with one single command. This section discusses only the most important Make options because there are enough to fill entire chapters.

The Make utility uses an input file (called a *makefile*) that describes the project (program) is has to make.

This makefile defines the project interdependencies to be checked by the utility. Listing 4.6 shows the makefile that can be used for the example program.

LISTING 4.6 A Makefile

```
#This is the makefile for Hello.c

OBJS = hello.o
LIBS =

hello: $(OBJS)
    gcc -o hello $(OBJS) $(LIBS)
```

You can now build the example program by simply typing make on the command line when the current directory contains the makefile. It is, of course, possible to put the project definition in a file with a different name, but the Make utility then has to be told explicitly which file to look for:

```
make -f mymakefile
```

This is useful when you want to create more than one project definition in the same directory (perhaps to build different versions of the software from the same directory of source files).

Let's look at Listing 4.6 line by line and see what is happening:

Line 1: This simply is a comment; it could have been any text that might be useful.

Line 2: This defines the objects needed for the target; it actually defines a variable OBJS which will be used in the makefile from now on.

Line 3: This defines the variable LIBS, which again can be used in the remainder of the makefile. Because the hello program is so simple, it is not actually needed.

Line 5: This is the definition of a rule that states that the target hello depends on the content of the variable OBJS.

Line 6: This line actually lists the command to build the target. There can be multiple command lines, as long as they always start with a tab.

For more makefile commands, you are referred to the appropriate manuals. and the section "The Profiler," later in this chapter, where a slightly more complex makefile is explained.

The Debugger

Bug searching is an activity every programmer will have to do sooner or later. And when saturating the sources with print statements has finally lost its charm, the next logical step is using the debugger. The power of the debugger lies in the fact that it allows the user to follow the path of execution as the program runs. And at any time during the execution, the user can decide to look at (and even change) the value of variables, pointers, stacks, objects, and so on.

The only precondition is that the executable contains special debugging information so that the debugger can make connections between the executable and the sources; it is more useful to look at the source code while debugging a program than to be presented with the machine instructions or the Assembly listings. Adding debug information will make the executable larger, so when a program is ready to be released, the whole project should be rebuilt once more but without debug information.

Adding debug information to the executable can be done by adding the -g option to the compile command:

```
gcc -g hello.c -o hello
```

The generated executable can now be run by the debugger. To start the GNU debugger, type

```
gdb hello
```

Countless debugging tools are available, but the terminology used is generally the same. The following sections provide an overview of important terms.

Run

Run starts the program execution. It is important to note that run will continue running the program until the end or until a breakpoint (see "Breakpoint," later in this chapter) is encountered. In general you set breakpoints and then run the program, or single step (see "Step") into the program to start debugging activities.

Step

A step executes a single source file statement. As opposed to run, a step executes only one statement and then waits for further instructions. Executing part of a program this way is called *single-stepping*.

Step Into/Step Out Of

When single-stepping through a program, you can decide between seeing a call to a function as a single instruction (and stepping, in effect, over the function call) or directing the debugger to step into the function and debug it. Once inside a function, it is possible to skip the rest of the statements of the function and return to the place where it was called. In that case, you decide to step out of the function.

Breakpoint

A breakpoint is a predefined point in a source file where you want the debugger to stop running and wait for your instructions. You generally set a breakpoint on a statement close to where you think the program will do something wrong. You will then run the program and wait for it to reach the breakpoint. At that point, the debugger will stop and you can check variables and single-step (see "Step") through the rest of the suspicious code.

Conditional Breakpoint

A conditional breakpoint is a breakpoint that is seen by the debugger only when a certain condition has been satisfied ($i > 10$ or $Stop \mathrel{!=} TRUE$). Instead of simply stopping at an instruction, you can tell the debugger to stop at that instruction only when a certain variable reaches a certain value. For example, say a routine goes wrong after 100 iterations of a loop. You would need 100 run commands to get to that program state using a normal breakpoint. With the conditional breakpoint, you can tell the debugger to skip the first 100 iterations.

Continue

Sometimes this is also called *Run*. The continue is a run from whatever place in the code you might have reached with the debugger. Say you stop on a breakpoint and take a few single steps, you can decide to continue to the next breakpoint (or the end of the program if the debugger encounters no more breakpoints).

Function Stack/Calling Stack

The calling stack is the list of functions that was called to arrive in the program state that you are examining. When the debugger arrives at a breakpoint it might be useful to know what the path of execution was. You might be able to arrive in function A() via two different calling stacks: Main() -> CheckPassword() -> A() and Main()->ChangePassword()-> A(). Sometimes it is even possible to switch to the program state of a previous call, making it possible to examine variables before the routine which is under investigation is called. By going back to CheckPassword() or even Main() you can see, for instance, what went wrong with the parameters received by A().

Watch

A watch is basically a view on a piece of memory. During debugging, it is possible to check the value of variables, pointers, arrays, and even pieces of memory by putting a watch on a specific memory address. Some debuggers will even allow you to watch the internal state of the microprocessor (registers and so on).

Effects When Debugging

A popular philosopher once remarked that it is impossible to observe anything without influencing that which is being observed, and sadly this is also true when debugging programs. A program that is being debugged will not behave exactly the same as when it is running normally. One reason for this is the fact that the binary image is different; because of the addition of debug information, the variables, constants, and even functions will reside at different relative addresses within the executable. This means that overwriting memory boundaries and using corrupted (function) pointers will have a different effect during debugging. The bug is still there, but its effect might be more (or even less) noticeable. Another reason why a program can behave differently during a debugging session is that single stepping through the code affects its timing. This is especially important to remember when debugging multi-threaded programs. But even during the running of the program, the timing will be slightly different because of the debugging overhead.

A final remark concerning debugging is the suggestion of using the debugger to do preventive maintenance, as mentioned in Chapter 3, "Modifying an Existing System." By single stepping through a few iterations of a complex routine, bugs might be found before they have a chance to go out into the world and celebrate.

The Profiler

The profiler is the most important tool related to performance optimizations. This tool can determine how often each function of a program is called, how much time is spent in each function, and how this time relates (in percentages) to the other functions. In determining which parts of a program are the most-important candidates for optimization, such a tool is invaluable. There is no point in gaining optimizations in functions which are not on the critical path, and it is a waste of time to optimize functions which are seldom called or are fairly optimal to begin with. With the profiler, you look for functions that are called often and that are relatively slow. Any time won in these functions will make the overall program noticeably faster. An important side note is that one should be careful in trying to optimize user input functions. These will mostly just seem slow because they are waiting for some kind of user interaction!

As with the debugger, the use of the profiler warrants some preparations made to the executable file. Follow these steps to use the profiler:

1. Compile the executable with the -pg option so the profiler functions are added. The command gcc -pg <source-name>.c -o <exe-name> will do this.

2. Run the program so the profiler output is generated. It should be clear that only data on functions that are called during this run will be profiled. This also implies that for the best results you need to use test cases that are as close to field use as possible.

3. Run the profile tool to interpret the output of the run.

Listing 4.7 will be run through the specified steps. Note that the new example program used is more interesting for the profiler.

LISTING 4.7   Program to Profile

```c
#include <stdio.h>

long mul_int(int a, int b)
{
        long i;
        long j=0;

        for (i = 0 ; i < 10000000; i++)
           j += (a * b);

        return(j);
}

long mul_double(double a, double b)
{
        long i;
        double j=0.0;

        for (i = 0 ; i < 10000000; i++)
           j += (a * b);

        return((long)j);
}

int main(int argc, char *argv[])
{
        printf("Testing Int    : %ld\n", mul_int(1, 2));
        printf("Testing Double : %ld\n", mul_double(1, 2));
        exit(0);
}
```

This program contains two almost-identical functions. Both functions perform a multiplication; however, they use different variable types to calculate with: mul_int uses integers and mul_double uses doubles. The profiler can now show us which type is fastest to calculate with.

Compile this program with the following command line:

gcc -pg test.c -o test

And run it with the command line:

test

The following output should appear onscreen:

```
Testing Int       : 20000000
Testing Double    : 20000000
```

The output file that was generated during the run is called gmon.out. It contains the results of the profile action and can be viewed with the following command line:

```
gprof test > test.out
```

This command will redirect the output of the profiler to yet another file called test.out, which is a normal text file that can be viewed with any editor. Because the test.out file contains a lot of information and explanation, only the most-important part is shown in Listing 4.8 and discussed in this section.

LISTING 4.8 Profile Output

```
Each sample counts as 0.01 seconds.
  %     cumulative    self              self     total
 time     seconds    seconds  calls   us/call   us/call   name
62.50      0.10       0.10      1    100000.00  100000.00  mul_double
37.50      0.16       0.06      1     60000.00   60000.00  mul_int
 0.00      0.16       0.00      1         0.00  160000.00  main
```

% time	the percentage of the total running time of the program used by this function.
cumulative seconds	a running sum of the number of seconds accounted for by this function and those listed above it.
self seconds	the number of seconds accounted for by this function alone. This is the major sort for this listing.
calls	the number of times this function was invoked, if this function is profiled, else blank.
self ms/call	the average number of milliseconds spent in this function per call, if this function is profiled, else blank.
total ms/call	the average number of milliseconds spent in this function and its descendents per call, if this function is profiled, else blank.

LISTING 4.8 Continued

```
name                the name of the function.  This is the minor sort
                    for this listing. The index shows the location of
                    the function in the gprof listing. If the index is
                    in parenthesis it shows where it would appear in
                    the gprof listing if it were to be printed.
```

The first column tells us that 62.5% of runtime was spent in function mul_double() and only 37.5% in the function mul_int(); the value for main seems to be negligible, and this is not so surprising as the main function only calls two other functions. The numbers are reflected again in column 3 but this time in absolute seconds. Note that the output is sorted by the third column, so it is fairly easy to find the most time-consuming function. It is up to the developer to decide whether this usage of time is acceptable or not.

Listing 4.9 shows what the steps for profiling look like when transformed into a makefile.

LISTING 4.9 Makefile with Different Targets

```
#This is the makefile for test.c

PROG    = ./test
PROFOPT = -pg
PROFCMD = gprof
COPT    = -O2
OBJS    = $(PROG).o
LDLIBS  = -L/usr/local/lib/


test:   $(OBJS)
        gcc $(COPT) -o $(PROG) $(OBJS) $(LDLIBS)

profile:$(OBJS)
        gcc $(COPT) $(PROFOPT) $(PROG).c -o $(PROG) $(LDLIBS)
        $(PROG)
        $(PROFCMD) $(PROG)

clean:
        rm $(PROG).o gmon.out $(PROG)

execute:
        $(PROG)
```

The makefile presented here has different targets, depending on how the Make is invoked:

make and make test	Generates a normal executable as shown in the previous sections
make clean	Removes all generated object files and profiler output
make execute	Runs the generated executable
make profile	Creates the profile output (hint: to store this in a file, redirect it again)

As with the debugger, the profiler will influence the program it profiles. This time, however, the implications are not as far reaching because all functions will be influenced almost exactly the same way. The relations between the functions are therefore useable.

The Runtime Checker

The runtime checker is used to detect irregularities during program execution. As with the profiler, the runtime checker will add routines to your program that gather and output information on your program while it is running. Again, it gathers information only on parts of the program that are actually activated during the run, so the test cases are very important here also.

Typical problems a runtime checker will detect are

- Memory leaks (memory is allocated but never released)
- Overflow of the stack (overly recursive function calls)
- File descriptors left open
- Reading from or writing to released memory
- Releasing already released memory
- Reading or writing beyond the bounds of an array or structure
- Using uninitialized memory
- Reading or writing via null pointers

Quite a few commercial runtime checkers are available, and there are freeware checkers available also: Electric Fence, mcheck, and mpr.

The Static Source Code Analyzer

Both the runtime checker and the debugger help you find bugs and irregularities while your program is running. This means you generally have a high level of control over the checking procedure (changing variable values during execution in the debugger, for instance), but you do only check the parts of the program that are activated. The static Source Code Analyzer differs in this respect. In essence, it looks at the source code (all the source code!) and remarks on constructions that it finds suspicious. This is very much like the task the compiler performs, and a lot of analyzer functionality can in fact be invoked by raising the warning levels of most compilers, but the analyzer goes beyond syntactical correctness of the code.

The following example will pass the compilation process with flying colors because it is syntactically correct; in fact, you might have even written this listing on purpose:

```
for (i = 0; i < 10; i++);
    DoWop();
```

But it is more that likely that the ; at the end of the first line was unintentional and you wanted the DoWop() function to be called 10 times instead of just once. The Static Source Code Analyzer would remark on this. Other constructions the Analyzer can warn us about are

- Program statements which are never reached:

```
{
    ~
    return pResult;
    pResult++;
}
```

- Variables which are used before being initialized:

```
int c;
return c++;
```

- Logical expressions with a constant value:

```
if (a = 1) {~}
```

It is also possible to compile your program with the -Wall option (warnings all) to get analyzer type functionality:

```
gcc -Wall hello.c -o hello
```

Beware that the output from the analyzer can be quite overwhelming, and not all its remarks will be justified. You will have to evaluate each remark on its own merits.

Your Own Test Program

One of the most important development tools you can use is most likely your own test program. Only this piece of software can be equipped with all the information needed for a good, non-generic test. It should be created early in the development process and be able to call all I/O functions of your program and evaluate all returned data/program states. Often this last part is forgotten, but it is as useful, if not more useful, to test the reaction to faulty data and conditions as it is to test whether the program can work under perfect conditions. Where possible, test programs should be able to run automatically, without needing constant user interaction, and even use a mechanism for regression tests (some kind of scripting, perhaps). The idea behind this is that when you add new functionality to a program, you should *always* retest *all* the old functionality. If it is possible to do this at night via an automatic script, all the better.

Other advantages to automatic testing:

- Running a test twice will guarantee it is conducted the exact same way; this means incurred problems are highly reproducible, which is important in finding out if a new build has solved the identified problem.
- Automatic testing can take place overnight and no development time needs to be invested.
- The test output can be logged and compared (automatically) to other test outputs; this is ideal to check regression tests.
- Tests can easily be expanded to include new test cases.

There are, of course, tools to aid you in creating test applications, but there is nothing wrong with spending time on writing a C or C++ program. The invested time will definitely pay itself back.

Optimizing with Help from the Compiler

It is possible to have the compiler perform optimizations on the executable code it generates. This is a very cheap form of optimization as no extra development effort is needed for finding places to optimize and performing the actual code optimizations. Only compiling the sources will possibly take longer, but this extra time is negligible. How and when to instruct the compiler to perform optimizations will be explained in the following sections.

Optimizing with Compiler Optimization Options

Most compilers will perform only basic code translation optimizations when invoked without specific optimization instructions. It is possible, however, to instruct compilers to do more optimization on the output they generate. For this the option -On is commonly used, where n is the level of optimization (-O3 will perform more optimizations than -O2 and so on). The exact range of n for the GNU compiler depends on the version used. The lowest level of optimization is of course obtained by completely omitting the -O compiler option. One compilation instruction for generating an optimized executable from the example program of the beginning of this chapter is

```
gcc -O2 myfile.c -o myfile
```

Before looking closer at what kind of optimizations the compiler can actually make (see the section "A Closer Look at What Actually Happens," later in this chapter), this section will explain why compilers do not perform the maximum level of optimization per default. Intuitively, you would expect that the more the compiler optimizes, the better off you are, but there are some practical reasons why this is not always the case.

Reasons why the compiler does not perform maximum optimization by default:

- The more the compiler optimizes, the more difficult debugging becomes. The compiler is able to combine segments of code which have a strong logical connection—for instance, segments that result in identical groupings of machine code. During debugging, it will seem as if single stepping causes the processor to jump from code segment to code segment at random.

- Compiler optimizations carry a certain amount of risk. In optimizing, the compiler will attempt to combine or skip as many code segments as possible. It can happen that the compiler does not correctly assess what the programmer is attempting to do and optimizes something important out of existence. For example, variables which are initialized but never used will probably be removed.

- Optimizing execution speed of a generated executable can cause this executable to become larger. Some optimizations make the generated executable faster but also larger, this happens when function calls are expanded (see Chapter 8). The compiler cannot assess easily where footprint and speed optimization priorities lie. For this it needs to be instructed. More about these instructions can be found in the following section "A Closer Look at What Actually Happens."

Taking into account the dangers specified in the preceding list, it becomes apparent that it is a good idea to make sure a program actually works before turning on the optimization option (for instance, on the release build), especially when a high level of optimization is attempted. The optimized executable will, of course, have to be tested again to evaluate whether any functionality was damaged and whether the program still adheres to footprint and performance requirements.

A Closer Look at What Actually Happens

The compiler can offer substantial help in optimizing executable code, especially where performance of the code is concerned. This section walks through some examples of optimizations made by the compiler and shows exactly what the compiler has done. First, here is a list of all the optimization options for the G++ and GCC compilers:

```
Optimization Options GCC and G++
                -fcaller-saves -fcse-follow-jumps -fcse-skip-blocks
                -fdelayed-branch -felide-constructors
                -fexpensive-optimizations -ffast-math -ffloat-store
                -fforce-addr -fforce-mem -finline-functions
                -fkeep-inline-functions -fmemoize-lookups
                -fno-default-inline -fno-defer-pop
                -fno-function-cse -fno-inline -fno-peephole
                -fomit-frame-pointer -frerun-cse-after-loop
                -fschedule-insns -fschedule-insns2
                -fstrength-reduce -fthread-jumps -funroll-all-loops
                -funroll-loops -O -O2 -O3
```

This list can be obtained on UNIX via the command line

```
man gcc
```

This section presents in-depth examples of what happens when you use several different optimization options. For an explanation of all the options, you are referred to the UNIX man pages on gcc.

To illustrate the optimization steps of the compiler, this section presents several Assembly files generated by the g++ compiler. It is not actually necessary to understand the Assembly code line-by-line to appreciate what happens as the general concepts will be explained in the accompanying texts.

Listing 4.10 presents the example program which is used in this section.

LISTING 4.10 Example Program for Compiler Optimization: test.cc

```
int main (int argc, char *argv[])
{
  int i, j=0;

  for (i = 1; i <= 10; i++)
    j+=i;

  exit(j);
}
```

4

This program simply adds the numbers 1–10 during a loop and returns the result (55) on exit.

Listing 4.11 shows the Assembly code generated without any optimizations turned on (g++ -S test.cc).

LISTING 4.11 Generated Assembly for Listing 4.10 Without Compiler Optimization: test.s (Not Optimized)

```
.file    "test.cc"
gcc2_compiled.:
___gnu_compiled_cplusplus:
    .def    ___main;    .scl    2;    .type    32;    .endef
.text
    .align 4
.globl _main
    .def    _main;    .scl    2;    .type    32;    .endef
_main:
    pushl %ebp
    movl %esp,%ebp
    subl $16,%esp
    call ___main
    movl $0,-8(%ebp)
    movl $1,-4(%ebp)
    .p2align 4,,7
L2:
    cmpl $10,-4(%ebp)
    jle L5
    jmp L3
    .p2align 4,,7
L5:
    movl -4(%ebp),%eax
    addl %eax,-8(%ebp)
L4:
    incl -4(%ebp)
    jmp L2
    .p2align 4,,7
L3:
    movl -8(%ebp),%eax
    pushl %eax
    call _exit
    addl $4,%esp
    xorl %eax,%eax
    jmp L1
    .p2align 4,,7
L1:
    movl %ebp,%esp
    popl %ebp
    ret
    .def    _exit;    .scl    3;    .type    32;    .endef
```

Listing 4.12 shows the Assembly code generated with optimization turned on; level -O2 looks like this (g++ -O2 -S test.cc).

LISTING 4.12   Generated Assembly for Listing 4.10 with Level 2 Compiler Optimization: test.s (Optimized with -O2) by gcc

```
.file    "test.cc"
gcc2_compiled.:
___gnu_compiled_cplusplus:
    .def    ___main;   .scl   2;   .type   32;   .endef
.text
    .align 4
.globl _main
    .def    _main;   .scl   2;   .type   32;   .endef
_main:
    pushl %ebp
    movl %esp,%ebp
    call ___main
    xorl %edx,%edx
    movl $1,%eax
    .p2align 4,,7
L5:
    addl %eax,%edx
    incl %eax
    cmpl $10,%eax
    jle L5
    pushl %edx
    call _exit
    .def    _exit;   .scl   3;   .type   32;   .endef
```

Even though this is a small, trivial program, you can already see substantial differences in efficiency and footprint. The optimized version of the example program is clearly much shorter and, when you look at the loop (the code between L2 and L3 in the first Assembly listing, and L5 in the second Assembly listing), you see a noticeable decrease in the number of compare instructions (cmp) and jumps (jmp, jle). In this example, the optimized code is, in fact, easier to read than the original code, but this is certainly not always the case. Also, note that -O2 takes care of several kinds of optimization in a single compilation.

More can be done with this example. There is a loop in the program and, having seen the available optimization options at the beginning of this section, you have undoubtedly spotted the option -funroll-loops.

Unrolling loops is a technique to make software faster by doing more steps inside a loop and doing fewer actual loop iterations. The following example demonstrates this principle:

Normal Loop	Unrolled Loop
execute loop ten times	execute loop 2 times
step A	step A
end loop	step A
	step A
	step A
	step A
	end loop

Both loops perform step A ten times. The unrolled code is definitely larger, but it is also faster because the overhead incurred by looping around (checking the end condition and jumping back to the beginning) is performed less often, thus taking up a smaller percentage of loop-execution time (Chapter 8 describes loops in more detail). Listing 4.13 shows what unrolling loops can do for the example program (g++ -O2 -funroll-loops -S test.cc).

LISTING 4.13 Generated Assembly for Listing 4.10 with Further Compiler Optimization by gcc: test.s (Optimized with -O2 -funroll-loops)

```
.file    "test.cc"
gcc2_compiled.:
___gnu_compiled_cplusplus:
    .def    ___main;    .scl    2;    .type    32;    .endef
.text
    .align 4
.globl _main
    .def    _main;    .scl    2;    .type    32;    .endef
_main:
    pushl %ebp
    movl %esp,%ebp
    call ___main
    pushl $55
    call _exit
    .def    _exit;    .scl    3;    .type    32;    .endef
```

Apparently, this was a very good choice. The generated file is now pretty small; notice that the loop has, in fact, completely disappeared! The only evidence remaining is the placement of the number 55 (the result of the ex-loop) on the stack. This means the compiler performed the loop during compilation and placed only the result in the generated code. This is possible only because the result of the loop is known at compile time; there was, in fact, a hidden constant in the program.

It seems that using compiler optimizations can already have benefits before you even begin thinking long and hard about what to do. Playing around with the other optimization options found at the beginning of this section will give more insight into what the compiler is willing and able to do.

The Language for the Job

Before implementation can start, an important decision needs to be made: Which programming language is actually going to be used? The choice of programming language will affect both performance and footprint. All programming languages have their own characteristics, their pros and cons, so choosing the language which fits the goals of your project best is therefore all but trivial. Although this book is essentially about optimizing C and C++, this section provides an overview of considerations to make when choosing between the programming languages that are currently most popular. The best optimization to make in C or C++ is perhaps not using it when another language will do better.

Assembly, C, C++, or...?

Before weighing specific language characteristics, it is important to analyze the project and its goals. It is impossible to say which programming language characteristics are positive or negative before you know what you want to do with the language. For instance, it makes no sense to say that C++ is *better* than Java simply because it allows the programmer more control over what happens inside the software. The statement holds true when talking about writing driver software or large and complicated applications, but quickly setting up an Internet tool which can be run on all hardware platforms without recompilation and which is never allowed to crash is a different story entirely. The following list contains questions that need to be asked to determine which qualities a project expects from a programming language. It also takes into account the environment in which the project is set up.

- *Approximate size of the software to be developed.* Is this going to be a *small* tool, a full-fledged application, or a large, multimodular project? The larger a program gets, the more complicated maintenance work and updates will be. A large project therefore needs a language that allows for readable lines of code and good levels of abstraction. The design should be transparent in the program. For small applications or tools, this is less important as implementers can *oversee* a much greater proportion of the project.

- *Available programming language knowledge.* This is a budget consideration because knowledge comes at a price. When none of the project team members has experience with a certain language, it might prove to be cheaper to choose a better-known language than sending everybody to courses or hiring external implementers.

- *Available software resources.* In the same vein as the previous point, you should consider not only knowledge gained on programming languages, but also the built-up software library. Do you have a lot of software parts you can use from other/previous projects? If so, probably little cost will be incurred when using those. When this is compared to rewriting the existing parts in the new language, a different cost picture emerges. You also need to consider development tools (compilers, debuggers, simulation software, and hardware) and the knowledge of using them, as well as existing documentation.

- *Available development time.* Some languages simply take up more development time than others. Think of printing a string onscreen either with BASIC or with Assembly. This involves not only the number of code lines that need to be typed to implement a certain action, but also the complexity of performing certain actions in a specific language. This extra time is incurred not only in thinking up and implementing a solution, but also during debugging and testing. Another time consideration is the amount of help and ready-made solutions that come with the different languages. BASIC and C++ come with a range of functional libraries, whereas Assembly comes with whatever you can find around you.

- *Target platform.* When this decision has already been made, one might find that the choice of programming language is perhaps artificially limited. This can be because of the availability of quality compilers for that hardware platform or even complexity of the hardware itself. Some systems simply do not invite you to write closely hardware-related solutions.

- *Future project development.* When you expect to upgrade the system and making new software versions in future, it is inadvisable to choose a programming language that is already becoming unpopular. When decreasing support (in the shape of compilers, third-party solutions, technical documentation, and so on) is given for a programming language, it is going to be increasingly difficult to maintain development in future. Similarly, it is then also inadvisable to *bet* on a new language for which there is not yet a lot of support, one that has not proven itself in the field, or one for which the syntax is not even completely standardized. Another advantage of using a more popular language is the increased chance of finding programmers in future to replace or strengthen the current development team. An entirely different, but no less important, future development issue is syntax readability. When you expect to be working on a system for an extended period of time, you want to choose a language that is easily readable and thus extendible. These risks lessen as the need for future development decreases. For one-time projects, it matters only if the current compiler and available documentation and human resources suffice.

- *Desired level of portability.* The question here is whether you are writing software for one specific target platform (be it embedded software or not) or whether you expect different hardware configurations to have to execute the software. With most programming languages, you have to recompile the sources to get an executable that runs on a system with a different microprocessor. This does not have to be a problem. Only system-specific parts used might need to be reinvented or bought for new platforms. Other languages are not simply ported. Trying to port the source might even be similar to rewriting the whole program. Clearly you have to decide in advance if the language will have the characteristics desired at *porting* time.

Table 4.1 shows how the characteristics of the programming languages C, C++, Pascal, (Visual) Basic, Java, and Assembly compare to each other:

TABLE 4.1   Programming Language Characteristics

Characteristics	C	C++	Pasc.	VB	Java	Asm.
Portability	++	++	+	-	+++	-
Speed of development	++	++	++	+++	+++	-
Ease of update/ enhancement	+	++	+	++	+++	-
Availability of knowledge	++	++	+	++	++	-
Standard solutions	+	++	+	++	+++	-
Code readability	++	+++	++	+++	+++	-
Possibility complex design	++	+++	+	+	+	-
Execution speed	++	++	+	-	-	+++
Execution footprint	+++	+	+	-	-	+++
Ease of optimization	++	++	+	-	-	+++
Time to learn language	++	+	++	++	++	-

4

TOOLS AND LANGUAGES

From this table you can draw the following conclusions on when to use which language:

- C

    The C programming language seems to be doing quite well in most categories. Only in the categories "complexity of design" and "ease of update/enhancement" does it look like there are better choices around these days. This is because C was basically developed before the object-oriented (OO) approach became so popular. This means that C is still an accessible, universally applicable language, as long as the projects do not become too large or too complex. When large numbers of developers need to update big chunks of each other's code, C can, in fact, easily become a mess.

    This is why C is a good choice for most kind of applications, as long as the programs do not become too large or complex.

- C++

    The C++ programming language has characteristics very similar to those of C, unsurprisingly, with the exception of being more readable and maintainable when the programs become larger or the development process is more dynamic. The price that is paid for this is the fact that C++ generally has a larger footprint and takes longer for programmers to learn, especially when they are expected to use it well.

    This is why C++ is a good choice for all kinds of applications, as long as the footprint is not too tight.

- Pascal

    The Pascal programming language is easy to learn, reasonably fast, and quite strict in runtime type checking. This programming language does have a few strange quirks that might have to be programmed around though (strings are limited to 255 characters by default, for example). Also, there are quite a few flavors of Pascal around, which make portability less than obvious. Pascal imitates C and C++ in characteristics, but seems to be less popular at the moment.

    This is why Pascal is seen as a good all-arounder, but watch out for future support.

- (Visual) Basic

    The Visual Basic programming language comes with a plethora of preimplemented functionality, and it is easy to learn, very stable in use, and has low development times. It is not too fast in execution, however, and the footprint can become somewhat large because of the extra software needed to run an executable (libraries, interpreter).

    This is why (Visual) Basic is a good choice for quickly building programs, user interfaces, and prototypes that aren't time critical (execution slowness is even a plus when writing those first prototypes).

- Java

    The Java programming language is easy to learn, has a lot of standard solutions, is robust in usage, has a relatively fast development time and, most importantly, is portable, even without recompilation. The price paid for this is that it is not that fast nor is it optimal in footprint.

Conclusion: Non–time-critical, portable applications; Internet software, downloadable executables, prototypes.

- Assembly

  The Assembly programming language is prominently fast, small, and easily optimizable, if used expertly. Development times, as learning times, are quite high, and this language does not lend itself to writing large programs with a complex design.

  Conclusion: Small, time-critical programs or program parts. Drivers, interrupt routines, close hardware interaction programs.

Two final remarks on choosing a programming language:

Remember that developers work better with languages they like. A developer using his favorite language will enjoy his work more and is prone to putting extra effort into producing quality software.

In some cases, it is possible, even advisable, to try to mix different programming languages. The next section discusses this in detail.

Mixing Languages

This section describes ways of mixing programming languages, allowing the choice of beneficial language characteristics to be taken on a lower or more modular level—per library or program module, for instance. Before unnecessary complicating matters, however, determine whether you actually need the different language segments to communicate within a single executable file. If not, you can opt for easier, external communication between components created from different languages. Think of using files, pipes, COM/CORBA, or network communication protocols (TCP/IP can also be used between two programs or processes that run on the same computer). For example, a program generated from Turbo Pascal could write data to a file that, in turn, is read by a program running on a Java engine. Similarly, as in Listing 4.14, a C program could route its output to STDOUT which is captured by a C++ program reading from STDIN.

LISTING 4.14 Routing Data from a C-Compiled Source to a C++-Compiled Source using an External File

```
/*
 C:
*/
void Send(char * buffer)
```

LISTING 4.14 Continued

```
{
    printf("%s", buffer);
}

//
// C++:
//
void Communicator::Read(char & buffer)
{
    cin >> buffer;
}
```

Using this kind of external communication does away with the need for more complex, in-executable communication. There are some cons to external communication to keep in mind, though:

- It is considerably slower than in-executable communication.
- It is dependent on the performance and availability of the external medium (disk, hard drive, network drive, and so on).
- Locking problems for read/write actions can be quite invisible and difficult to solve.

For some problem domains, then, it is necessary to look for in-executable solutions. This section looks at two mixing techniques closely related to optimizing C and C++: mixing C and C++ and mixing C (or C++) with Assembly.

Mixing C and C++

This example of mixing C with C++ takes a C object containing a single function and links it with a C++ program. The C++ program contains a main function that calls the linked C function. The C object looks like the code in Listing 4.15.

LISTING 4.15 A Simple C Program my_c.c

```
#include <stdio.h>

void my_c_fn()
{
    printf("It's 'C' that we're talking!\n");
}
```

As this object does not have a main function, there is no point in trying to create an executable. Therefore, create an object file using the command

```
gcc -c my_c.c
```

The result of this command is the file my_c.o.

Listing 4.16 shows the C++ program that will use the C object.

LISTING 4.16   Invoking C Functions from C++—my_cpp.cpp

```
#include <streams.h>

extern "C" void my_c_fn();              // declare our C function

int main(int argc, char *argv[])
{
    cout << "We're in C++ now!" << endl;
    my_c_fn();
}
```

Create an executable containing both the C++ and C functionality by compiling the file with the command

```
g++ my_cpp.cpp my_c.o -o my_cpp
```

Note that both files need to be located in the same directory for the build to work.

When you run the generated executable (my_cpp) the following output will be displayed:

```
We're in C++ now!
It's 'C' that we're talking!
```

It is possible to incorporate C functions in C++ by declaring them as external. Moreover, you do not have to declare every single function as external, as in Listing 4.17. Instead, you can declare a whole (source) file external in one go.

LISTING 4.17   A File of C Functions for C++

```
#ifdef __cplusplus
extern "C" {
#endif

/* The C-functions here... */


#ifdef __cplusplus
}
#endif
```

4

TOOLS AND LANGUAGES

Now let's look at how to tackle Assembly.

Mixing C/C++ and Assembly

Some C compilers allow the use of Assembly statements in the source code, effectively mixing C and Assembly within a single source file (Aztec C, Turbo C, GNU C, and so on). This use of Assembly statements within other programming languages is called *inline Assembly*. To notify the compiler that it should switch to parsing Assembly, a keyword is used. Depending on the compiler, the keyword will be something like asm, #asm, or asm(code). It is possible that the compiler also needs an extra option to ensure it will recognize the Assembly statements.

Turbo C example of mixing C and Assembly:

```
mul(int a, b)
{
    asm    mov ax, word ptr 4[bp]
    asm    word ptr 6[bp]
}
```

gcc example of mixing C and Assembly:

```
void do_nothing()
{
    asm("nop");
}
```

gcc allows only a single Assembly statement per line so a function with multiple lines looks like Listing 4.18.

LISTING 4.18   Multiple Inline Assembly Lines Within a C++ Source for gcc

```
#include <stdio.h>

void change_xyz (int x, int y)
{
   int z = 3;

   printf("x.y.z %d %d %d\n", x, y, z);
   asm("
       movl $4,8(%ebp)
       movl $5,12(%ebp)
       movl $6,12(%esp)
   ");
   printf("x.y.z %d %d %d\n", x, y, z);
}
```

LISTING 4.18 Continued

```
int main(int argc, char *argv[])
{
    change_xyz(1,2);
}
```

This program can be compiled with the command:

```
gcc asm_examp.cpp -o asm_examp
```

Although small, this example does a number of interesting things. The function change_xyz() will change the value of x and y via the "base pointer", and the value of z (created locally) via the "stack pointer." Note that line 10, movl $6, 12(%esp) can be replaced by movl $6, -4(%esp), which does the same. The result of executing this program is the output

```
x.y.z 1 2 3
x.y.z 4 5 6
```

But what does all that %ebp and %esp stuff actually mean? It all has to do with the way of accessing the variables in Assembly. As the variables x and y are passed to the function by value, they reside on the stack in the order in which they are declared—from left to right, first x and then y. You get to the stack via the base pointer, which points to the memory address eight bytes below the first variable. Where you say *x* in C, you have to say *8(%ebp)*. And *y* in this example becomes *12(%ebp)*. Note that the variables are placed four bytes apart as the integer size is four bytes.

The variable *z* is a local variable and is placed under the base pointer, *-4(%ebp)*. If there had been a second local variable (*int z, q*) this second variable would be placed directly after *x*, so *q* would be *-8(%ebp)*. Refer to chapter 8, "Functions," for more detail.

Now let's look at what happens to variables which are passed by reference. The reference variables are, in fact, placed on the stack exactly the same way as the variables that are passed by value. So the following example

```
void TestObject::PassByRef(int & a){..}
```

locates a reference to a at *8(%ebp)*. However, because this is still a reference, you need to read the value of this address to find the address of the actual object (a in this case). The statement a = 5 thus becomes

```
asm("
movl 8(%ebp), %eax
movl $5, (%eax)
")
```

%esp has not been mentioned yet though. Similar to the base pointer used in the explanations, *%esp* is a pointer to the stack. The only difference is that esp and ebp point to different positions within the stack. It is left as an exercise to the reader to determine the difference between esp and ebp; you already know that -4(%ebp) is equal to 12(%esp).

The Assembly statements used as inline Assembly do not have to be written completely from scratch. Instead, you can ask the compiler to generate an Assembly listing for you (gcc -S). This way, you can write a first setup of a function in C or C++, have the compiler translate it, and reuse the generated Assembly in the source files. This process allows you to make optimizations to generated Assembly with the added advantage that the optimizations will not be lost the next time you compile your sources!

Remember, though, that the use of inline Assembly will make your sources less portable because the Assembly statements are written for one specific processor (not, however, one specific operating system, this depends on whether you use OS calls). The Assembly used in this chapter, for example, will run only on 80x86 compatible processors.

Inline Assembly in Developer Studio

As the examples are slightly different when using Microsoft's Developer Studio C++ compiler, this section briefly highlights the main differences.

The inline Assembly keyword Developer Studio is __asm. Assembly statements can be written individually when preceded by the keyword

```
__asm mov eax,2 ; move the number 2
__asm add eax,2 ; add the number 2
```

or even

```
__asm mov eax,2     __asm add eax,2
```

Assembly statements can also be grouped with a single keyword:

```
__asm
{
        __asm mov eax,2 ; move the number 2
        __asm add eax,2 ; add the number 2
}
```

Referring to function parameters is child's play as the symbolic names can simply be used inside the Assembly code as in Listing 4.19.

LISTING 4.19 Referring to Function Parameters from In-lined Assembly Within a C++ Source for DeveloperStudio

```
int DoWop(int dow, int op)
{
        __asm
        {
                mov eax, dow    ; retrieve dow
                add eax, op     ; retrieve op
                ; leave result in eax to be returned.
        }
}
```

The C/C++ call int a = DoWop(1,2); will now result in the freshly created variable a receiving the value 3.

Summary

This chapter discussed preliminaries of working on actual code optimizations. It introduced development and optimization tools and discussed the importance of choosing the correct programming language for a project.

The tools discussed were

- The compiler tool which transforms a program written in a high-level programming language into an executable binary file

- The preprocessor tool that takes care of several processes before the compiler starts its big task

- The assembler tool that translates human understandable mnemonics into microprocessor instructions (executable code)

- The linker tool that takes all the libraries and object files you have created and links them together

- The Make utility tool that aids in checking up on dependencies and recompiling all objects that are effected by a change in one or more source files

- The Debugger tool that allows the user to follow the path of execution as the program runs

- The Profiler tool that determines how often each function of a program is called, how much time is spent in each function, and how this time relates (in percentages) to the other functions

- The Run Time Checker tool that is used to detect irregularities during program execution

4

TOOLS AND
LANGUAGES

- The Static Source Code Analyzer tool that looks at the source code (all the source code!) and remarks on constructions which it finds suspect
- The test program, which is probably the most important development tool you can use

The programming languages discussed in this chapter are

- *C.* Usable for most kind of applications, as long as the programs do not become too large or complex.
- *C++.* Usable for all kinds of applications, as long as the footprint is not too tight.
- *Pascal.* A good all-arounder, but watch out for future support.
- *Visual Basic.* Usable for quickly building programs, user interfaces, and prototypes that are not time critical (execution slowness is even a plus when writing those first proto- types).
- *Java.* Usable for portable applications that aren't time critical, Internet software, down- loadable executables, and prototypes.
- *Assembly.* Usable for small, time-critical programs or program parts. Drivers, interrupt routines, close hardware interaction programs.

Measuring Time and Complexity

IN THIS CHAPTER

In previous chapters, you have seen how to identify parts of programs that are likely candidates for optimization. You have also seen that it is necessary to determine whether it is worth optimizing an existing algorithm, or whether a completely new algorithm is necessary to achieve the necessary performance goals. However, when you have a choice between a large number of algorithms, how do you decide which will be fastest? Do you implement all of them and do speeds tests or can something intelligent be said beforehand? Also, how exactly can you perform speed comparisons easily between different algorithms?

This chapter introduces you to the tools and background information you will need when optimizing your software. The concepts laid out here are used throughout this book to prove and demonstrate the presented theory. The subjects covered in this chapter are: a notation of algorithm complexity, a handy timing function to use in your code, system influences to look out for when performing timing tests and tips to decrease the influence of the system.

The Marriage of Theory and Practice

This section introduces two techniques for providing efficiency information on algorithms. The first technique is a theoretical description of the complexity of an algorithm, the O(n) notation. It can be used to compare the merits of underlying concepts of algorithms. This can be done without doing any implementation. The second technique introduced in this section is a timing function that can be used to time implemented code. It is used throughout this book to time suggested coding solutions.

Algorithm Complexity (the O Notation)

The O notation is used to compare the efficiency of different algorithms. This notation expresses the mathematical complexity of an algorithm. It tells you, for example, how the number of elements that is stored in a database influences the amount of time that sorting the data base will take. So, by looking at the O notation of a sorting algorithm, you can determine the impact on sorting time when the number of elements increases. In the O notation the letter *O* is followed by an expression between brackets. This expression contains the letter *n* which denotes the number of elements on which the algorithm is to be unleashed.. Here are some example complexities:

> O(n)
>
> O(n^2)

In the first example—*O(n)*—the algorithm complexity is a direct function of the number of elements on which the algorithm will be unleashed. This means, for example, that if searching through a database of 1,000 elements takes one second, it will take two seconds to search through a database of 2,000 elements. It also means that three times the number of elements to search will take three times as long. An example of an O(n) algorithm is an algorithm that handles each element the same number of times during processing. Traversing a linked list or an array from beginning to end is an example of this.

In the second example—$O(n^2)$ —the time taken by an algorithm increases with the square of the number of elements; twice as many elements to handle will take four times as long and so on.

Of course these notations can only serve as indications, the exact amount of time that an algorithm will take depends on many variables. Think of how close a base of information already is to being sorted. Also, some searching algorithms use starting assumptions; the closer these are to the actual truth, the faster searching will be. The O notation is therefore used to express general characteristics of algorithms: worst case time, best case time, average time.

So how can you use this notation? Think of a sorting algorithm: When sorting small bases of information you will hardly notice any difference between the performance of different sorting algorithms. However, as data size increases, choosing the right sorting algorithm can easily mean the difference between waiting 500 seconds or 24 hours. This may sound extreme but it can and does happen. The following table demonstrates this by comparing five different complexities found in sorting algorithms (For examples of algorithms refer to Chapter 10):

Elements	O(log2 n)	O(n)	O(n log2 n)	O(n^2)	O(2^n)
10	3	10	33	100	1024
100	7	100	664	10,000	too large
1000	10	1000	9966	1,000,000	too large
10,000	13	10,000	132,877	100,000,000	too large

The first column of the previous table indicates the number of elements to sort. The remaining columns represent worst-case sorting times for algorithms with different complexities. Let's say the base time is one minute. This means that sorting 10,000 elements with an algorithm with an O(log2 n) complexity takes 13 minutes. Sorting the same number of elements with an algorithm with an O(n^2) complexity takes 100,000,000 minutes, which is over 190 years! That is something you probably do not want to wait for. This also means that choosing the right algorithm will improve performance far greater than tweaking the wrong algorithm ever could. What you do when tweaking an algorithm is changing its base time, but not the number of algorithmic steps it needs to take. In the example given by the previous table, this could mean optimizing the O(n^2) algorithm to perform sorting in 100,000,000 * 30 seconds instead of 100,000,000 * 60 seconds. Which means the new implementation is twice as fast, but sadly, it still takes over 80 years to complete its task in worst case, and it still does not compare to the 13 minutes of the O(log2 n) algorithm. What you are looking for is thus an algorithm with as low a complexity as possible.

You have already seen an example of an algorithm with O(n) complexity. But what about those other complexities? Algorithms with O(n^2) complexity are those which, depending on the number of elements, need to do some processing for all other elements. Think of adding an element to the back of a linked list. When you have no pointer to the last element, you need to traverse the list from beginning to end each time you add an element. The first element is added to an empty list, the fifth element traverses the first four, the tenth element traverses the first nine, and so on.

Other complexities you are very likely to come across in software engineering are O(log2 n) and O(n log2 n). The first *n* in *nlog2 n* is easy to explain; it simply means that something needs to be done for all elements. The *log2 n* part is created by algorithmic choices that continuously split in half the number of data elements that the algorithm is interested in. This kind of algorithm is used, for instance, in a game in which you have to guess a number that someone is thinking of by asking as few questions as possible. A first question could be, Is the number even or odd? When the numbers have a limited range, from 1 to 10 for instance, a second question could be, Is the number higher than 5? Each question halves the number of possible answers.

Algorithms with O(1) complexity are those for which a processing time is completely independent of the number of elements. A good example of this is accessing an array with an index: int a = array[4]; no matter how many elements are placed into this array, this operation will always take the same amount of time.

Final remarks on the O notation:

- Constants prove to be insignificant when comparing different O(n) expressions, and can be ignored; O(2n^2) and O(9n^2) are both considered to be O(n^2) compared to O(n) and so on.
- Linking algorithms of different complexities creates an algorithm with the highest of the linked complexities; when you incorporate a step of O(n^2) complexity into an algorithm with O(n) complexity the resulting complexity is O(n^2).
- Nesting algorithms (in effect multiplying their impact) creates an algorithm with multiplied complexity; O(n) nested with O(log2 n) produces O(n log2 n).

The Timing Function

This section introduces a timing function which is used throughout this book to time different solutions to performance problems. It shows how and why it can be used. The source code for the timing function can be found in the accompanying files: BookTools.h and BookTool.cpp.

Consider the Mul/Shift example program in Listing 5.1:

LISTING 5.1   Mul/Shift Example

```cpp
#include <iostream.h>
#include "booktools.h"

long MulOperator()
{
    long i, j = 1031;

    for (i = 0 ; i < 20000000; i++)
    {
        j *= 2;
    }
    return 0;
}

long MulShift()
{
    long i,  j = 1031;

    for (i = 0 ; i < 20000000; i++)
    {
        j <<= 1;
    }
    return 0;
}


void main(void)
{
    cout << "Time in MulOperator:   "<< time_fn(MulOperator,5) << endl;
    cout << "Time in shiftOperator:   "<< time_fn(MulShift,5) << endl;
}
```

This Mul/Shift example program uses two different techniques for multiplying a variable (j) by two. The function MulOperator() uses the standard arithmetic operator *, whereas the function MulShift() uses a bitwise shift to the left <<. Performance of both multiplication functions is timed with a function called time_fn(). This function is explained later in this chapter.

You will agree that the choice between writing j *= 2 or j <<= 1 has no real impact on code reliability, maintainability, or complexity. However, when you write a program that at some point needs to do this kind of multiplication on a large base of data, it is important to know beforehand which technique is fastest (or smallest). This is especially true when multiplication is used widely throughout the sources you write for a certain target system.

5

MEASURING TIME
AND COMPLEXITY

So how does this test help you? The result expected of the Mul/Shift example by anyone with a technical background would be that the logical shift is much faster than the multiplication, simply because this action is easier for (most) microprocessors to perform. However, when you run this test using Microsoft's Developer Studio on an x86-compatible processor, you will see that both techniques are equally fast. How is this possible? The answer becomes clear when you look at the assembly generated by the compiler—how to obtain assembly listings is explained in Chapter 4.

The following assembly snippets show the translations of the two multiplication techniques for Microsoft's Developer Studio on an x86-compatible processor.

```
// Code for the multiplication:
; 16   :              j *= 2;
    shl    DWORD PTR _j$[ebp], 1

// Code for the shift:
; 36   :              j <<= 1;

    shl    DWORD PTR _j$[ebp], 1
```

Without even knowing any assembly, it is easy to see why both multiplication functions are equally fast; apparently the compiler was smart enough to translate both multiplication commands into a bitwise shift to the left (shl). So, in this situation, taking time out to optimize your data multiplication routines to use shifts instead of multipliers would have been a complete waste of time. (Just for fun, look at what kind of assembly listing you get when you multiply by 3; j *= 3;) Similarly, if you had run the Mul/Shift example on a MIPS, you would have noticed that for this particular processor the multiplication is in fact faster than the shift operator. This is why it is important to find out specific target and compiler behavior before trying to optimize in these kinds of areas.

The Mul/Shift example introduced a second method for you to time your functions (the first method, using profiling as a means of generating timing information, was introduced in Chapter 4.) The Mul/Shift example uses the function time_fn(). You can find the definition of this timing function in the file BookTools.h.

You can find the implementation of the timing function in Listing 5.2 and in the file BookTools.cpp.

The best way to use the timing function is to simply add both booktools files to the makefile of your software project.

LISTING 5.2   The Timing Function

```
unsigned long time_fn(long (*fn)(void), int nrSamples = 1)
{
    unsigned long average = 0;
    clock_t tBegin, tEnd;

    for (int i = 0; i < nrSamples; i++)
    {
        tBegin = clock();
        fn();
        tEnd = clock();

        average += tEnd - tBegin;
    }
    return ((unsigned long)average / nrSamples);
}
```

The `time_fn()` function receives two parameters: The first is a pointer to the function which it has to time; the second is the number of timing samples it will take. In the Mul/Shift example, you see that the `time_fn()` function is called first with a pointer to the multiplier function, and then again with a pointer to the shift function. In both cases, five samples are requested. The default number of samples is just one.

The actual timing part of the function is done via the `clock()` function. This function returns the number of processor timer ticks that have elapsed since the start of the process. By noting the clock value twice—once before executing the function which is to be timed, and once after it is finished—you can approximate quite nicely how much time was spent. The following section explains how to minimize external influences to this timing. Note that the overhead created by the `for` loops in the `MulOperator()` and `MulShift()` functions of the MUL/Shift example is also timed. This is of no consequence to the timing results as you are interested only in the relation between the results of the two functions and both functions contain the exact same overhead.

The `clock()` function is not part of ANSI C++, so its usage can be slightly different per system. This is why several `#ifdef` compiler directives can be found in the booktools files. The example systems (Linux/UNIX and Windows 9x) used in this book are separated by the fact that the Developer Studio automatically creates a definition `_MSC_VER`. When using the `time_fn()` for systems other than the example systems used in this book, you should consult the relevant manuals to check whether there are differences in the use of the `clock()` function.

5

MEASURING TIME
AND COMPLEXITY

System Influences

When doing timing tests as proposed in the previous section, it is important to realize that you are in fact timing *system behavior* while you are running your code. This means that, because your piece of code is not the only thing the system is dealing with, other factors will influence your test results. The most intrusive factors are other programs running on the system. This influence can of course be minimized by running as few other programs on your system as possible while performing timing tests, and increasing the priority of the process you are timing as much as possible. Still some influences will remain because they are inherent to the operating system. This section discusses the remaining system influences and how to deal with them.

Cache Misses

Cache is memory that is used as a buffer between two or more memory-using objects. The cache that is referred to in this section is the buffer between the CPU and the internal memory of a computer system. Most CPU architectures split this cache into two levels. Level 1 cache is located physically in the CPU itself, and level 2 cache is located outside, but close to, the CPU. Level 1 cache is usually referred to as l1 in technical literature, level 2 cache is usually referred to as l2. Figure 5.1 depicts the two-level cache concept.

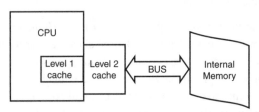

FIGURE 5.1

CPU level 1 and level 2 cache.

The reasons for splitting the cache into two levels have to do with the different characteristics of the cache locations. In general, available space for cache inside a CPU is smaller than outside, with the added advantage that accessing cache inside the CPU is often faster. On most architectures l2 has to be accessed with a clock frequency which is a fraction of the CPUs clock frequency. So, as a rule of thumb: l1 is smaller and faster than l2.

Usage of caching means that a CPU does not need to retrieve each unit of data from memory separately; rather, a block of data is copied from memory into cache in one action. The advantage of this is that part of the overhead of transferring data from memory to CPU (for example, finding an address and doing bus interaction) is incurred only once for a large number of memory addresses. The CPU uses this cached data until it needs data from a memory address that is not cached. At this point a *cache miss* is incurred and a new block of data needs to be transferred from memory to cache. Of course data is not only read, it can be changed or overwritten as well. When a cache miss occurs, it is often necessary to transfer the cache back to internal memory first, to save the changes. Each time a cache miss is incurred, processing halts while the copy actions take place. It would, therefore, be unfortunate if a cache miss causes a block of cached data to be switched for a new block, after which another cache miss switches the new block back for the original block again. To minimize these kind of scenarios occurring, further refining caching concepts are often introduced in system architecture, as the following two sections explain.

Using Cache Pages

With cache paging the available cache resource is divided into blocks of a certain size. Each block is called a page. When a cache miss occurs, only one page (or a few pages) is actually overwritten with new data, and the rest of the pages stay untouched. In this scenario, at least the page in which the cache miss occurred has to stay untouched. This does mean that for each page, a separate administration is needed to keep track of the memory addresses that the page represents and whether changes have been made to the data in the page.

Using Separate Data and Instruction Caches

With separate data and instruction caches the available cache resource is split into two functional parts: one part for caching CPU instructions, which is a copy of part of the executable image of the active process; and another part for caching data, which is a copy of a subset of the data that is used by the active process.

These strategies are, of course, very generic as they cannot take into account any specific characteristics of the software that will run on a certain system. Software designers and implementers can, however, design their software in such a way that cache misses are likely to be minimized. When software is designed to run on a specific system, even more extreme optimizations can be made by taking into account actual system characteristics—such as l1 and l2 cache sizes.

Different techniques for minimizing cache misses and page faults are presented in a later section titled "Techniques for Minimizing System Influences."

Page Faults

The concept of using paging, as discussed in the previous , can also be used on internal memory. In this case, internal memory acts as a *cache* or buffer between the CPU and a secondary storage device—for example, a hard disk. When this concept is applied to internal memory it is called *virtual memory management*. Figure 5.2 depicts the virtual memory concept.

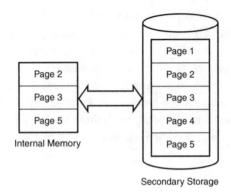

FIGURE 5.2
Virtual memory.

When virtual memory is used, the internal memory is divided into a number of blocks of a certain size. Each block is called a page. The memory management system can move these pages to and from the secondary storage. On the secondary storage, these pages are stored in something called a *page file* or a *swap file* (for maximum performance, even a swap partition can be created). In general this page file can contain more pages than can fit in memory. The size of available internal memory is thus virtually increased by the usage of the larger page file. However, whenever an active process refers to data or an instruction which is located in a page that is not at that time in internal memory, a page fault occurs. The page which is referred to has to be transferred from secondary storage to internal memory. In the worst case another page has to be transferred from internal memory to the page file first, to make room for the new page. This is the case when some of the data of the page that will be replaced was changed.

Other OS Overhead

Apart from overhead which is directly related to your process, the OS itself can also generate more overhead which is related to other activities.

Task Switching

Unless your target is an embedded system with a very straightforward architecture, chances are that your target is multitasking.

In practice this means there are always other processes (daemons, agents, background processes, and so on) running alongside your testing process. Some will be small, whereas others might be fairly large compared to your tests. What the OS does is give all these processes some CPU time to do their job, based on their individual priorities. This is called *task switching* and it can bring along overhead varying from simply saving CPU registers on stack to swapping entire pages in and out of internal memory.

IO

When a process on your system is performing IO this will generally be a large influence on system time spent. This is because IO to secondary storage or external devices is generally many times slower than CPU-to-memory interaction. Similarly, when your test program uses a lot of IO, it might not perform exactly the same during two separate test runs. A later run could use data that was buffered during an earlier run.

General OS Administration

An OS will, from time to time, do some administration. This can be anything from updating some kind of registry to doing active memory management. On some systems this is done only after a certain amount of idle time; however, the OS can still decide to do this just as you are about to run your test.

User Interaction

When a user interacts with the system, chances are that some kind of background process will suddenly become very active to deal with all the new input. It is generally a good idea to interact as *little* as possible with the system while running your tests. This includes not moving the mouse, playing with the keyboard, or inserting floppy discs or CDs as the OS might do more than you expect (like displaying ToolTips, looking for environment variables, checking status/validity, switching focus, and so on).

Techniques for Minimizing System Influences

Before starting tests, you should ensure that OS overhead is set to a minimum by running as few other programs on your system as possible and by setting the priority of the process doing the test as high as possible. This will minimize task switching and OS administration overhead. Also it might be a good idea to start tests on a clean computer—that is, one which was just booted. This way the legacy of old programs, such as a certain level of memory fragmentation, can be minimized. Then, to get a good picture of how a certain algorithm or part of a program performs, several tests should be run. From these test results, you can eliminate those results with inordinately high values (caused by cache misses, page faults, and so on) or inordinately low values (caused by buffered IO and so on). A clean average should prevail. However, for certain influences it is best to minimize their occurrence by writing better code in the first place—for example, for cache misses and page faults. It is possible to design software in such a way that cache misses and page faults are likely to be minimized, even without necessarily taking specific system architecture information into account. This remainder of this section presents these kinds of techniques.

Minimizing Data Cache Misses and Page Faults

• Group Data According to Frequency of Use

Place data that is used most frequently, closely together in memory. This increases the change of having at least some of it at hand almost continuously.

• Group Data According to Time/Space Relations

Place data that is often needed simultaneously or consecutively closely together in memory. Creating this kind of grouping of related data increases the chance that data is available when it is needed.

• Access and Store Data Sequentially

When data is accessed sequentially, chances increase that a miss or a fault will retrieve several of the data elements which are needed in the near future. If the data structure consists of some kind of linked elements (linked list, tree, and so on) this only works when sequential elements are stored closed together and in sequence in memory. This is because otherwise a linked element can basically be anywhere in memory.

• Perform Intelligent Prefetching

When it is possible to determine with reasonable accuracy what data is needed in future, a deliberate miss or fault can be generated during idle time to facilitate a kind of prefetching mechanism. This kind of strategy can be inefficient when it is impossible to determine which pages will be used for the prefetch. You will most likely want to combine this strategy with the following.

• Lock Frequently Used Data

When data is needed on a frequent or continual basis during some stage of a program, it could be worth while to find out whether the page it is in can somehow be locked. For more information, consult system and compiler documentation.

• Use the Smallest Working Set Possible

On most systems, it is possible to influence the working set of a process. This could aid in battling page faults as the working set determines how much memory will be available to a process. The closer this working set matches the maximum memory needs of a program, the closer its data and instruction are packed together. For more information, consult system and compiler documentation.

Minimizing Instruction Cache Misses and Page Faults

• Group Instructions According to Frequency of Use

Place functions or sets of instructions that are used most frequently closely together in memory. This increases the change of having at least some of them at hand almost continuously.

- Group Related Instructions Together

  Place functions or sets of instructions that are often needed simultaneously or consecutively closely together in memory. Grouping related instructions in this way increases the chance that instructions are available when they are needed. In effect this means that you try to determine chains of functions that are likely to call each other and place them together and in order.

- Lock Frequently Used Instructions

  When a function or group of instructions is needed on a frequent or continual basis during some stage of a program, it could be worth it to find out whether the page they are in can somehow be locked. For more information on this consult system and compiler documentation.

Note that not all strategies given here are always possible or even desirable. Implementing a certain strategy can sometimes have more cons than pros. For each separate situation the strategies should be weighed on their merits. Note also that some strategies are not particularly suited to be combined.

Most standard platforms have tools which help you determine the number of cache misses and page faults that occur during the running of a piece of software, and the time that is lost during a certain kind of cache miss (l1/l2) or page fault. For more information, consult system and compiler documentation.

Summary

By using the O(n) notation to describe the behavior of an algorithm in relation to the number of elements of data it needs to handle, a lot can be said about algorithm efficiency even before it has been implemented. Algorithms that have already been implemented can easily be pitted against each other using a timing function as is described in this chapter. When performing this second kind of speed tests, however, you should realize that you are effectively timing system behavior while your test is running. There are several things you can do to minimize the influence of system overhead during testing. To minimize the side effects caused by other processes and OS administrative tasks you can

- Run as few other processes on the system as possible
- Increase the priority of the testing process
- Run on a clean (rebooted) system
- Perform several test runs and average only least contaminated results

To minimize cache misses and page faults while your software is running, you can use several optimization strategies:

- Group data and functions according to frequency of use
- Group data and functions which are related to each other
- Access and store data sequentially
- Perform intelligent prefetching
- Lock frequently used data and functions
- Adjust the working set of a process
- Take specific system information into account

How fast data and instruction access can be, is dependant on where it must come from. Figure 5.3 provides an overview.

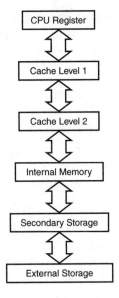

FIGURE 5.3

Overview of locality.

This diagram shows the different places from which the CPU can get data and instructions. This diagram orders the places by proximity to the CPU, where the registers are closest to the CPU and the external storage is furthest away. In general it can be said that the closer a storage is to the CPU, the smaller and faster it is.

The Standard C/C++ Variables

IN THIS CHAPTER

This chapter examines some simple and effective ways to achieve optimizations through the use of standard C/C++ variables. It shows in depth when, how, and why performance or footprint issues can arise.

Variable Base Types

The standard C/C++ variables consist of base types (char, short, int, and so on), which can be grouped together to form user-defined types (struct, union, bitfield, and so on). This chapter looks at base types and grouped types separately, starting with the base types.

Size and Range of Variables

Although most compilers these days use the same memory mapping of base types, this is still not always the case. Furthermore, not all programmers are always fully aware of the implications of choosing a certain base type. This section therefore takes a closer look at the size—number of bytes—that each variable type takes up and the range of values they can contain.

Determining variable type size is easily done with the C/C++ `sizeof()` function. Although the range of a variable can be deducted from the size of the variable, for some types (such as float or double) it is best to consult the relevant compiler documentation. Table 6.1 presents the sizes and ranges of variable types for the two example environments of this book.

TABLE 6.1 Variable Sizes and Ranges

Base Type	W/D		U/G	Range
	(Size in Bytes)		(Signed)	(Unsigned)
char	1	1	−128 to 127	255
short	2	2	−32,768 to 32,767	65,535
short int	2	2	−32,768 to 32,767	65,535
long	4	4	−2,147,483,648 to 2,147,483,647	4,294,967,295
int	4	4	−2,147,483,648 to 2,147,483,647	4,294,967,295
float	4	4	3.4E ± 38 (7 digits)	..
double	8	8	1.7E ± 308 (15 digits)	..
long double	8	8	*1.2E ± 4932 (19 digits)*	..

TABLE 6.1   Continued

Base Type	W/D		U/G	Range
	(Size in Bytes)		*(Signed)*	*(Unsigned)*
struct	1	1	..	..
bit field	4	4	..	..
union	1	1	..	..
long long/__int64	8	8	– 9,223,372,036, 854,775,808 to 9,223,372,036, 854,775,807	14,757,395,258,967,641,292

The first column of sizes is valid for Windows with Developer Studio (W/D). Some documentation for this compiler claims the `long double` to be ten bytes in size instead of eight, in which case the larger range would be valid. A 64-bit integer is called `__int64` by Developer Studio.

The second column of sizes is valid for UNIX and Linux with the GNU compiler (U/G). When we use the GNU compiler the 64-bit integer is called a `long long`.

Careful readers might notice the `struct`, `bit field`, and `union` types appearing in this list. These are included because the smallest possible size of these types is not always apparent. It is possible to determine the sizes of these types by checking an instance containing the smallest possible element—for example,

```
struct Small {char c;}; struct Bitfield {unsigned bit:1;}; union Un {char a;}
```

These types are discussed in more detail at the end of this chapter.

When you are using a different target environment from the two dealt with above, it is a good idea to run some size tests. A function which does just that is included in the book tools on the Web site: `BaseTypeSizes()` (see Chapter 5, "Measuring Time and Complexity"). To prevent cryptic descriptions of types, the remainder of this book refers to the variable types as they are specified in the column U/G. So, when a reference is made to a 64-bit integer, the type name `long long` will be used.

After the sizes and ranges of variable types have been determined, implementers select variable types with the best fit for their variables. In the instance of more visible variables, the design should aid in this selection. Examples include elements that occur as database fields (the amount of characters possible in a name; the maximum value of a ZIP code or postal box number), global definitions (number of possible application states, range of error codes), and return types of interface functions. And always consider whether variables are allowed to contain only positive values or both negative and positive values. As shown earlier in Table 6.1, the positive range of a type is halved when negative values are also allowed. For strictly positive variables use the unsigned keyword:

```
unsigned short bigAl;          // 0–65,535

signed   short littleAl;       // 0–32,767 (and –32,768–0)
```

Performance of Variables

When choosing between base type variables, it also makes sense to think about the performance implications of using the different types. When you run the three functions below—Float(), Double(), Int()—in the timing test of Chapter 5, the reason becomes quite clear, as shown in Listing 6.1.

LISTING 6.1   Performance of Base Types

```
long Float()
{
    long i;
    float j = 10.31, k = 3.0;

    for (i = 0 ; i < 10000000; i++)
    {
      j *= k;
    }
    return j;
}

long Double()
{
    long i;
    double j = 10.31, k = 3.0;

    for (i = 0 ; i < 10000000; i++)
    {
      j *= k;
    }
    return j;
}

long Int()
{
    long i;
    int j = 1031, k=3;

    for (i = 0 ; i < 10000000; i++)
    {
        j *= k;
    }
    return j;
}
```

Although the difference in speed between multiplying floats and doubles is negligible, using integers is many times faster. So it makes sense to use integers where possible and simply adjust the meaning of the value to accommodate the use of fractions. In the Int() example, by effectively multiplying the variable j by 100, the decimal point was no longer needed. Of course it is possible that the decimal point will be needed again—when generating application output, for instance—and in that case it will be necessary to convert the value of j. However, the idea is that this conversion will only have to be done a few times (possibly only once), whereas the rest of the application can use much faster calculations. It is still necessary to examine other calculations though. Consider these examples, where the arithmetic is substituted in the three functions for

```
j *= k;            // original statement.

j -= k;            // alternative 1.

j += k;            // alternative 2.

j /= k;            // alternative 3.
```

Notice that the integer is a speed demon in all cases but one—the division. This is because the integer is converted several times during a division. So, to judge whether to replace floats and doubles with integers, an implementer must determine how often the different arithmetic functions are likely to be used. An application that uses a certain floating point variable mostly in multiplication, addition, and subtraction is thus an ideal candidate for integer replacement.

Scope of Variables and Objects

When using variables and object instances, be aware of their scope. The scope of a variable or object has implications for both footprint and performance. This section discusses variable and object scope in three important contexts: lifetime, initialization, and use.

Lifetime

Generally, a variable is created within its specified scope and destroyed when this scope runs out of existence. So it makes sense to ensure that no unnecessary overhead is incurred for creating a variable. Listing 6.2 shows some examples.

LISTING 6.2   Variable Scope Example 1

```c
void Scope1()
{
    for (int a1 = 0; a1 < 10; a1++)
    {
        char arr[] = "pretend this is a long string";
        int b2 = (int)arr[a1];
    }
}
```

Apart from not actually doing anything, it seems as if this example also contains a few serious scoping flaws. Integer a1 is defined in a for statement header, whereas array arr and integer b2 are defined inside the scope of a for loop. It would appear that at least arr and b2 generate overhead by being created and destroyed for each iteration of the loop. However, the setup of this loop is pretty straightforward and most C/C++ compilers will assign a stack space to each of the three variables. (See Chapters 4, "Tools and Languages," and 8, "Functions," for more information about stack space for variables.) So the generated code should be no different from that shown in Listing 6.3.

LISTING 6.3   Variable Scope Example 2

```
void Scope2()
{
    int a1, b2;
    char arr[] = "pretend this is a long string";

    for (a1 = 0; a1 < 10; a1++)
    {
        b2 = (int)arr[a1];
    }
}
```

However, when you make things a little more complicated, you will see that it makes sense to try to declare variables and objects only once. What if the compiler is unable to predefine a variable outside of its scope? This situation occurs when you allocate variables dynamically or need to call a constructor to create a type, as shown in Listing 6.4.

LISTING 6.4   Variable Scope Example 3

```
void Scope3()
{
    for (int a1 = 0; a1 < 10; a1++)
    {
        char *arr = new char[20];
        Combi *b2 = new Combi;
        b2->a = (char) a1;
```

In this case, variable b2 seems to be a structure or a class, and array arr is now also dynamically created. This generates a lot of overhead because reserving and releasing heap memory occurs in every loop iteration. This sort of overhead can be avoided in situations where it is possible to reuse object instances. In those cases objects such as b2 and arr are instantiated once, outside the loop, and they are only *used* by statements inside the loop body. Obviously, when objects are dynamically created inside a loop to be stored away for later use (filling an array, list, or database) you have no choice but to create different instances.

Listing 6.4 is shown because, although in small loops it can be pretty apparent when dynamic creations are wasted, in larger and more-complex algorithms it is not. So it's good standard programming practice to consider using dynamic objects in limited scopes such as loops and even complete functions. Often implementers use dynamically allocated variables to contain temporary values, perhaps retrieved from a list or a database and so on.

Initialization

A similar problem to that described in the previous paragraph can occur when variables or objects are initialized with function results. Consider the following example, shown in Listing 6.5.

LISTING 6.5   Initialization Example 1

```
void IncreaseAllCounters(DB *baseOne)
{

    for (int i = 0; i < baseOne->GetSize(); i++)
    {
        DBElem * pElem = baseOne->NextElem();
```

This piece of code will iterate over all the elements of object baseOne. To make sure no element is missed, the function GetSize() is called in order to determine the number of elements in baseOne. Because of the implementation choice to call GetSize() in the header of the for statement, a lot of needless overhead is incurred. This piece of code will call the GetSize() function as many times as there are elements in baseOne. A single call would have sufficed as shown in Listing 6.6.

LISTING 6.6   Initialization Example 2

```
void IncreaseAllCounters(DB *baseOne)
{
    int bSize = baseOne->GetSize();

    for (int i = 0; i < bSize; i++)
    {
        DBElem * pElem =baseOne->NextElem();
        ~
```

Again, this is a simple example, but not that many programmers take the time to determine which information is *static* for an algorithm and calculate or retrieve it beforehand. It seems that the more complex algorithms become, the less time is spent on these kinds of matters. This is ironic because these are exactly the kind of algorithms that implementers end up trying to optimize when the application proves to be too slow.

Use

A similar slowdown, as described in the previous paragraph, can occur with the use of variables. Listing 6.7 demonstrates how not to use member variables.

LISTING 6.7   Using Member Variables Example 1

```
class DB
{
    ~
    int dbSize;
    int i;
    ~
};

void DB::IncreaseAllCounters(int addedValue)
{
    for (i = 0; i < dbSize; i++)
    {
        ~
```

The variables i and dbSize are member variables of the DB class. They can, of course, be used in the way described earlier, but accessing member variables can easily take twice as long as accessing local variables . This is because the this has to be used in order to retrieve the base address of a member variable. A better way to use this information might be to create local variables and initialize them (once!) with member variable values as shown in Listing 6.8.

LISTING 6.8   Using Member Variables Example 2

```
void DB::IncreaseAllCounters(int addedValue)
{
    int iSize = dbSize; // use iSize in the rest of the function.
    ~

    for (i = 0; i < iSize;  i++)
    {
        ~
```

Grouping Base Types

6

This section looks at ways to achieve optimizations in grouped C/C++ types. The way in which grouped types are created has an impact on the footprint as well as the performance of the type.

Structs

The use of structures as data containers seems pretty straightforward, which it is really, when you take one or two things into account before using structures for large sets of data. Listing 6.9 demonstrates several ways of creating a grouped type.

LISTING 6.9 Structure Sizes

```
// Structure Size example
#include    <iostream.h>

struct A  { char a; long b; char c; long d; };

struct B  { char a; char c; long b; long d; };

#pragma pack(push,1)
struct C  { char a; long b; char c; long d; };
#pragma pack(pop)

void main(void)
{
    cout << "Size of A: " << sizeof(A) << " bytes." << endl;
    cout << "Size of B: " << sizeof(B) << " bytes." << endl;
    cout << "Size of C: " << sizeof(C) << " bytes." << endl;
}
```

Listing 6.9 defines three structures that contain identical information: two long words—called d and b—and two characters—called a and c. When you run this program on a Windows system using Developer Studio, you get the following output:

> Size of A: 16 bytes.
>
> Size of B: 12 bytes.
>
> Size of C: 10 bytes.

The reason these structures are not the same size has to do with alignment. Normally, a compiler will force long words to be placed at the next long word boundary; this means a new long word can be specified only every four memory addresses. Thus, the memory presentation of the beginning of structure A is:

Address	Content
00	char a
01	stuffing
02	stuffing
03	stuffing
04	long b, byte 0
05	long b, byte 1
06	long b, byte 2
07	long b, byte 3*

Actual byte order within a long is system dependent.

Structure B is more compact because, although `long b` still starts at the same address relative to the beginning of the structure, some of the stuffing is replaced by `char b`:

Address	Content
00	char a
01	char b
02	stuffing
03	stuffing
04	long b, byte 0
05	long b, byte 1
06	long b, byte 2
07	long b, byte 3*

Actual byte order within a long is system dependent.

Looking at these examples, it should not surprise you to find out that the two structures shown in Listing 6.10 are exactly the same size.

LISTING 6.10   Structure Stuffing

```
struct Full                          struct NotSoFull
{                                    {
    char a, b, c, d;                     char a;
    long e;                              long e;
};                                   };
```

So it makes sense to think about variable order when designing structures. When you use only a few instances of a structure at a time, the footprint impact of the extra stuffing bytes is of course marginal, but it is a different story entirely when you use structures to store elements of an expansive database. It is generally good practice to always use well-thought-out structure design not only because—as explained in previous chapters—software (modules) are reused in ways not always anticipated, but also because it is a good idea to make these kinds of techniques second nature.

Now let's look at our *wunderkind.* How did structure C manage to squeeze itself into a 10-byte hole? You have seen the #pragma pack compiler commands so you have a pretty good idea how, but what exactly happens? The #pragma pack compiler command for Developer Studio tells the compiler to temporarily adjust alignment. In the example program the alignment is set to one byte, creating the following memory mapping:

Address	Content
00	char a
01	long b, byte 0
02	long b, byte 1
04	long b, byte 2
05	long b, byte 3
06	char c
07	long d, byte 0
08	long d, byte 1
09	long d, byte 2
10	long d, byte 3*

* Actual byte order within a long is system dependent.

Using push and pop ensures that the alignment for the rest of the program is not affected. Basically you *push* the current alignment onto some compiler stack, force the new alignment in place, and later *pop* the old alignment back into action. For more information on alignment consult the manual of the compiler used (look up the /Zp compiler option for Microsoft Developer Studio, or consult the manpages for the GNU compiler—man gcc or man g++).

Of course alignment is an issue for all types. Table 6.2 is an alignment table for the Windows and UNIX/Linux OSes.

TABLE 6.2   Base Type Alignment Table

Type	Windows/ Dev Studio	UNIX, Linux, GNU
char	1	1
word	2	2
short	2	2
long	4	4
int	4	2
pointer	4	4
float	4	4
double	4	4
long double int64/	8	4
long long	8	4
struct	alignment of largest member type.	
union	alignment of largest member type.	
bit field	4	4

For specific alignment details of other systems or various compilers, consult their respective documentation, or perform an alignment test. This can be as easily done as creating a structure of required types, interspersed with character variables (to make sure the compiler will actually force alignment for every type). Alternatively, use the booktool function: `alignment_info()` to perform this job for you.

NOTE

Alignment exists for a reason: Some processors simply have difficulty using odd memory addresses. When you port code that uses adjusted alignment, the new footprint of the program can thus differ, and variable access can even become somewhat slower. The implementer should therefore be aware that alignment adjusting is a system-specific optimization that needs to be tweaked to the target system (OS, hardware, and compiler combination).

Bit Fields

This section discusses the use of structures as bit fields. Bit fields are discussed in the following contexts:

- Footprint implications
- Performance implications
- Pitfalls
- Final remarks

Footprint Implications

Bit fields allow you to use even more-extreme alignment of variables. Essentially, the bit field of C++ makes it possible to declare several variables within a base type, making full use of the range of the base type. Let's say you need to create data base elements that contain six variables, four of which have a range of 0–2031 and two of which have a range of 0–1011. Without using bit fields, you will need a structure as defined in Listing 6.11.

LISTING 6.11 Structure Without Bit Fields

```
struct NoBitField
{
    short     rangeAOne, rangeATwo, rangeAThree, rangeAFour;
    short     rangeBOne, rangeBTwo;
};
```

For the range 0–2031 you need 11 bits and for the range 0–1011 you need 10 bits; the smallest base type that can contain this information is the "word" (2 bytes), which is called a "short" by most C++ compilers. The size of the NoBitField structure is thus 12 bytes. However, when using bit fields our structure could look like Listing 6.12.

LISTING 6.12 Structure with Bit Fields

```
struct BitField
{
    unsigned rangeAOne    : 11;    // long 1;
    unsigned rangeATwo    : 11;
    unsigned rangeBOne    : 10;
    unsigned rangeAThree  : 11;    // long 2;
    unsigned rangeAFour   : 11;
    unsigned rangeBTwo    : 10;
};
```

The compiler will pack this whole structure into two long words. The size of the BitField structure is thus eight bytes. The compiler can do this because it was told to use only 11 bits for the rangeAxx variables and only 10 bits for the rangeBxx variables. And by ordering the variables intelligently within the structure (11+11+10=32) you ensured optimal storage. The reason this order is important has again to do with alignment. Bits of the base type are assigned to the fields in the order in which they are declared, however, when a field is larger than the number of bits left over in the base type, it is "pushed" to the next base type alignment. The base type for bit fields is a long word for most compilers so when you look at the placement of rangeAOne, rangeATwo, and rangeBOne in the first long word, you will see this:

```
0000 0000 | 0000 0000 | 0000 0000 | 0000 0000
|  rangeBOne  |   rangeATwo   |   rangeAOne  |
```

With a less-optimal ordering, as in the following structure, you see

```
struct WastingBitField
{
    unsigned rangeAOne      : 11;     // long 1;
    unsigned rangeATwo      : 11;
    unsigned rangeAThree    : 11;     // long 2;
    unsigned rangeAFour     : 11;
    unsigned rangeBTwo      : 10;
    unsigned rangeBOne      : 10;
};
```

rangeAOne and rangeATwo take up 22 bits of the first long word. This means there are 32–22=10 bits left for the following field; however, because you declared another 11-bit field, that field is moved to the next long word alignment, leaving 10 bits of the first long word unused. As a consequence, the size of the WastingBitField structure is 12 bytes.

Performance Implications

In fact, forcing boundaries on variables makes perfect sense. By putting a little thought into designing your bit fields you can easily take advantage of the space gained, and because variables are set at their closest alignment borders, the compiler can generate relatively fast code. To set a value in a bit field at most two bit operations are needed, see Listing 6.13.

LISTING 6.13 Operations Necessary to Set Values in a Bit Field

```
// C code:
BitField inst;
inst.rangeBOne = 2;

// pseudo code to implement the C code:
register = long0 AND 0x003fffff
register =   register OR 0x00800000
```

The AND masks off everything but the bits of the rangeBOne variable, and simultaneously resets the bits of rangeBOne which need to be reset for the value 2. The OR then sets the bits that need to be set for the value 2.

But you do not always use constant values, or values from which the compiler can derive constants at compile time. When a variable is used for setting, or doing arithmetic with, a bit field, considerably more overhead is incurred. Listing 6.14 demonstrates this.

LISTING 6.14 Speed of Bit Fields

```
// C++:
struct Bitfield  { unsigned num : 11; };
struct Structure { short    num; };

void main(void)
{
    Bitfield  a; Structure b;

    for (int i = 0; i < 100; i++)
    {
        a.num = i; b.num = i;
    }

}

// Relevant Assembly:

; 11   :          a.num = i;

    mov    eax, DWORD PTR _a$[ebp]
    and    eax, -2048              ; fffff800H
    mov    ecx, DWORD PTR _i$[ebp]
    and    ecx, 2047               ; 000007ffH
    or     eax, ecx
    mov    DWORD PTR _a$[ebp], eax

; 12   :          b.num = i;

    mov    eax, DWORD PTR _i$[ebp]
    mov    WORD PTR _b$[ebp], ax
```

You do not have to know Assembly to see that about three times as many instructions are needed to process the bit field (label 11) compared to the short (label 12). The exact overhead depends on the compiler and target system used. If speed and footprint tradeoffs become important when using structures, it is a good idea to test the implication for the destined target system using test cases such as the one in Listing 6.14.

Pitfalls

When you look at Listing 6.11, you see that in the NoBitField structure more than one variable was declared on a single source line. This is also possible for bit field structures but take care not to make the following mistake shown in Listing 6.15.

LISTING 6.15   Pitfall in Using Bit Fields

```
struct FaultyBitfield
{
    unsigned a, b : 4; // INCORRECT!
};
```

Instead of creating two bit fields of four bits, listing 6.15 creates a bit field of 32 bits a and a bit field of four bits b. The correct way to group names is shown in Listing 6.16.

LISTING 6.16   Correct Use of Bit Fields

```
struct CorrectBitfield
{
    unsigned a : 4, b : 4;        // correct.
};
```

It is also possible to use bit fields and *normal* base types together in the same structure as shown in Listing 6.17, however, this is not recommended.

LISTING 6.17   Bad Use of Bit Fields

```
struct CombinedFields
{
    char        a;              // Bad idea.
    unsigned    b : 4;
};
```

Sadly, whenever a base type follows a bit field or vice versa, the continued memory mapping is aligned on the next long word boundary. The CombinedFields structure thus uses four bytes for the character and another four bytes for the bit field. It would be better to write the character out as a bit field of eight bits, this way the entire structure will fit into a single long word (remember; bit field structures use the long word as a base unit.)

Final Remarks

It is possible to use signed bit fields as shown in Listing 6.18. Use either int or unsigned as the bit field type.

LISTING 6.18 Signed Bit Fields

```
struct SignedBitFields
{
    int         a : 10;
    unsigned    b : 10;
};
```

Remember that using signed values (int) effectively decreases the positive range of the variable.

Finally, there are two things we simply cannot do with bit fields. It is impossible to use the address of a bit field, or to initialize a reference with a bit field.

Unions

Unions are used to combine the memory space of several variables when only one of the variables will be used at a time. Consequently, the size of a union is that of the largest element it contains. Listing 6.19 shows that when the contained elements are roughly the same size, unions are a wonderful tool for saving space while maintaining strong type checking.

LISTING 6.19 Union Size Match

```
union PerfectMatch
{
    char    text[4];
    int     nr;
};

void main(void)
{

    PerfectMatch a;

    a.text[0] = '0';
    a.text[3] = '0';
    ~
    // Somewhere else in the code:
    a.nr = 9;
}
```

Listing 6.19 creates two different ways to approach the same memory, allowing the use of different types.

When the elements of a union have vastly different sizes, you need to reevaluate how you use unions. Consider Listing 6.20, which represents a data base object.

LISTING 6.20   Union for Database Fields

```
struct Address
{
    char    *streetName;
    char    *zipCode;
    short    houseNumber;
};

union Location
{
    Address    adr;
    int        poBox;
};

struct Client              // sizeof(Client) = 20 bytes
{
    char    *name;
    short    cityCode;

    char        locationSelector;
    Location    loc;
};
```

These structures are used to store client information. They register the name of a client, a code for the city she lives in, and her address. However, some clients are known by their post-office box number (PoBox) and others by their full address. The union Location combines this information so the space needed for the PoBox is reused for the address. The locationSelector in the Client structure tells us which kind of address is being used by an instance of the Client structure.

This example works fine, but the Client structure is 20 bytes large and when clients are known by their PoBox number, only 12 of the 20 bytes are actually necessary. This might not be a problem for a small database—it might not even be a problem when most clients are known by their address—but when you have a large number of "PoBox" clients, you are simply wasting space. Listing 6.21 gives an example of splitting the Client structure into two (observing structure alignment as discussed in the previous sections).

LISTING 6.21   Structures Replacing a Union

```
struct ClientAdr            // sizeof(ClientAdr) = 16 bytes
{
    char      *name;
    char      *streetName;
    char      *zipCode;
    short      houseNumber;
    short      cityCode;
};

#pragma pack(push,2)
struct ClientPoBox          // sizeof(ClientPoBox) = 10 bytes
{
    char      *name;
    short      cityCode;
    int     poBox;
};
#pragma
```

For every instance of `ClientPoBox` that is placed in the database, 10 bytes are effectively won; without the pragmas the structure is 12 bytes, winning eight bytes. For every instance of `ClientAdr`, four bytes are won.

Of course you create a minor problem when using two `stucts` instead of one, namely that of *typing* the database elements. Workarounds for this are as diverse as

- Creating separate containers (lists, arrays, and so on) for address-client objects and PoBox-client objects

- Adding a selector to the structure or object referring to a client object and then casting client pointers to either `ClientAdr` or `ClientPoBox`

- Using polymorphism—that is, classes instead of structs. More about this can be found in Chapter 8.

Summary

Although most compilers now use the same memory mapping of base types, this is not always the case, and not all programmers are fully aware of the implications of choosing a certain base type. That is why it is important for implementers to familiarize themselves with the sizes, ranges, and accessing speed of the standard C/C++ variables of their target environment. This chapter discussed ways to evaluate variable characteristics and gave practical examples of optimal use.

- Speed of variables

  Not all base types are equally fast in access and arithmetic. It is possible for the integer to be much faster than the float and double in all arithmetic operations except division, depending on the characteristics of the target platform. Also bit fields can be quite fast until you try to do arithmetic with them. The scope and lifetime of a variable also has impact on the speed of use.

- Design of structures and unions

  Because of alignment issues, the size of structures depends on the order in which their elements are declared. This alignment can be tweaked in several ways. Unions are always at least as large as their largest member; however, there are techniques for determining optimal use of unions.

Basic Programming Statements

IN THIS CHAPTER

This chapter looks closely at how choices between basic programming statements—that do essentially the same thing—can affect your programs. Often, it is not very clear what the performance and footprint repercussions are of choosing a certain solution. In this chapter, different solutions are presented together with useful data on their performance. This will provide the necessary insight into what actually happens when a program executes and how to determine an optimal implementation solution. Ready-to-use solutions are, of course, offered for the more common implementation problems.

Selectors

This section focuses on selector statements. As there are a variety of different C/C++ statements to enable a program to choose between a set of execution paths, you might wonder what the actual differences between the selector statements are. Certainly almost any selection implementation can be rewritten to use a different statement—replacing a `switch` with an `if..else` construction, for instance. However, each statement does have its own specific strengths and weaknesses. When these statement characteristics are understood, it becomes possible to intuitively choose an efficient implementation solution.

This section presents the characteristics of the different selector statements, after which a performance comparison between the different statements is made.

`if..else` Statement

- `if` as an expression evaluator

The `if` check can be used to check several expressions at once. The expressions can be concatenated with logical operators—and (&&), or (||), not (!), and so on. Here is an example of concatenated expressions within an `if` statement:

```
if ((lights_out == TRUE) && (response_to_doorbell != TRUE))
  nobody_is_home = TRUE;
```

There are two very important things to remember with concatenated expressions:

- The expressions are evaluated from left to right.
- No further expressions are evaluated when the result has been determined.

The reason why this is important to realize is that you can take advantage of the time that is won when certain expressions are not evaluated. For instance, when expressions are concatenated with a logical 'and', expression evaluation will stop with the first expression that is false. Remember, for an 'and' to be true, *all* expressions concatenated into that 'and' have to be true. So, in the preceding example, the expression (`response_to_doorbell != TRUE`) is never evaluated when `lights_out` equals `FALSE`. Similarly, the evaluation of expressions that are concatenated with a logical 'or' will stop after the first expression that is found to be true. Remember, for an 'or' to be true, at least one expression needs to be true. It makes sense, therefore, to order concatenated expressions according to their evaluation speed, with the fastest expression to evaluate being the leftmost (or the one most likely to be false as the leftmost). The following example demonstrates this for a simple if with 'and'-ed expressions:

```
char a[]="this is a long string of which we want to know the length";
int b    = 0;

// inefficient and.
if ( (strlen(a) > 100) && (b > 100) )
{
    d++;
}

// efficient and.
if ( (b > 100) && (strlen(a) > 100) )
{
    d++;
}
```

Calculating the length of a string takes time because a function needs to be called and an index and a pointer need to be instantiated, after which a loop will determine the end of the string. Comparing the value of an integer variable with a constant takes considerably less time. This is why the second if in the preceeding example is easily 200 times faster than the first when the expression (b > 100) is not true.

The following example demonstrates the same theory for a simple if with 'or'-ed expressions:

```
char a[]="this is a long string of which we want to know the length";
int b    = 101;

// inefficient or.
if ( (strlen(a) > 100) || (b > 100) )
{
        d++;
}

// efficient or.
if ( (b > 100) || (strlen(a) > 100) )
{
        d++;
}
```

Again, when the fastest expression to evaluate is placed first, the if can be many times faster. Because this example uses an 'or' this time, the second if of the preceeding example is easily 200 times faster then the first when the expression (b > 100) is true.

Note that when all expressions of an 'and' are true, evaluation time is no longer influenced by expression order as all expressions are evaluated anyway.

Note that when none of the expressions of an 'or' are true, evaluation time is no longer influenced by expression order as all expressions are evaluated anyway.

Note also that the rules of expression evaluation hide a sneaky pitfall. Often you can be inclined to test and set a variable in an expression:

```
for (int i = 0; i < MAX; i++)
    if ( (i >= BuffSize) || (EOF == (c = GetNextChar())) )
```

The second expression in this `if` will attempt to get a new character from some input and test whether the input has run dry. However, because there is another expression placed to its left, you cannot guarantee that `GetNextChar()` is called for every loop iteration!

- `if` as a selector

The `if` (`else`) statement is probably the most straightforward selector of C/C++. Via an `if` an expression is evaluated, after which either the statements belonging to the `if` itself, or those belonging to the `else`, are executed. The following example demonstrates this:

```
if (a < 10)
{
    DoLittle();         // execute when a < 10.
}
else if (a < 100)
{
    DoMore();           // execute when  10 <= a < 100.
}
else if (a < 1000)
{
    DoDa();             // execute when  100 <= a < 1000.
}
```

First variable a is compared to 10. When a is lower than 10, the function `DoLittle()` is called. Only when a is equal to or larger than 10 is the second comparison made (a < 100). Similarly, only when a is equal to or larger than 100 is the third comparison made. This means that the more comparisons are specified, the more statements need to be executed in order to reach the final comparison. In the preceeding example, the call to the function `DoDa()` is reached only after three comparisons have been made. It stands to reason that the implementation of a large number of choices made with the `if..else` technique can thus result in a rather sluggish piece of code. The first comparisons in the `if..else` construction are still quite fast, but the deeper you get, the slower the response becomes. This means that the statements that need to be executed most often should be placed as high up in the `if..else` construction as possible. It also means that the default instructions—the ones executed when none of the other comparisons match—will take the longest to reach.

```
if (a == 1)
{
    Do1();          // fastest code to reach.
}
else if (a == 2)
{
    Do2();          // still pretty fast.
}
~
~
else if (a == 1000)
{
    Do1000();            // very slow to reach.
}
~
~
else
{
    DoDefault();    // slowest to reach.
}
```

The power of the if..else really lies in the fact that complicated expressions can be used as the basis of a choice.

Jump Tables

When the range of conditions for the choices can be translated to a continuous range of numbers (0, 1, 2, 3, 4, and so on), a jump table can be used. The idea behind a jump table is that the pointers of the functions to be called are inserted in a table, and the selector is used as an index in that table. The following code example implements a jump table that does much the same thing as the previous example where if..else is used:

```
// Table definition:
typedef long (*functs)(char c);
functs JumpTable[] = {DoOne,DoTwo,DoThree /* etc*/};

// some code that uses the table:
long result = JumpTable[selector](i++);
```

The first two lines of code in this example define the jump table. The typedef determines the layout of the functions that will be contained by the jump table—in this case, a function which receives a single character as input and which returns a long as a result. The array definition of JumpTable actually places the pointers of the functions in the table. Note that the functions

`DoOne()`, `DoTwo()`, and `DoThree()` must be defined elsewhere and should take a character as input parameter and return a long.

The last line of code demonstrates the use of the jump table. The variable `i` is input for the function that is selected via the variable `selector`. The variable `result` will receive the long returned by the selected function. In short, when `i` contains the character `a` and `selector` has the value 2, the following function call is actually made:

```
long result = DoThree('a');
```

The implementation of a jump table solution is equally fast for each possible selection (table entry). The drawback is that the range of selections has to be continuous and a default has to be encoded by hand. It is, of course, possible to specify continuous ranges that do not start at zero. This is done by decreasing the selector in value before accessing the jump table:

```
// Range 19-56

selector -= 19;
long result = JumpTable[selector](i++);
```

It is also possible to use several table entries per selector value, by using multiplication of the selector value as in this example:

```
// 2 functions per selection:

int tabEntry = selector * 2;

long result  = JumpTable[tabEntry](i++);
long result += JumpTable[Tabentry+1](i++);
```

`switch` Statement

The `switch` statement presents a number of cases which contain programming statements. A case can be chosen and executed when its constant expression matches the value of the selector expression that is being evaluated by the `switch` statement. Listing 7.1 demonstrates this:

LISTING 7.1   A Simple Switch

```
switch(b)
{
    case 1:  DoOne();  break;
    case 4:
    case 2:  DoEven(); break;
    default: DoError();
}
```

Depending on the value of the selector expression (here, variable b), a certain function is called. When b equals 1, DoOne() is called; when b equals 2 or 4, DoEven() is called; and for all other values of b, the function DoError() is called. By adding or omitting the break command, the implementer can decide whether a single case is executed exclusively (break) or whether one or more of the following cases are evaluated (and possibly executed) also (omitting the break).

The implementation of the switch statement is not fixed though. Depending on how it is used in a piece of source code, the switch statement is translated by the compiler using one of the following techniques:

- switch as a Jump Table

A switch without holes in the case continuity will be implemented as a jump table. When, for instance, the following cases are specified

```
{case 0, case 1, case 2, case 3, case 4, case 5, case 6, default}
```

the value of the selector expression can be used as the index in the jump table. Each jump table entry is, of course, a pointer to the implementation of a certain case; however, these cases are not implemented as functions, but as branches. Here it is sufficient to mention that a microprocessor incurs much less overhead when it executes a branch compared to when it executes a function call; the reason for this is that during a branch no context needs to be pushed to, and later popped from, the stack. More will be explained about function calling overhead in Chapter 8, "Functions." For now, it is important to understand only that the overhead of a switch case is a lot less than that of our own jump table, as long as the switch cases directly contain the statements that should be executed. When the cases delegate to other functions, however, as in Listing 7.1, the overhead increases as first a jump to the specific case, and then a call to a function, needs to be executed.

But this switch is even sneakier than you might think. Before reaching the actual jump table, the selector expression is first compared with the maximum of the range of cases. This is done in order to determine if the default should be executed. In this example, a quick if (b > 6) will determine the validity of the default, making it perhaps unnecessary to even consult the jump table. As you would thus expect, the default is the fastest decision this kind of switch can make.

Even when the continuous cases start at a random number, a jump table can still be used. When the following cases are specified

```
{case 19, case 20, case 21, case 22, case 23, default}
```

the value of the selector expression is simply decreased with the starting number (19) and then used as jump table index.

Of course, the implementation of a jump table introduces a certain overhead; this is why switch statements with a small number of cases will still be implemented by a compiler as an if..else, simply because this is faster.

- switch as an if..else

You will appreciate that a jump table cannot as easily be used for a switch with cases that have seemingly random constant expressions. Consider the following cases:

```
{case 55, case 300, case 6, case 12, case 79, case 43, case 3, default}
```

For this set of cases it is necessary for the compiler to use a number of if..else statements in order to determine exactly which case should be executed. However, not all is lost yet. Although this technique does introduce some overhead, a good compiler will group the if..else values in such a way as to minimize the number of comparisons that need to be made. When the first comparison determines that the selector expression is larger than that for the first case (55), there will, of course, be no need to compare the expression with cases 6, 12, and 3. The if..else construct will contain expressions grouped in such a way that unnecessary comparisons are not done.

When the switch is represented by an if..else construct, the default case will not be the fastest decision made by the switch.

Conclusion: It pays to design a case statement in such a way as to allow the cases to be presented as a continuous range. Then, when possible, the default case should be used for the selection that is executed most often.

Comparing Selector Performance

Now that the workings of the different selectors has been discussed and their strengths and weaknesses are known, let's look at some practical examples and see just how different implementation strategies measure up to one another.

This section uses three test cases to analyze different kinds of implementation:

- Comparing without function call overhead
- Comparing with function call overhead
- Array look-up

The sources used in this section can be found on the Web site. Also, the following paragraphs will highlight the most important concepts used by the sources and explain what exactly is being done.

The examples of this section make use of selectors with numeric values with a continuous range; this way all techniques can be used and thus compared fairly.

- Comparing without function call overhead

This paragraph looks at the execution of selectors that do not delegate to other functions. By this is meant that all the statements to be executed upon selection are included in the body of the selected `if` or `case`:

```
// switch without function delegation:
switch(j)
{
    case 1:
            k+=1;       // Statements to be executed.
            break;
    case 2:
            k+=3;       // Statements to be executed.
            break;
    ~~

// if..else without function delegation:
if (j==1)
{
    k+=1;                   // Statements to be executed.
}
else if (j == 2)
{
    k+=3;                   // Statements to be executed.
~~
```

As shown in the previous paragraphs, delegating to functions creates extra (function call) overhead; it is therefore treated in a separate test case. This is also why jump tables are not included in this test case: Jump tables always use function calls.

The program 07Source01.cpp that can be found on the Web site, uses the timing function `time_fn()` from the book tools—as discussed in Chapter 5, "Measuring Time and Complexity"—in order to time the differences between the `if..else` and `switch` implementations. Although the exact timing results will differ per system, the relations between the `if..else` measurements and `switch` measurements should not. Table 7.1 shows the relations discovered with 07Source01.cpp:

TABLE 7.1   Test Results of 07Source01.cpp (No Function Call Overhead)

Selected Case	Switch Results	If..Else Results
1	1400	700 // 'if' is 2 times faster than 'switch'
2	1400	1050
3	1420	1400

TABLE 7.1 Continued

Selected Case	Switch Results	If..Else Results
4	1410	1760
5	1390	2110
6	1420	2460
7	1400	2810 // 'switch' is 2 times faster than 'if'
8	1410	3170
9	1400	3520
Default	890	3480 // 'switch' is 4 times faster than 'if'

Table 7.1 shows timing values of a `switch` implementation (column 2) and a similar `if..else` implementation (column 3). The timing values denote the relative time it takes for a certain case to be reached. For instance, in order to reach case 7, the `if..else` construct needs twice as much time as the `switch` does. What else do can you see in these results? Apparently, the `if..else` is faster for the first three cases, after which it starts to lose ground. The `switch` has a relatively constant value for each of the non-default cases. Remember that the `switch` is implemented as a branching table in this example, as the number of cases is relatively high. Another prominent number in this table is that for the default `case`; the `switch` is clearly much faster than the `if..else` construct there.

Conclusion: Where possible, the default `case` of a `switch` should be the most used case. The cases used most often in an `if..else` construct should be placed as the first `if`s of that construct. Sometimes it might even be a good idea to precede a `switch` by one or two `if..else` statements.

When neither the design nor the requirements make clear which cases are most important—that is, which cases are executed most often when the program is being used—some static debug counters could be inserted in the various cases in order to determine how often a case is executed during field tests. This information can then be used to optimize case order and implementation. Once again, though, the profiler can give us this information as well (see Chapter 4, "Tools and Languages").

- Comparing with function call overhead

Now that you will be looking at selectors that delegate to other functions, it is fair to add the jump table technique to our set of selectors to examine. The following excerpt shows how the different techniques will be tested:

```
// switch with function delegation:
switch(j)
```

```
{
   case 1: k+=aa();      // Function call.
           break;
   case 2: k+=bb();      // Function call.
           break;

~~

// if..else with function delegation:
if (j==1)
{
  k+=aa();              // Function call.
}
else if (j == 2)
{
  k+=bb();              // Function call.
}
~~

// jump table with functions:
k+=table[j-1]();         // Function call.
~~
```

The program 07Source02.cpp that can be found on the Web site uses the timing function `time_fn()` from the book tools—as discussed in Chapter 5—in order to time the differences between the `if..else`, `switch`, and `jump table` implementations. Although the exact timing results will differ per system, the relations between the results for the different techniques should not. Table 7.2 shows the relations discovered with 07Source02.cpp.

TABLE 7.2   Test Results of 07Source02.cpp (Test with Function Call Overhead)

Selected Case	Switch Results	If..Else Results	Jump Table Results
1	2630	1940	1920
2	2640	2290	1980
3	2640	2620	1930
4	2640	2980	1930
5	2620	3350	1930
6	2620	3700	1920
7	2650	4010	1930
8	2620	4360	1920
9	2650	4730	1920
Default	1930	4740	1930

Table 7.2 shows timing values of a `switch` implementation (column 2), a similar `if..else` implementation (column 3), and a `jump table` implementation (column 4). The timing values denote the relative time it takes for a certain case to be reached.

As expected, both the `switch` and the `jump table` have constant results for the non-default cases. The `if..else` is still faster than the `switch` for the first two cases but it does not outdo the `jump table`. Do not forget, however, that the `jump table` technique creates some extra overhead that is not represented by this timing data. This overhead is incurred when the jump table is initialized with the function pointers. However, this is done only once and most likely at some point during the start of the program.

Conclusion: When the number of statements to be executed in each case becomes large enough to warrant delegation to functions, the `jump table` technique is clearly the fastest choice, with the `switch` coming a close second.

Conclusion 2: When constant lookup time is important, the jump table is definitely the way to go.

- Array lookup

This final bullet examines array lookup. It is not really a fair comparison to set array lookup times next to selector times, which is why it is placed in a separate bullet; however, array lookup is still a very interesting technique simply because it is incredibly fast.

The principle of array lookup is basically creating an array containing results. Then, instead of calling a function in order to obtain a result, the array is simply indexed. Of course, this technique can only be used when all possible function results can be calculated beforehand and an indexing system can be used. A popular and very useful implementation of a lookup array is one containing sine, cosine, or tangent results. Instead of calling an expensive `tan()` function, an array is created containing the tan results with the needed resolution. The following example illustrates this:

```
// Look-up Array definition:
short tan[] = {0,175, 349,524,698,872,1047,1221,1396,1571,1746};
~~
// Use of array as if function:
short res = tan[a];
```

Note that this example also puts into practice some techniques concerning efficient use of variables as explained in Chapter 6, "The Standard C/C++ Variables." Table 7.3 shows some timing results.

TABLE 7.3 Test Results of Array Lookup

Selected Case	Array Lookup Results
1	340
2	340
3	340
4	330
5	340
6	340
7	330
8	340
9	340
Default	330

The fastest times yet, obviously. And, of course, each case (array index) is equally fast. The consideration to be made concerning array lookup is whether its use measures up to the amount of space the array takes up. In this example the decision is clear: Any tan function would be considerably larger than this small array of shorts. And even when the array does become impressively large, it might still justify its existence when the data it contains is needed very often, is very expedient, or both.

Loops

This section focuses on loop statements. Loops have a way of making a source code listing look relatively compact as repetitions of statements are coded only once. This is where loops present a danger to performance as well; any small inefficiency in the body of a loop will be incurred as many times as the loop body is iterated over. A loop that has one superfluous statement and that is iterated over 10,000 times will, of course, cause 10,000 superfluous statements to be executed. Consequently, loops are the places where most often a lot of performance can be won. This section presents several techniques that can be used to optimize loops.

Aborting Loops

Often, loops are implemented with termination conditions, as shown in the following examples:

```
// typical loop termination conditions:
for (j = 0; j <  arraySize; j++)
{~~}

while (q < nrOfElems )
{~~}

do {~~}
while (countDown > 0);
```

These are typical uses of loops for iterating over the elements of arrays, databases, and lists. They are syntactically correct, of course, but can be wildly inefficient. Consider an array of which each element is, on average, accessed an equal amount of times during program execution; a loop as specified like this will thus, on average, execute 50% of its iterations in vain. Only when the element that the loop is "looking for" happens to be the last element in the array does the loop actually have to iterate over *all* the array elements. This is why often a second stop clause is added to the loop, enabling it to stop when it has found what it is looking for. Listing 7.2 demonstrates this.

LISTING 7.2   Aborting a Loop with a Flag

```
void DB::FindId(int searchId)
{
    int Found = 0;

    for (int i=0; i<Index && !Found; i++)
    {
        if (base.GetId(i) == searchId)      // abort criteria.
        {
            //Found.
            Found = 1;
        }
        ~~ other loop statements ~~
    }

    base.ExecuteElement(i);
~~
```

The flag Found is added to the stop condition of the for loop in order to abort further iteration when the job has been done. As can be seen in this example, two comparisons are needed to determine an early stop. The first comparison is made in the body of the loop in order to determine whether you have found what you are looking for—in which case the Found flag is set. The second comparison is made in the header of the loop in order to check up on the status of the Found flag. This already gains us some performance as the average number of iterations is now brought down by 50% (for loops in which each element is used the same number of times on average). However, when the loop does not find what it is looking for, all iterations are, of course, still performed and two statements of overhead were added to every iteration! A better way to abort a loop is presented in Listing 7.3.

LISTING 7.3   Aborting a Loop with a Break

```
void DB::FindId(int searchId)
{
    for (int i=0; i < Index ; i++)
    {
        if (base.GetId(i) == searchId)      // abort criteria.
        {
            //Found.
            break;
        }
        ~~ other loop statements ~~
    }

    base.ExecuteElement(i);
~~
```

By using break (Listing 7.3), you can eliminate one of the two comparisons used in Listing 7.2.

When the abort criterion is satisfied (GetId(I) == searchId), the break takes program execution to the first statement following the loop, which is base.ExecuteElement(i) in Listing 7.3. Not only does the code in Listing 7.3 use fewer comparisons per iteration, it is also faster when the abort criterion is reached. This is because the break causes the rest of the statements in the loop to be skipped (~~ other loop statements ~~), and the loop header is not evaluated a last time.

Note that the stop criterion in the header of the loop itself could also be replaced by an if..break combination; however, this is unlikely to affect the loop performance as compilers will generate the same, or very similar, code for both solutions.

In practice, complicated loops will often take up most of a function, with the function result being a pointer (or reference) to the found element. In these cases, it is, of course, best to abort the loop by immediately returning the found object. The following example illustrates this:

```
void DB::FindId(int searchId)
{
    for (int i=0; i < Index ; i++)
```

7

BASIC
PROGRAMMING
STATEMENTS

```
    {
        if (base.GetId(i) == searchId)     // abort creteria.
        {
            //Found.
            return base.GetObjectRef(i);
        }
        ~~ other loop statements ~~
    }
}
```

Skipping Parts of the Loop

In the previous section, you saw how to speed up loops by skipping unnecessary iterations.
This section will explain how to speed up loop iteration by skipping unnecessary statements
within the loop body. Basically, it comes down to finding out whether the iteration will be useful as early on as possible. If it is not, the rest of the statements of the loop body are skipped
and the next iteration is started. This technique is a valuable time saver; it should especially be
considered for large or work-intense loops. The code in Listing 7.4 looks very similar to that of
Listing 7.3, where break was used to abort a loop. The results, however, are fundamentally different.

LISTING 7.4   Aborting an Iteration of a Loop

```
void DB::ServiceProblems(int threshold)
{
    int size = baseSize;          // local copy of a member variable.

    for (int i=0; i < size ; i++)
    {
        EL *element = GetObject(i);    // local pointer.

        if (element->GetPressure() < threshold)     // skip criteria.
        {
            // not an interesting element.
            continue;
        }
        ~~ other loop statements ~~
    }
}
```

The example in Listing 7.4 iterates over all database elements and performs some actions
for each element that has a pressure value greater than that of the specified threshold. An
if..continue combination was added to discard any element with a safe pressure value.

Consequently, for safe elements the ~~ `other loop statements` ~~ will be skipped, as the `continue` forces the next iteration to be started immediately. Notice that, in this example, the `if..continue` could have easily been replaced by an `if..else` construct. This is basically always the case; however, more complex loops can become much easier to read when `continue` is used instead. Notice also that some techniques discussed in Chapter 6 are used here.

Summary

There are different techniques for implementing selectors and loops. Depending on the aim of a piece of code, a certain technique will be more useful than another. This chapter explained the characteristics of different techniques and showed where to use each.

- Selectors

`if..else` constructions are very fast for the first few cases and increasingly slower for the rest, with the default case being the slowest. Use `if..else` constructions for evaluating complex expressions that cannot be reduced to a numbered range for a selector, and either/or situations that are unlikely to be augmented with additional cases in the future.

The `switch` statement is equally fast for all selectable cases, except for the `default` case, which is faster than the other cases. `switch` is slower than `if..else` only when there are a minimal number of cases. Use the `switch` statement wherever the selector can be reduced to a numbered range—preferably a continuous one—and the number of (expected) cases is higher than 3 or 4.

Jump tables are equally fast for each selectable function they contain. Defaults need to be coded by hand. When cases delegate all the work to a function, a jump table is even faster than a `switch`, as long as the selector range is continuous. Use jump tables when the selector can be reduced to a continuous numbered range and cases immediately delegate to functions.

Array lookup is the fastest technique to obtain a result based on the value of a selector. The memory usage of the array is best when the selector range is continuous. Array lookup can be used only when the selectable results can be calculated beforehand. Use array lookup when the selector can be reduced to a continuous numbered range, the footprint of the array is not a problem, and the selectable results can be calculated beforehand.

- Loops

It is very important to keep an eye on the performance of the body statements of loops. Loops often perform hundreds of iterations, which means that each statement that can be optimized is, in effect, optimized hundreds of times over. This chapter has shown some techniques for optimizing loops and highlighted places where loops can often be optimized. It is a good idea for implementers to always keep the efficiency of their loops in mind when writing software, even when writing seemingly trivial loops. In many cases, the number of loop iterations depends on the number of elements in an array, list, or database. This number will grow over time. In other cases, loops with an initially small number of iterations are enlarged when a program is updated or reused. This means you cannot assume that a small loop will always stay a small loop.

Where possible the size and number of iterations of loops should be honed with the use of `break` and `continue` statements.

Functions

IN THIS CHAPTER

This chapter focuses on different ways of invoking functions and passing function parameters. It introduces several calling techniques and compares their characteristics. An in-depth view is given of what exactly is involved with calling functions via the different techniques and when best to use which technique.

Invoking Functions

Let's first look at what actually happens when a function call is made. Previous chapters have already hinted at function-call overhead and now seems to be the ideal time to discover exactly what this so-called overhead is. Consider therefore the simple C/C++ function presented in Listing 8.1.

LISTING 8.1   A Simple Add Function

```
int MyAddFunct(int a, int b, int c)
{
    return a + b + c;
}

void main(void)
{
    int a = 1, b = 2 , c = 3;
    int res = MyAddFunct(a,b,c);
}
```

The function MyAddFunct in Listing 8.1 takes three integers as input and returns as a result the sum of the three. By compiling this source with the assembly output option turned on (see Chapter 4, "Tools and Languages"), you can look at what the processor actually has to do to execute this function. The assembly listings presented in this section were generated with Developer Studio for Windows, but other compilers will give similar results. A column of line numbers has been added to the output to facilitate referencing from the explanatory text. The first line(s) in each listing depicts the original C/C++ statement. Listing 8.2 shows the assembly generated for the call to MyAddFunction.

LISTING 8.2   Assembly for Calling MyAddFunct()

```
// MyAddFunct(a,b,c);

00    mov eax, DWORD PTR _c$[ebp] ; place value of 'c' in register eax.
01    push eax                    ; push register eax onto the stack.
02    mov ecx, DWORD PTR _b$[ebp] ; place value of 'b' in register ecx.
03    push ecx                    ; push register ecx onto the stack.
04    mov edx, DWORD PTR _a$[ebp] ; place value of 'a' in register eax.
05    push edx                    ; push register eax onto the stack.
06    call ?MyAddFunct@@YAHHHH@Z  ; call MyAddFunct()
```

As can be seen in Listing 8.2, before a function is even called a lot of work is already done. In lines 00–05 the three variables that are input for the function (a, b, and c) are placed on the top of the stack, so they become part of the function's local parameter set. Then, in line 06, the function is actually called. This causes the value of the program counter to be placed into the stack also. At any time, the program counter points to the memory address from which the processor is retrieving instructions. In calling the function, the program counter is set to point to the address of the first instruction of the function. Because the previous value of the program counter resides safely on the stack, execution can continue with the instruction after the function call when the function has ended.

Note that this part of the function call overhead (placing variables on the stack) will grow larger when more (or larger) parameters are passed to a function, and smaller when fewer (or smaller) parameters are passed. Now let's look at what happens inside the function. Listing 8.3 shows what happens on entry of the function.

LISTING 8.3   Assembly for Entering MyAddFunct()

```
// int MyAddFunct(int a, int b, int c)
// {

07  push ebp            ; place the base pointer on the stack.
08  mov ebp, esp        ; new base pointer value.
```

The statements in Listing 8.3 are executed before the actual function body statements. So what exactly is the overhead that is incurred when entering a function? Basically it is more stack work. The base pointer (ebp)—which tells the processor where to find local variables—is pushed onto the stack. Its value will be needed when the function ends and access is needed to the local variables of the calling context. After the base pointer is placed onto the stack, the base pointer receives the value of the stack pointer. Now pointing at the top of the stack, the base pointer can be used to retrieve (albeit via a negative index) the function parameters. This is logical, as the base pointer now points at the stack frame containing the function's local variables.

This part of the function call overhead is pretty standard. It basically saves the current context onto the stack so it can be used again when the function ends. The more registers that are used inside the function, the more registers will have to be pushed onto the stack for safekeeping. This means two things. First, the function MyAddFunct is obviously not going to use a lot of different registers. Second, the more *complicated* a function is, the more overhead will be incurred on function entry. Figure 8.1 shows what the stack looks like at this point inside the function call.

8

FUNCTIONS

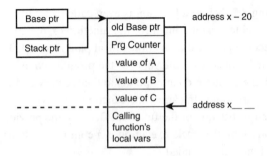

FIGURE 8.1
Stack frame when inside a function call.

Arriving at the instructions that form the function body, Listing 8.4 shows the assembly statements that make up the body of the MyAddFunct function.

LISTING 8.4   Assembly for the Body of MyAddFunct()

```
// return a + b + c;

09   mov eax, DWORD PTR _a$[ebp] ; value of 'a' in register eax.
10   add eax, DWORD PTR _b$[ebp] ; add value of 'b' to eax.
11   add eax, DWORD PTR _c$[ebp] ; add value of 'c' to eax.
```

The body statement is represented by three assembly lines (09–11). The register eax, which is used for returning values from functions, is loaded with the value of the variable a, after which the values of b and c are added. It should be clear from this example exactly how parameters are passed to functions; for more information, see Chapter 4.

So is this it then? No, not exactly; there is still the exiting of the function and returning the result. Listing 8.5 shows what happens when MyAddFunct terminates.

LISTING 8.5   Assembly for Exiting MyAddFunct()

```
// }

12   pop    ebp        ; return ebp to its original value.
13   ret    0          ; return from the function.
```

Basically this is the opposite of Listing 8.2; saved register values are taken from the stack in reverse order, line 12. At this point all that remains on the stack are the three parameters and the program counter. Line 13 returns from the function and effectively pops the program counter from the stack and causes execution to continue at the instructions right after the function call. Listing 8.6 shows how the returned result of function MyAddFunct is captured by the calling function.

LISTING 8.6 Assembly for Capturing the Result of `MyAddFunct()`

```
// int res = ...

14  add esp, 12                    ; pop 3 variables * 4 bytes.
15  mov DWORD PTR _res$[ebp], eax  ; eax contains the function
                                   ; result.
```

The three variables were still on the stack so the stack pointer is adjusted by 12 bytes (as the stack grows downwards in memory an add is used instead of a sub).

So all in all quite a lot of instructions had to be executed to make this calculation, which itself was only *three* instructions long.

When a function is used often, and it does not contain that many statements, it would be great if it were possible to somehow skip the overhead shown in this section, while still keeping the level of abstraction created by the function call. The rest of this section will discuss techniques to do just that, as well as some other useful techniques.

Macros

One way to avoid function-call overhead is by using macros. You can define a macro in both C and C++ with the `#define` keyword. Just as with any other use of the `#define` keyword, a macro basically tells the precompiler to substitute a specified sequence for an identifier:

```
#define TRUE 1
```

With the definition above, the precompiler is told to replace all occurrences of the word TRUE in the source with the character 1, before handing the source over to the compiler (for more information on the precompiler, see Chapter 4). With function macros we take things a little further as we are able to use function-like arguments. Listing 8.7 shows a few much-used macro definitions.

LISTING 8.7 Macro Examples

```
#define MAX(a,b)   ((a) < (b) ? (b) : (a))
#define MIN(a,b)   ((a) < (b) ? (a) : (b))
#define ABS(a)     (a) < 0 ? -(a) : (a)

#define TSTBIT(a,b) ((a & (1<<b)) ? (true): (false))
#define SETBIT(a,b) ((a | (1 << b)))
#define CLRBIT(a,b) ((a & (~(1 << b))))
#define FLIPBIT(a,b) (TSTBIT(a,b) ? (CLRBIT(a,b)) : (SETBIT(a,b)))
```

8

FUNCTIONS

When you look at the MAX macro in Listing 8.7, you see that the identifier part—MAX(a,b)—contains the parameters a and b. These parameters are repeated in the replacement string. The precompiler will thus be able to make a parameterized substitution by taking whichever parameters it finds between the brackets and placing them in the appropriate spots within the substitute string. Listing 8.8 uses this macro and demonstrates immediately why macros are not always a good idea.

LISTING 8.8   Unexpected Macro Results

```
#define MAX(a,b) ((a) <(b) ? (b):(a))

void main(void)
{
        int   a= 10;
        char b = 12;

        short c = MAX(a,b);   // a = 10, b = 12, c = 12 (ok)
        c = MAX(a++,b++);     // a = 11, b = 14, c = 13   (not ok)
}
```

The first use of the macro in Listing 8.8—MAX(a,b)—seems to work fine; it returns the larger of the two given parameters and places it in variable c. The second call, however, is expanded a little differently than the implementer might have intended:

```
MAX(a++,b++);    =>   ((a++) < (b++) ? (b++) : (a++))
```

The variables a and b are incremented on evaluation; variable b is incremented once more when it is returned. This demonstrates how cryptic the use of macros can be, particularly when you are using functions written by a third party. You might not even be aware that the function you are calling is in fact a macro and therefore has some peculiarities. Moreover, both macro calls in the example use different types of variables; MAX can return either a character or an integer but the result is stored in a short, and the compiler does not complain about this.

It seems it is time to list the advantages and disadvantages of using macros:

The following is the advantage of using macros:

- They can make function execution faster by eliminating function call overhead.

The following are disadvantages of using macros:

- Often macro descriptions are very cryptic and hard to read.
- Use of macros increases footprint as macro bodies are expanded wherever they are used.
- Finding compiler errors in macros can be a difficult task.

- Debugging a source with macros can be problematic, because debuggers (as other development tools) do not always know exactly how to handle macros.
- Macros do not facilitate type-checking.

Conclusion: Although the use of macros can certainly speed up code that uses small functions repetitiously, you should be wary of using them. Most often there are other ways to solve the problems. Use macros only if and when you really feel you have to.

Inline Functions

Another way of avoiding function call overhead is the use of inline functions. Inline functions are a C++ feature and therefore cannot be used in C. They operate under a principle similar to that of macros—namely that the function call is actually substituted by the function body during compile time. This can be a great timesaver for short functions which are called frequently. Think of class member functions for accessing private data; they appear very often in C++ sources but usually do nothing more than return a pointer or variable value. Every time such an access function is called, though, function-call overhead is incurred that is many times larger than the actual function body. An ideal situation for optimization it seems.

There are two ways of declaring inline functions: first, by adding the keyword `inline` to the function definition, and second, by adding the function body in the definition of a member function of a class. Listing 8.9 shows the two methods of declaring inline functions.

LISTING 8.9   Two Ways to Inline Functions

```
inline int MyAddFunct(int a, int b, int c)  // inlining a non class
                                            //   member function.
{
    return a + b + c;
}

class Client
{
private:
    char                *name;      // Private data.
    unsigned char       age;
    char                gender;

public:
    char *GetName() { return name;} // inlining access to name.
    int  GetAge() { return age;}    // inlining access to age.
    char GetGender();
};
```

LISTING 8.9 Continued

```
inline char Client::GetGender()      // inlining access to gender.
{
    return gender;
}
```

Let's look at the advantages and disadvantages of inlined functions:

Inlining offers the following advantages:

- Faster function calls
- Easy optimization as only a keyword has to be added, or a definition moved to a header file
- Retains the benefit of type-checking for parameters

Inlining also offers the following disadvantage:

- Increased footprint as the function body appears everywhere where the inlined function is called

Conclusion: Use inlining only for short functions that are called frequently or that are part of a time-critical piece of code.

Sadly, however, for practically all compilers the inlining of functions is merely a suggestion made by the programmer. This means that making a function inline is no hard guarantee that the compiler will in fact substitute function calls for function bodies. It is possible that some or all inlined functions are treated like normal function definitions. For more information on inlining implementation, consult the documentation provided with the compiler you use.

Iteration Versus Recursion

A third way of avoiding function-call overhead is by simply expanding a function by hand. This way you have none of the dangers of macros, none of the uncertainty of inline functions, and most definitely all the work to do. The main part of this work is making sure the expanded functionality is correct every time, so this means no copy and paste mistakes! Still, sometimes it can be worth considering, especially where a function is called many times in the same place. This section examines a function expanded within an iterative process, compared to using the same functionality recursively. The thing to note here is that, although the expanded function is called many times, the expansion is only coded in one place in the source. This means no copy/paste dangers and no footprint issues.

Iteration is simply repeating a certain functionality over and over again until some stop condition is met. Think, for example, of a `for` or `while` loop iterating over array elements.

Recursion basically comes down to using a function that at some point makes a call to itself. This second invocation can of course call itself also and so on. It's a bit like standing between two mirrors and looking at your reflection.

This section will use the mathematical factorial function—denoted by the ! sign in mathematics—as an example. The factorial for number n is defined as the product of all integers between 1 and n itself. For example

> 5! equals 5×4×3×2×1=120
>
> 4! equals 4×3×2×1=24

Looking at the example calculations it becomes apparent that 5! equals 5 * 4!, or, to put it more generically:

> n! = n(n-1)!
>
> where n > 0

Having defined n! in terms of simpler cases of itself, it is now possible to write a recursive implementation. Listing 8.10 shows what such an implementation can look like.

8

LISTING 8.10   Recursive Example of n!

```
long FactRec(int n)
{
    if (n == 0)
        return 1;
    else
        return (n * FactRec(n-1));
}
```

Note that as multiplication is used, the result of a factorial grows rapidly. When the function `FactRec()` of Listing 8.10 is called with `int result = FactRec(3);` the function will keep calling itself, passing a smaller version of n each time.

```
FactRec(3) -> FactRec(2) -> FactRec(1).
```

Eventually the final function call will receive a value of n which is 1. This deepest `FactRec()` in the recursion returns the value 1. The `FactRec()` that called it—`FactRec(2)`—receives the 1 and multiplies it by its own value of n which is 2. The result is again returned to the calling `FactRec()` invocation.

Now let's look at how n! can be made iterative. Listing 8.11 shows an iterative version of n!.

LISTING 8.11   Iterative Example of n!

```
long FactIter(int n)
{
    int prod = 1;

    while (n != 0)
    {
        prod *= n;
        n--;
    }
    return prod;
}
```

The iterative function in Listing 8.11 is a bit longer in lines of code than the recursive function in Listing 8.10, but perhaps more intuitive to read. When you run both examples through the time_fn() test as described in Chapter 5, "Measuring Time and Complexity," you uncover the following results:

Recursive	5
Iterative	2.2

These relative numbers tell you, even without more precise measurement, or looking at the generated assembly, that the recursive function is a lot slower than the iterative function. This should come as no surprise as you have seen in the beginning of this chapter that function calls—of which a lot are used in recursion—cause considerable slowdown for relatively small functions. Moreover, the recursive function actually uses more runtime memory as it repeatedly places function call overhead on the stack. The factorial of 10 will in fact result in 11 calls to the FactRec() function. This touches on a major drawback of recursive functions: Their use is limited by the amount of stack that is available. This means predictions have to be made at implementation/design time; when using recursion you simply have to guarantee that the function will never be called with a parameter (or parameters) that will cause a stack overflow, or an unallowable system slowdown.

Summarizing, the following rules of thumb can be defined for when to use recursion:

- When a function can be defined in terms of itself and cannot easily be made iterative.
- When repetitive actions have to be done on a varying set of data (like walking through subdirectories or traversing a tree—see the example in Chapter 11, "Storage Structures.")
- When you can guarantee that the recursive call will never cause system interference.

Passing Data to Functions

When function calls have to be made, it becomes important to find out how this can be done as efficiently as possible. When you look at how functions receive their parameter data, there are basically three options to choose from:

- Passing parameters by value
- Passing parameters by reference
- Using global data

This section examines in detail how to get data to functions via these three methods.

Pass by Reference Versus Pass by Value

As was shown in the previous section, parameters which are passed to a function are placed onto the stack before the function call is made. If a parameter is an integer, the integer is placed on the stack. If a parameter is a pointer to an integer, a pointer to an integer is placed on the stack. So the distinction between passing a parameter by reference or passing it by value lies in what happens to the stack when the function is called. A parameter which is passed by value is copied onto the stack in its entirety. A parameter which is passed by reference is not copied at all but a pointer containing its address is placed on the stack. Listing 8.12 shows the different ways of passing function arguments by value and reference.

8

LISTING 8.12 Declaration and Use of Reference and Pass-by-Value Function Arguments

```
// Passing by value:

void FunctValue(int input1, int input2)
{ input1 += input2;}

// Passing by reference:

void FunctRef(int &input1, int &input2)          // using references.
{ input1 += input2; }

void FunctPoint(int *input1, int *input2)        // using pointers.
{ *input1 += *input2; }


void main(void)
{
   int a = 6, b = 7;
```

LISTING 8.12   Continued

```
    FunctValue(a, 5);    // values 6 and 5 placed on stack.
    FunctRef(a, b);  // addresses of 'a' and 'b' placed on stack.
    FunctPoint(&a, &b);  // addresses of 'a' and 'b' placed on stack.
}
```

Note that passing an object by reference does in fact exactly the same thing as passing an object by a pointer; the only difference is in the notation of the function call and the way the implementer can refer to the object in the body of the function: input1 versus *input1.

There are two reasons why you want to be able to pass a parameter by reference:

- When an object is relatively large it is a much better idea to place its address on stack than the entire object itself. Placing a large object on stack not only costs runtime footprint, it also costs time.

- When a function receives a reference to an object, it can permanently change the value of that object. In Listing 8.12 the functions FunctRef() and FunctPoint() will change the value of variable a in the scope of the calling function, in this case main(). After FunctRef(a,b) the variable a equals 13, then. After FunctPoint(&a, &b) the variable a equals 20 (13 + 7). The first call—FunctValue()—however, does not change the value of variable a. In fact, FunctValue() does nothing—that is, it changes the value of input1 which is a variable on the stack and which disappears after FunctValue() ends.

There is another implication to consider, namely the access to parameters. When a parameter is passed by value, it is part of the local function stack. This means its value can be accessed directly. A parameter which is passed by reference has to be dereferenced before its value can be accessed. This means the pointer of the variable is taken and used to find the value of the variable. Accessing value parameters is thus faster than accessing pointer/reference variables. Listing 8.13 shows this through the assembly that is generated for Listing 8.12.

LISTING 8.13   Assembly Listing Showing Parameter Access for Value Arguments Versus Reference Arguments

```
// FunctValue Body.
input1 += input2;

    mov eax, DWORD PTR _input1$[ebp]     ; get value of input1.
    add eax, DWORD PTR _input2$[ebp]     ; add value of input2.
    mov DWORD PTR _input1$[ebp], eax     ; place addition back in
;    input1.
; value of input1 is subsequently lost.
```

LISTING 8.13   Continued

```
// FunctRef & FunctPoint Bodies.
input1 += input2; or *input1 += *input2;

    mov eax, DWORD PTR _input1$[ebp]    ; get pointer to 'a'.
    mov ecx, DWORD PTR [eax]            ; get value of 'a'.
    mov edx, DWORD PTR _input2$[ebp]    ; get pointer to 'b'.
    add ecx, DWORD PTR [edx]            ; add value of 'b'.
    mov eax, DWORD PTR _input1$[ebp]    ; get pointer to 'a'.
    mov DWORD PTR [eax], ecx            ; place result back in 'a'.
; value of input1, as well as original variable 'a', has been changed.
```

Choosing between passing parameters by reference or by value to time-critical functions is perhaps not as trivial as you might think. Certainly a reference or a pointer must be used when the passed parameter should be permanently changed by the function. When a parameter is passed for read-only use, a choice needs to be made which is based on the following two characteristics:

- Size of the parameter to be passed

  When our parameter is a compound object (structure, array, class, and so on) it will most often be large enough to warrant passing it by reference; a quick `sizeof(object_to_pass)` will tell you exactly how many bytes will be pushed onto stack when you pass `object_to_pass` by value. However, it is not a fair conclusion that passing a parameter by pointer or reference is *always* better where stack footprint is concerned. Passing a character by value causes only a single byte to be placed on stack, for instance, where passing a character by reference causes at least four bytes to be placed on stack!

- Number of times the parameter is accessed.

  When a read-only parameter—or any of its compounded members—is accessed frequently within the function, accessing overhead as demonstrated by Listing 8.13 will begin to influence function performance. In some cases it might be better to make a local copy of the values which are accessed most often:

```
int in = *input1;    // make a local copy of the value pointed to by
                     //  input1.
```

But when the whole parameter—or many of its compounded members—is accessed frequently, it becomes a performance/footprint tradeoff whether or not to pass the parameter by value.

Global Data

The previous section demonstrated how the kind and number of parameters passed to a function can influence function performance. The use of global data makes it possible to decrease the amount of data placed on the stack for a function call. Global data is data that can be accessed by all functions of a program; thus, global data does not have to be passed in a function call. This makes the call itself faster as well as the access to the data, compared to data that is passed by reference. When this globally defined data is used by several functions (but does not become the subject of a multiple access dispute between threads), defining the data globally is even more useful.

Listing 8.14 takes a structure with authentication data—consisting of a username, a password and a registration code—and checks whether this data is valid. For this, four different functions are created:

- `int CheckAuthentication_Global()`

  Takes a globally defined instance of the authentication structure and evaluates its validity. No stack data is used.

- `int CheckAuthentication_ByValue(Authentication value)`

  Takes an authentication structure by value and evaluates its validity. This instance of the structure is copied completely to stack.

- `int CheckAuthentication_ByReference(Authentication &ref)`

  Takes an authentication structure passed by reference and evaluates its validity. A pointer to the instance of the structure is placed into the stack.

- `int CheckAuthentication_ByPointer(Authentication *ref)`

  Takes an authentication structure passed via a pointer and evaluates its validity. A pointer to the instance of the structure is placed into the stack.

The timing results of the different functions are presented at the end of this section:

LISTING 8.14   Comparing Calling Techniques

```
#define OFFSET 10        // secret value used in authentication check.

// Structure to pass as data to the functions.
struct Authentication
{
    unsigned char regCode[21];
    unsigned char user[7];
    unsigned char password[7];
};
```

LISTING 8.14   Continued

```
// Globally defined instance of data, used in the global version of the
//   CheckAuthentication function.
Authentication glob =
        {{0,3,1,0,0,4,0,4,2,1,0,5,0,2,1,0,5,0,2,}, "Bond01","shaken"};


// Global function.
int CheckAuthentication_Global()
{
    int result = 1;

    glob.user[result] = result;
    for (int i = 0; i < 7; i++)
    {
        if (glob.user[i] + glob.password[i] !=
            (glob.regCode[i*3]-OFFSET))
        {
            result = 0;
            break;
        }
    }

    return result;
}

// Pass-By-Value function.
int CheckAuthentication_ByValue(Authentication value)
{
    int result = 1;

    value.user[result] = result;

    for (int i = 0; i < 7; i++)
    {
        if (value.user[i] + value.password[i] !=
            (value.regCode[i*3]-OFFSET))
        {
            result = 0;
            break;
        }
    }

    return result;
}
```

8

FUNCTIONS

LISTING 8.14   Continued

```
// Pass-By-Reference function.
int CheckAuthentication_ByReference(Authentication &ref)
{
    int result = 1;

    ref.user[result] = result;
    for (int i = 0; i < 7; i++)
    {
        if (ref.user[i] + ref.password[i] !=
            (ref.regCode[i*3]-OFFSET))
        {
            result = 0;
            break;
        }
    }

    return result;
}

// Pass-By-Reference -using a pointer- function.
int CheckAuthentication_ByPointer(Authentication *ref)
{
    int result = 1;

    ref->user[result] = result;
    for (int i = 0; i < 7; i++)
    {
        if (ref->user[i] + ref->password[i] !=
            (ref->regCode[i*3]-OFFSET))
        {
            result = 0;
            break;
        }
    }

    return result;
}
```

A program using Listing 8.14 can be found in the file 08Source04.cpp on the Web site. The result of the program is a list of relative numbers indicating the execution speed of the various data passing techniques used. Table 8.1 shows these timing results.

TABLE 8.1 Calling Technique Timing Results

Technique	Relative Time Spent
Calling by reference	220
Calling via a pointer	220
Calling by value	380
Using global data	170

The results presented in Table 8.1 take into account different calling methods as well as variable access for the different calling methods. From this table, you see that calling by pointer and calling by reference are indeed equally fast. As expected, calling by value is quite a lot slower. The clear winner is the function which uses global data.

Early Returns

As with loops, it is possible to optimize function execution by implementing a function in such a way as to allow the optional skipping of body statements. Using early returns is a method of checking as many reasons as possible for not continuing to execute the function. What you basically want to do is make sure that reserving memory, doing complex calculations and calling other functions is only done when it is clear that the efforts will be useful. Listing 8.15 shows an example function that uses no early returns.

LISTING 8.15 No Use of Early Returns

```
struct Object
{
    int  color;
    int  material;
    int  city;
    char *name;
};


Object *CreateObject(char *name)
{
    Object *pObj = new Object;
    strcpy(pObj->name, name);

    pObj->color    = CurrentStatus->FashionColor();
    pObj->material = CurrentStatus->FashionMaterial();
    pObj->city     = CurrentStatus->CurrentCity();
```

LISTING 8.15   Continued

```
if (    pObj->city     == UNDEFINED ||
        pObj->color    == UNDEFINED ||
        pObj->material == UNDEFINED)
    {
        delete [] pObj->name;
        delete pObj;
        return NULL;
    }

    return pObj;
}
```

The function `CreateObject()` endeavors to create a new object with a given name. This new object will take its other values (`color`, `material`, and `city`) from a global database that should contain current status information. This way the new object will have the color and material which are most fashionable at the moment of creation, and will be produced in the city with the best plants. It is possible, however, that some status information is not defined at object creation time, in which case it is not necessary to create a new object yet.

Listing 8.15 shows the way functions are often used in the field. When you look closely at the fail conditions, found at the end of the function, you notice that it is possible to speed up function execution considerably in the case when no object is created. This becomes increasingly useful as likelihood of failure increases. By evaluating fail conditions earlier, it is possible to skip time-consuming object creation and deletion. Listing 8.16 demonstrates this for the `CreateObject()` function of Listing 8.15.

LISTING 8.16   Using Early Returns

```
Object *CreateObject(char *name)
{
    int col, mat, cit;

    if (UNDEFINED == (col = CurrentStatus->FashionColor()))
        return NULL;
    if (UNDEFINED == (mat = CurrentStatus->FashionMaterial()))
        return NULL;
    if (UNDEFINED == (cit = CurrentStatus->CurrentCity()))
        return NULL;

    Object *pObj = new Object;
    strcpy(pObj->name, name);
    pObj->city     = cit;
```

LISTING 8.16 Continued

```
    pObj->color    = col;
    pObj->material = mat;

    return pObj;
}
```

Note the complete absence of a delete instruction from Listing 8.16. Also, a call to `strcpy` is made only when necessary.

Functions as Class Methods

This section looks at functions which are part of classes—that is, class methods. Classes are a concept of C++ and cannot be used in C; consequently this section will probably not be of great interest to C-only programmers.

Classes make application design and code reuse easier by allowing more intuitive and orderly grouping of source code functionality into reusable objects. However, with the added ease of use come also additional performance and footprint considerations. These considerations are different depending on the way in which class methods are actually used. This section looks in detail at the implications of different techniques of using class methods and provides guidelines on when and where to use which technique.

Inheritance

Inheritance can be a very good way of safely reusing existing functionality. Typically, inheritance is used where related objects share some common functionality. Consider two objects that retrieve information from the Internet. The first object retrieves pictures to display on screen, and the second retrieves music to play over audio speakers. The data manipulation done by these objects will be quite different but they have some common functionality: Internet access. By moving this common functionality into a base class, it can be used in both objects but the actual code for Internet access needs to be written, tested, and, most importantly, maintained, only in one place. This is a great advantage where development time is concerned. The design becomes more transparent and the problems tackled by the base class need to be solved only once. Moreover, when a bug is found and fixed, there is no danger of overlooking a similar bug in similar functionality. Listing 8.17 shows a class with which we will demonstrate different ways of using inherited functionality.

LISTING 8.17 Base Class Definition of an Example Class

```
#define unknownOS  0
#define OS2        1
#define WINDOWS    2
```

LISTING 8.17   Continued

```cpp
#define LINUX      3


class ComputerUser
{
public:

  // constructor
  ComputerUser()
  {
    favouriteOS = unknownOS;
  }

  ComputerUser(char *n, int OS)
  {
    strcpy(name, n);
    favouriteOS = OS;
  }

  // destructor
  ~ComputerUser()
  {
  }

  // interface
  void SetOS(int OS)
  {
    favouriteOS = OS;
  }

  void SetName(const char *s)
  {
    strcpy(name, s);
  }

private:

  // data
  int favouriteOS;
  char name[50];
};
```

The ComputerUser class will be our base class for storing information about a computer user. Each computer user can have a name and a favorite OS. The class implementation is pretty straightforward, but note that the constructor is overloaded. When a computer user's name and favorite OS are known at construction time, this information will be initialized immediately.

Now let's assume that for a specific type of computer user, you want to store more information. For instance, of computer users who have access to the Internet you want to know what their favorite browser is. Not all computer users have Internet access but all people with access to the Internet use a computer; therefore, it is possible to derive an `Internetter` from a `ComputerUser`. Listing 8.18 shows how this can be done.

LISTING 8.18 Deriving from the Example Base Class

```
#define unknownBROWSER   0
#define NETSCAPE         1
#define EXPLORER         2

class Internetter: public ComputerUser
{
public:

  // constructor
  Internetter()
  {
     favouriteBrowser = unknownBROWSER;
  }

  Internetter(char *n, int OS, int browser)
  {
    SetName(n);
    SetOS(OS);
    favouriteBrowser = browser;
  }

  // destructor
  ~Internetter()
  {}

  // interface
  void SetBrowser(int browser)
  {
    favouriteBrowser = browser;
  }

private:

  // data
  int favouriteBrowser;
};
```

The Internetter class also has an overloaded constructor for passing initialization data. Because Internetter is a derived class, it needs to initialize not only its own data but also that of its base class. This is can be seen in its second constructor.

Now that you have seen an example of a base class and a derived class, let's look at some different techniques of using their member functions.

Inefficient Object Initialization

One way of creating an instance of the Internetter class could be

```
Internetter *p = new Internetter;

p->SetName("John");
p->SetOS(LINUX);
p->SetBrowser(NETSCAPE);
.........
delete p;
```

Though this construction of an Internetter is functionally correct, it is far from efficient. In fact this example of class method use would not have been shown were it not for the fact that it is used in the field often in some form or other. What happens in this example is that a class is first instantiated, after which (three) separate methods are called to initialize it. This can be done sometimes because initializing data needs to be retrieved from different places, but it would be more efficient to gather the data first and then create the class instantiation with a single constructor call:

```
Internetter *p = new Internetter("John", LINUX, NETSCAPE);
```

Inefficient Base Class Initialization

More inefficiencies lurk in Listings 8.17 and 8.18. To find them, you have to take a closer look at what happens when you create an Internetter instantiation. To create an Internetter, you first need to create a ComputerUser; the constructor of the ComputerUser is thus called. Similarly, the destructor of the ComputerUser will be called when the Internetter is deleted; however, as constructors and destructors are called in a stacklike fashion, first the Internetter destructor is called and then the ComputerUser destructor. As the Internetter constructors do not explicitly call any ComputerUser constructor, the default constructor is used. Again several method calls are needed to initialize the class. In this case, two calls are made to ComputerUser, namely SetName() and SetOS(). It would be better to have the Internetter class explicitly use the ComputerUser constructor, which allows member initialization. Listing 8.19 shows such a class.

LISTING 8.19   Better Use of Base Class Construction

```
class Internetter2: public ComputerUser
{
public:
  // constructor
  Internetter2()
  {
    favouriteBrowser = unknownBROWSER;
  }

  Internetter2(char *n, int OS, int browser)
  : ComputerUser(n, OS)              // base class construction.
  {
    favouriteBrowser = browser;
  }

  // destructor
  ~Internetter2()
  {
  }

  // interface
  void SetBrowser(int browser)
  {
    favouriteBrowser = browser;
  }

private:

  // data
  int favouriteBrowser;
};
```

8

FUNCTIONS

Without Inheritance Overhead

Before looking at actual timing data of the different techniques, you should examine what happens when you do not use inheritance. Certainly in this example, where so few members are found in the base class, it is worth considering coding the base class functionality directly into the derived class. For objects of which the use is time critical (which are used/accessed often during search actions and so on), it might prove to be a good idea to do just this. Listing 8.20 shows how Internetter functionality can be combined with ComputerUser functionality.

LISTING 8.20 Not Using Inheritance

```
class ExtendedComputerUser
{
public:

  // constructor
  ExtendedComputerUser()
  {
    favouriteOS = unknownOS;
  }

  ExtendedComputerUser(char *n, int OS, int browser)
  {
    strcpy(name, n);
    favouriteOS = OS;
    favouriteBrowser = browser;
  }

  // destructor
  ~ExtendedComputerUser()    {}

  // interface
  void SetOS(int OS)
  {
      favouriteOS = OS;
  }

  void SetBrowser(int browser)
  {
      favouriteBrowser = browser;
  }

  void SetName(const char *s)
  {
      strcpy(name, s);
  }

private:

    // data
  int favouriteOS;
  int favouriteBrowser;
  char name[40];
};
```

Timing Data

The timing data for Table 8.2 was gathered using a program which can be found in the file 08Source01.cpp on the Web site. The result of the program is a list of relative numbers indicating the execution speed of the various object construction methods described in this section:

TABLE 8.2   Timing Data on Different Uses of Inheritance

3200	Inefficient initialization of `Internetter`	(1)
3180	Efficient initialization of `Internetter`	(2)
2480	Efficient initialization of base class by `Internetter2`	(3)
2150	Without inheritance overhead by `ExpandedComputerUser`	(4)

Note that the first two results are quite close; this is because the overhead incurred in initializing the derived class in test 1 is still incurred in initializing the base class in test 2. Test 3 initializes both the derived class and the base class more efficiently and is noticeably faster. Not using inheritance at all is, unsurprisingly, the fastest method of the four. It should be noted also that slowdown increases as more levels of inheritance are added. Each time a class is derived from another, a layer of constructor and destructor calls is added. However, when constructors and other member functions are actually inlined by the compiler the overhead of derived constructors is, of course, negated.

Summarizing, it can be said that for time-critical classes the following questions should be asked concerning the use of inheritance:

- Is using inheritance actually necessary?
- What is the actual price to be paid when avoiding inheritance (not only where application footprint is concerned but also in terms of application maintainability)?
- When inheritance is used, is it used as efficiently as possible?

Virtual Functions

Before looking at the technical implications of using virtual functions, a small set of samples will demonstrate what exactly virtual functions are used for.

To the classes of Listing 8.19 is added another class describing Internetters who also happen to be multiplayer gamers. As not all Internetters are multiplayer gamers and certainly not all computer users are multiplayer gamers, the `MultiPlayer` class will be a derivative of the `Internetter2` class. Of a multiplayer gamer we are interested in his or her favorite game and the nickname used when playing. Listing 8.21 shows what the `MultiPlayer` class looks like.

Listing 8.21   MultiPlayer Class

```
#define unknownGAME      0
#define QUAKE        1
#define DESCENT      2
#define HALFLIFE     3

class MultiPlayer: public Internetter2
{
public:

    // constructor
    MultiPlayer()
    {
        favouriteGame = unknownGAME;
    };

    MultiPlayer(char *n, int OS, int browser, int game, char *nName)
    : Internetter2(n, OS, browser)
    {
        favouriteGame = game;
        strcpy(nickName, nName);
    }

      // destructor
    ~MultiPlayer()
    {}

      // interface
    void SetGame(int game)
    {
        favouriteGame = game;
    }

private:

      // data
    char nickName[50];
    int favouriteGame;
};
```

Now let's assume you have a group of computer users of which you want to know the names. To this end you can add a `PrintName` function to the base class `ComputerUser`

```
void ComputerUser::PrintName() { cout << name << endl;}
```

and create an array of `ComputerUser`s:

```
ComputerUser *p[4];
p[0] = new ComputerUser("John", WINDOWS);
p[1] = new Internetter("Jane", LINUX, NETSCAPE);
p[2] = new Internetter2("Gary", LINUX, EXPLORER);
p[3] = new MultiPlayer("Joe", LINUX, NETSCAPE, QUAKE, "MightyJoe");
```

The following fragment of code will print the names of the ComputerUsers in the array:

```
for (int i =0; i < 4; i++)
    p[i]->PrintName();
```

However, multiplayers decide they do not like this approach one bit and demand to be addressed by their nicknames. This implies creating a separate PrintName function for the MultiPlayer class which will print the nickname instead of the computer user name:

```
void MultiPlayer::PrintName() { cout << nickName << endl;}
```

Sadly, the print loop does not recognize this function. It takes pointers to ComputerUsers and calls only their print methods. The compiler needs to be told that we are thinking about overriding certain base class functions with a different implementation. This is done with the keyword virtual. Listing 8.22 shows the new and improved base class, which allows us to override the print method.

LISTING 8.22 Virtual PrintName Function

```
class ComputerUser
{
public:

  // constructor
  ComputerUser()
  {
    favouriteOS = unknownOS;
  }

  ComputerUser(char *n, int OS)
  {
    strcpy(name, n);
    favouriteOS = OS;
  }

  // destructor
  ~ComputerUser()
  {

  }
```

8

LISTING 8.22   Continued

```
// interface
void SetOS(int OS)
{
  favouriteOS = OS;
}

void SetName(const char *s)
{
  strncpy(name, s, 40);
}

virtual void PrintName()
{
  cout << name << endl;
}

private:

// data
int favouriteOS;
char name[50];
};
```

Now when you run the printing loop once more, the multiplayer gamer will be identified by his nickname.

By adding the keyword `virtual` you tell the compiler that you want to use something called *late binding* for a specific function. This means that it is no longer known at compile time which function will actually be called at runtime. Depending on the kind of class being dealt with, a certain function will be called. Note that

- By specifying a function as virtual in the base class, it is automatically virtual for all derived classes.
- When calling a virtual function via a pointer to a class instantiation, the implementation that is used is from the latest derived class that implements the function for that class instantiation.

The second bullet describes something called *polymorphism*. The example print loop uses pointers to `ComputerUsers`. When it becomes time to print the name of the `Joe` instantiation of `MultiPlayer`, it takes the `PrintName()` implemented by `Multiplayer`. This means that at runtime the program can see it is handling a `MultiPlayer` and not just a normal `ComputerUser` and calls the appropriate function implementation.

So how does this actually work? Two things are done at compile time to allow the program to make a runtime decision about which implementation of a virtual function to actually call. First, virtual tables (VT) and virtual table pointers (VPTR) are added to the generated code. Second, code to use the VTs and VPTRs at runtime is added.

Virtual Table (VT)

For every class that is defined and that either contains a virtual function or inherits a virtual function, a VT is created. A VT contains pointers to function implementations. For each virtual function there will be exactly one corresponding pointer. This pointer points to the implementation that is valid for that class.

In our previous example classes, the VTs of `ComputerUser`, `Internetter`, `Internetter2`, and `Multiplayer` all contain a single function pointer that points to an implementation of `PrintName`. As neither `Internetter` nor `Internetter2` define their own `PrintName()`, their VT entry will point to the base class implementation (`ComputerUser::PrintName()`). `MultiPlayer` does have its own `PrintName()` function and thus its VT entry points to a different function address (`MultiPlayer::PrintName()`).

The footprint implications are clear: The more virtual functions are defined within a class, the larger become the VTs of all derived classes. Note also that derived classes can define additional virtual functions; by doing this they again increase VT size for their own derivatives. However, when different classes have the same VT (as `Internetter` and `Internetter2` do in the examples) the compiler can decide to create only a single VT to be shared by the classes.

Virtual Table Pointer (VPTR)

When an instantiation of a class is made, it needs to be able to access the VT defined for its class. To this end, an extra member is added to the class which points to the VT. This member is called the virtual table pointer.

For example, the instantiation `Joe` contains a VPTR that points to the VT of `Multiplayer`. Through it, it can access the `PrintName()` function of `Multiplayer`. Similarly, `Jane`, an `Internetter`, contains a VPTR that points to the VT of `Internetter`, which in turn contains a pointer to `ComputerUser::PrintName()`.

The footprint implications are clear: To every instantiation made of a class that has a virtual table, an extra member is added—that is, a pointer that is automatically initiated with the address of the VT of the class at construction time. Figure 8.2 shows how virtual functions are called.

Note that Figure 8.2 depicts a possible VTable implementation. Depending on which compiler is used, the actual implementation may differ somewhat.

- Code to use the virtual table and virtual table pointer at runtime.

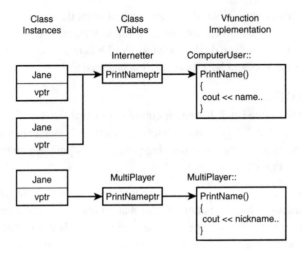

FIGURE 8.2

Calling virtual functions.

To call a virtual function at runtime, the VPTR of the instantiation needs to be dereferenced to find the class VT. Within this VT an index is used to find the pointer to the actual function implementation. This is where performance implications become clear. The following piece of pseudo-code shows how the MultiPlayer MightyJoe has his PrintName() function called:

```
// get vptr from class instance.
vtable *vptr = p[3]->vptr;

// get function pointer from vtable.
void (*functionPtr)() = vptr[PrintNameIndex];

// call the function.
functionPtr();
```

This may look like quite a bit of overhead but depending on the system used, it could easily translate into two or three machine instructions, which makes the virtual function overhead as small as the overhead incurred when you add an extra parameter of a base type (int for example) to a function call.

A program for testing calling overhead is included in the file 08Source02.cpp that can be found on the Web site. The result of the program is a list of relative timing values for

- Calling a non-virtual member function
- Calling a virtual member function
- Calling a non-virtual member function with an extra parameter

- Calling a member function from a base class via a derived class
- Calling a non-virtual member function via a pointer
- Calling a global function

Templates

Templates are used to describe a piece of functionality in a generic way. There are class templates and function templates. With function templates you can generically describe a function without identifying the types which are used by the function, whereas with class templates you can generically describe a class without identifying the types which are used by the class. These generic descriptions become specific when the templates are actually used; the types with which the templates are used determine the implementation. Listing 8.23 contains a function template.

LISTING 8.23   Function Template "Count"

```
template <class Type, class Size>
Size Count(Type *array, Type object, Size size)
{
    Size counter = 0;
    for (Size i = 0; i < size; i++)
    {
        if (array[i] == object)
        {
            counter++;
        }
    }
    return counter;
}
```

This template can be used to count the number of occurrences of a specific object, in an array of objects of the same type. To do this it receives a pointer to the array, an object to look for, and the size of the array. Note that the type of the object (and that of the array) has not been specified. The symbol Type has been used as a generic identifier. Note also that the type for holding the size of the array has not been specified. The symbol Size has been used as a generic identifier. With this template, you can count the number of occurrences of a character in a character string, but, just as easily, you can count the number of occurrences of number in a number sequence:

```
// Type = char, Size = short.

char a[] = "This is a test string";
```

8

FUNCTIONS

```
short cnt = Count(a,'s',(short) strlen(a));


// Type = int, Size = long.

int b[] = {0,1,2,3,4,0,1,2,3,4,0,0};
long ct = Count(b,0,12);
```

In fact, you could use this `Count()` function for any type imaginable, even your own structures and classes, as long as you make sure that the used type has an appropriate == operator. The reason this is possible is that the compiler actually generates a different implementation to deal with each different type for which the template is used. This means that in the preceding example two different `Count()` functions are created at compile time: one for counting characters in a character string, and the other for counting integers in an integer string. Clearly the use of templates does not solve any footprint problems. Although the source files can become smaller because the different functionality instantiations do not all need to be typed in, the executable size does not (that is to say, some compilers may be able to optimize certain template usage for types which are very similar: long versus int, signed versus unsigned, and so on). Templates do, however, obscure their footprint implications as you cannot easily assess how much code will be generated at compile time just by looking at the template definition. It is a common misconception, though, that templates are footprint inefficient. No more code will be generated from a template than you would create yourself by coding each used function out by hand.

Another misconception concerning templates is that their use is slower than that of "hand-carved" functionality. This is equally untrue. An implementation of a template is as efficient as the template was written to be. In fact, inefficiencies are more likely to pop up when you try to write out a function to be as generic as possible, in order not to have to use templates. Sometimes it can be rewarding to try this though, for instance, when a high number of template instantiations can be replaced with a single generic function. Listing 8.24 demonstrates this.

LISTING 8.24 Generic Functions and Templates

```
// Generic swap using a template.
template <class T>
inline void Swap(T &x,  T  &y)
{
  T w = x;
  x = y;
  y = w;
}

// Generic swap without template.
```

Listing 8.24 Continued

```
void UniversalSwap(void **x,  void  **y)
{
  void *w = *x;
  *x = *y;
  *y = w;
}
```

Listing 8.24 contains two functions that swap around the values of their arguments. The template version (`Swap()`) will cause an implementation to be created for every type you want to be able to swap around, whereas the non-template version (`UniversalSwap()`)will generate a single implementation. The non-template version is harder to read and maintain though, and you should consider whether a shallow copy via object pointers as used here will always suffice.

Another possibility is capturing a generic piece of functionality within a template. This way you have all the benefits of a generic implementation but its use becomes easier:

```
template <class UST>
inline void TSwap(UST &x, UST &y)
{
    UniversalSwap((void **)&x, (void **)&y);
}
```

Now the casting activities are captured within a template. For larger functions and classes, this kind of template wrapper makes perfect sense; the only piece of functionality that is instantiated for every used type is the small part that does the casting.

When you think of what the template mechanism actually does—generating different instances of functionality at compile time—you might wonder if you can somehow misuse this mechanism to save some valuable typing time. And indeed, evil things are possible if you are inventive enough. How about some compile-time calculation or loop-unrolling? You have already seen the factorial function (n!) in this chapter. Listing 8.25 shows code which will generate a list of factorial answers at compile time.

Listing 8.25 Misusing Templates

```
template <int N>
class FactTemp
{
    public:
      enum { retval = N * FactTemp<N-1>::retval };
};
```

8

FUNCTIONS

LISTING 8.25   Continued

```
class FactTemp<1>
{
  public:
    enum { retval = 1 };
};

void main()
{
    long  x = FactTemp<12>::retval;
}
```

Of course, the speed of this `Fact<>` function is unprecedented simply because it is not actually a function at all. This sort of template misuse is only possible when the compiler can determine all possible template instances at compile time. Listing 8.25 will probably no longer work when you ask it to produce the factorial of 69; the compiler will run into trouble and even if it did not, the answer would not even fit in a long. The interesting thing about using compile-time calculation is that you do not have to calculate a list of new values when, for instance, the resolution of your needed values changes. When you are using a list of cosine values and a newer version of your software suddenly needs one more decimal of precision, you can simply adjust the template to generate a different list.

In conclusion:

- Templates are not necessarily slower than "hand-carved" functionality.
- Templates can save a lot of development time as similar functionality for different types does not need to be written and tested separately.
- Templates can obscure their actual footprint size.
- Templates can be avoided by coding all different instances of functionality yourself, or writing generic functionality by using, for instance, pointers and references.

Look at the file 08Source03.cpp on the Web site for testing the speed of the different template techniques discussed in this section.

Summary

This chapter dealt with different techniques of calling and using functions.

One way to avoid function overhead for a certain type of function is to use macros. Although the use of macros can certainly speed up code that uses small functions repetitiously, you should be wary of using them because of the possibility of unexpected behavior. Most often there are other ways to solve the problems. Use macros only when you feel you really have to.

Another way of eliminating function call overhead is to inline functions. Use inlining only for short functions which are called frequently or are part of a time-critical piece of code. Sadly, however, for practically all compilers the inlining of functions is merely a suggestion made by the programmer.

One of the choices to make when implementing certain algorithms is whether to use recursion or iteration. Recursion is likely to incur a lot more function-calling overhead. Part of the function-calling overhead is the placement of parameters on the stack. When choosing whether to pass parameters by reference or by value you should consider the size of the parameters to be passed and the number of times the parameter is accessed.

For time-critical classes you should consider whether an implementation should use inheritance and virtual functions.

Finally, when considering templated functions and classes, you should be aware of the fact that templates, apart from saving development time, also obscure their footprint size.

Efficient Memory Management

This chapter focuses specifically on the performance and footprint aspects of memory management. It also explains memory fragmentation and memory leakage and how to avoid these in your software. Resizable data structures are discussed as easy to use and efficient mechanisms to manage large amounts of data.

Memory Fragmentation

This section deals with memory fragmentation. When free memory for use by programs becomes fragmented, programs will experience slowdown and might even stop working altogether. This is obviously a serious problem, especially where programs are concerned which should run for longer periods of time.

What Exactly Is Memory Fragmentation?

Memory is said to be *fragmented* when the blocks of memory that are not in use—free memory—are interspersed with blocks of memory that are in use—used memory. Strictly speaking, memory is almost always fragmented; however, fragmentation becomes a problem only when the levels of fragmentation are high. This is the case when the average size of the blocks of free memory becomes increasingly small. For instance, a system might have over 5MB of free memory for programs to use during runtime, but still be unable to allocate a continuous block of 1MB. This could happen when memory is so badly fragmented that there are hundreds of small blocks of free memory every one of which is no larger than 500KB.

When Is Memory Fragmentation Likely to Occur?

Memory fragmentation occurs when programs use memory dynamically. When blocks of memory are allocated and released during runtime, it is unlikely that this will be done in such a manner that released blocks of memory will again form continuous, larger, memory blocks. This is true not only because of the way memory is used within a single program, but also because of the way that different programs use the same memory resources simultaneously, as shown in Figures 9.1 and 9.2.

Let's say we have an application that allocates three blocks of memory (blocks A, B, and C) in close succession. After these allocations, memory usage could appear as shown in Figure 9.1.

At some point, block B is no longer needed and is released while blocks A and C are still in use. When new memory is requested, block B can be used only to satisfy claims for memory with a size equal to, or smaller than, the size of block B. The situation described here can occur recursively, creating continuously smaller blocks of memory. Figure 9.2 shows what memory usage could look like after a new block of memory is allocated (block D), which is smaller than block B.

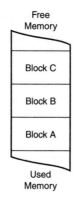

FIGURE 9.1

Memory before fragmentation.

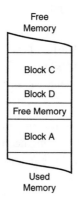

FIGURE 9.2

Memory after fragmentation.

Released blocks of memory can become increasingly small in this manner, making them less and less useful in the process.

Memory fragmentation is sped up when programs allocate and release memory at a high rate, especially when different block sizes are used. The chances of a released block being used up completely for a new memory claim is smaller when blocks of varying sizes are being used. Think of linked lists and trees used for storing data; most of the time, a large number of small objects is used for containing links and temporary information.

Characteristics of Memory Fragmentation

With what has been discussed about memory fragmentation so far, the following list of characteristics can be compiled:

- Memory fragmentation is often hidden; although the total amount of free memory might be sufficiently large to accommodate a certain program, fragmentation can cause the blocks that the free memory consists of to be too small to be usable.

- Memory fragmentation gets worse over time; as released blocks are often split into smaller pieces to satisfy further memory requests, fragmentation can easily become problematic.

- Memory fragmentation can slow down or even halt programs; depending on the OS used, different scenarios are executed when the OS is unable to allocate blocks of memory of sufficient size. OS responses can range from invoking some kind of garbage collecting, to swapping memory to and from the hard drive, to simply placing programs into holding patterns until memory becomes available.

- Memory fragmentation can happen when you least expect it; when using memory blocks that are as small as possible and releasing these blocks as soon as they are no longer needed, memory fragmentation can still occur. This is simply because not only is the total amount of memory used important, but also the dynamic behavior of the programs using it.

To guarantee a certain typical performance, it is important to consider memory fragmentation issues during the different phases of software engineering (requirements, design, and implementation), especially when a program will use relatively large parts of the memory resources available, or when a program is meant to run over extended periods of time. Early in development, it should therefore become clear whether special efforts will be needed to combat fragmentation. When fragmentation forms an immediate danger and the target OS does not implement a memory management scheme that suits the program or system requirements, it is likely that a dedicated memory manager needs to be incorporated into the software. The following section discusses theories and techniques that can be used by memory management software.

Memory Management

Memory managers (MMs) can be added to programs or systems to improve on the memory management scheme implemented by the target OS. Typical improvements include memory access and allocation speed, combating memory fragmentation, and sometimes even both. The implementation of dedicated MMs can range from a simple indirection scheme such as a suballocator that resides between program and OS, to full-blown applications that completely take over the OS role in memory management. This section discusses theories and techniques that can be used by MM software.

Suballocators

Suballocators are MMs that are placed between a piece of software and the operating system. Suballocators take their memory from, and (eventually) return their memory to, the OS. In between they perform MM tasks for the software.

Quick and Dirty MM

The simplest form of a suballocator MM is one that actually only *provides* memory. The following example demonstrates this:

```
// DIRTY MM
unsigned char membuf[512000];
unsigned char *memptr = (unsigned char *)membuf;

inline void *DirtyMalloc(long size)
{
    void *p = (void *)memptr;
    memptr += size;
    return(p);
}
```

When an application requests memory from this providing function, a slice of a preallocated block is returned. Although not a memory *manager* to take seriously, this `DirtyMalloc` does have some interesting characteristics: It is incredibly fast (MMs do not come any faster than this) and it will not give you any fragmentation. The downside to this `DirtyMalloc` is that memory is not actually *managed* at all; instead, only the whole initially claimed block can be freed at once (on program termination). But still there is some use for this kind of DirtyMalloc. Imagine you have to build a gigantic list of tiny blocks, sort it, print it, and then exit. In that case, you do not actually need a full memory manager as all the memory is used only once and can be thrown away immediately after usage. This code will be several times faster than a nicely implemented program that uses dynamic allocators such as `malloc` or `new`.

The Freelist MM

Dynamic memory is memory that your program can allocate and release at any time while it is running. It is allocated through the OS from a portion of the system memory resources called the *heap*. To obtain dynamic memory, your program has to invoke OS calls. Then, when that memory is no longer needed, it should be released. This is done again through OS calls. When your program frequently uses dynamic memory allocation, slowdown will be incurred through the use of those OS calls. This is why it is interesting to consider not releasing all memory back to the OS immediately, but rather keeping some or all of it on hand within your program for later use. A list, which we will refer to as the *freelist*, will keep track of the free memory blocks. This technique is particularly effective when memory blocks of the same size are allocated and released in quick succession. Think of the use of structures as elements of a list or array. Memory that was used to house a deleted list element can be used again when a new list element needs to be created. Thistime, however, no OS calls are needed.

Listing 9.1 presents the functionality you need to create a freelist. The functionality is presented in the form of a base class so it can be explained in a small separate listing and used in further listings in this section. The freelist is not exactly a normal base class though. Later in this section you will see why.

LISTING 9.1   Freelist Basic Functionality

```
#include <stdio.h>
#include <stdlib.h>

//Base class definition.
class FreeListBase
{
    static FreeListBase* freelist;       // pointer to free list

    FreeListBase* next;

public:
    FreeListBase()  {};
    ~FreeListBase() {};

    inline void* operator new(size_t);  // overloaded new()
    inline void operator delete(void*);    // overloaded delete()
};

inline void* FreeListBase::operator new(size_t sz)
{
  if (freelist)
  {
        // get memory from the freelist if it is not empty.
        FreeListBase* p = freelist;
        freelist = freelist->next;
        return p;
  }
  return malloc(sz);  // call malloc() otherwise
}

inline void FreeListBase::operator delete(void* vp)
{
```

LISTING 9.1 Continued

```
        FreeListBase* p = (FreeListBase*)vp;
        // link released memory into the freelist.
        p->next = freelist;
        freelist = p;
}
// Set the freelist pointer to NULL.
FreeListBase* FreeListBase::freelist = NULL;
```

The class `FreeListBase` overloads two important C++ operators, namely `new` and `delete`. Because `FreeListBase` has its own implementation of these operators, the standard `new` and `delete` operators are not invoked when you create or destroy `FreeListBase` objects. So, for example, when you do the following:

```
FreeListBase *pointerToAFreeList = new FreeListBase;
delete pointerToAFreeListBase;
```

the `new` and `delete` implementations of `FreeListBase` itself are invoked. You can easily test this by single stepping through this sample with a debugger. This setup provides you with a hook to do whatever you want at the moment a new instance of your class is created. The `FreeListBase` takes this opportunity to do two things:

- When a `FreeListBase` object (or an object derived from a `FreeListBase`) is deleted, a pointer to its memory address is placed at the front of the freelist. The pointer `freelist` always points to the first piece of released memory in the freelist. A new piece of memory that is added to the list will have its `next` pointer pointing to the object that was previously at the front of the list.

- When a new `FreeListBase` object is created, the freelist is consulted. If the freelist is not empty, a pointer to the piece of memory at the front of the freelist is returned. The pointer `freelist` is set to point at the next piece of memory in the list. If, however, the freelist is empty, memory is allocated via the OS through the use of the OS call `malloc`. The reason you will want to use `malloc` here is that you need a piece of memory of a certain size (as provided by the parameter given in the call to `new`). This way any class derived from `FreeListBase` (which will have a different size) will still receive the correct amount of memory. In fact, the standard `new` operator itself also uses `malloc` functionality.

For this to work, however, the `freelist` pointer has to be set to `NULL` at some time before it is used, to indicate that the list is still empty. As the same `freelist` pointer should be accessible for all—future—instances of `FreeListBase`, it is a static member of the `FreeListBase` class. It therefore needs to be set globally—that is, outside the member functions of the class. This is what is done in the last line of Listing 9.1.

```
FreeListBase* FreeListBase::freelist = NULL;
```

Note that the constructor of `FreeListBase` is still called when a new `FreeListBase` object is created. You cannot use the constructor to implement the freelist functionality, however, as it is invoked *after* memory allocation for the new object has taken place.

Now let's start using `FreeListBase` and compare its speed to that of using only conventional OS calls.

Listing 9.2 shows two classes with which it is possible to store information on different temperatures. One class uses the `FreeListBase` as a base class; the other does not.

LISTING 9.2   Using the `FreeListBase`

```
class TemperatureUsingFreelist : public FreeListBase
{
public:
    int     ID;
    int     maxTemp;
    int     minTemp;
    int     currentTemp;

    int average() {return (maxTemp + minTemp)/2;}
};

class TemperatureNotUsingFreelist
{
public:
    int     ID;
    int     maxTemp;
    int     minTemp;
    int     currentTemp;

    int average() {return (maxTemp + minTemp)/2;}
};
```

When an instance of `TemperatureUsingFreeList` is deleted, its freelist will remember the memory address of the instance and save it for future use. When an instance of `TemperatureNotUsingFreeList` is deleted, however, its memory is returned to the OS. A newly created `TemperatureNotUsingFreeList` instance will therefore again claim memory via the OS call `new`.

You can time both techniques (freelist memory management versus OS memory management) with two loops. One loop repeatedly creates and destroys `TemperatureUsingFreeList` instances, the other loop repeatedly creates and destroys `TemperatureNotUsingFreeList`. You can use these loops in the timing setup introduced in Chapter 5, "Measuring Time and Complexity." Here is an example loop:

```
for (int i = 1 ; i < 1000000; i++)
{
    TemperatureUsingFreelist*  t1;      // or TemperatureNotUsingFreelist

    t1 = new TemperatureUsingFreelist; // or TemperatureNotUsingFreelist
    delete t1;
    t1 = new TemperatureUsingFreelist; // or TemperatureNotUsingFreelist
    delete t1;
}
```

Although the exact timing results will differ per system, the relations between timing the above loop with TemperatureUsingFreeList instances and timing the above loop with TemperatureNotUsingFreeList instances should look something like this:

```
Using freelist      160
Not using freelist  990
```

This shows that using a freelist is significantly faster when memory is actively reused. Timing results will be equal for both classes when no instances are deleted within the timing loop as the freelist is not used in that case.

As you know, the freelist functionality was placed in a base class to explain its functionality clearly in a separate listing. When you use the freelist technique in practice, however, it is best to incorporate its functionality directly into the class that uses it. This is important as the FreeListBase class contains a static pointer to the available memory blocks. This same pointer would be used by all classes derived from FreeListBase. When you inherit from the FreeListBase class, the freelist can at some point contain blocks of different sizes, placed there by different classes. Clearly this is undesirable as the new operator simply returns the first available block, regardless of its size.

When you do decide you want to use a general freelist that is shared between different classes, simply augment the FreeListBase with a size parameter (which must be set during the delete operator) and a size check (which must be done in the new operator). Note, however, that the extra *set* and *check* will add some overhead to your FreeListBase. This means you have a tradeoff between speed (using a freelist per class is fastest) and footprint (using a shared freelist makes the code smaller).

Similarly, you could decide to expand the delete operator to be more intelligent. It could, for example, start to release memory back to the OS when the list reaches a certain size.

An example of a freelist can be found in the companion file 09Source01.cpp.

Simple Stack Memory Management

This section shows how a simple-but-effective MM scheme can be integrated into a class which provides stack functionality. Listing 9.3 shows a simple implementation of a `stack` class that relies on the OS for memory management.

LISTING 9.3 Stack Without Dedicated Memory Management

```
#define MAXSIZE 100000

class Stack
{
 struct elem
 {
  elem  *previous;
  char  *name;
  int   size;
  int   id;
 };


public:
    Stack() { last = NULL; totalSize = 0;}

    // store {name,id}
    void push(const char *s, const int nr);

    // retrieve {name,id}
    void pop(char *s, int &nr);

private:
    elem     *last;
    int      totalSize;
};


inline void Stack::push(const char *s, const int nr)
{ // add new item to the top of the stack

    int newSize = strlen(s) + 1;
    if (totalSize + newSize > MAXSIZE)
    {
        cout << "Error, Stack Overflow!!" << endl;
    }
    else
    {
```

LISTING 9.3   Continued

```
        elem *newElem = new elem;
        newElem->name = new char [newSize];

        strcpy(newElem->name, s);
        newElem->id        = nr;
        newElem->previous   = last;
        newElem->size       = newSize;

        last                = newElem;
        totalSize           += newSize;
    }
}

inline void Stack::pop(char *s, int &nr)
{ // return item from the top of the stack and free it
    if (last != NULL)
    {
        elem *popped = last;

        strcpy(s, popped->name);
        nr  = popped->id;
        last   = popped->previous;

        totalSize -= popped->size;
        delete [] popped->name;
        delete popped;

    }
    else
    {
        cout << "Error, Stack Underflow!!" << endl;
    }
}
```

This stack class can be used for storing strings and corresponding IDs. Storage is done in a last-in first-out (LIFO) fashion. Usage can be as follows:

```
Stack           q;
char            name[NAME_SIZE];
unsigned long   id;

q.push("Myname", 123);  // Push name + ID on stack
q.pop(name, id);        // Pop name + ID from the stack.
```

When this class is used intensely, memory will slowly start to fragment as small blocks of memory are allocated and released repeatedly. Even though it might seem that the memory blocks used by this stack are found in a continuous block of memory because the class behaves as a stack, this is not the case. Typically, different parts of a program will call this kind of storage class at different times. In between, other classes will also use memory resources, which makes it extremely unlikely that allocated memory will be found in a continuous block.

BigChunkStack MM

As the fragmentation caused by the stack class of the previous section is a direct result of the dynamic nature in which it deals with memory requests, the simplest solution for combating fragmentation in this case is to allocate a large chunk of memory immediately and divide this according to incoming requests. Listing 9.4 shows a class that does just that.

LISTING 9.4   Stack with Dedicated Memory Management

```
#include <stdio.h>
#include <string.h>
#include <iostream.h>

#define MAXSIZE 100000


class BigChunkStack
{
 struct elem
 {
  int   id;
  int   previousElemSize;
  int   nameSize;
  char  name;
 };


public:
    BigChunkStack()
    { totalSize = 0;
      emptyElemSize = sizeof(elem); lastElemSize = 0;}

    // store {name,id}
    void push(const char *s, const int nr);

    // retrieve {name,id}
    void pop(char *s, int &nr);

private:
    char   pool[MAXSIZE];
    int    totalSize;
    int    emptyElemSize;
```

LISTING 9.4 Continued

```cpp
    int     lastElemSize;
};


inline void BigChunkStack::push(const char *s, const int nr)
{ // add new item to the top of the stack

    int newStringSize   = strlen(s) + 1;
    int totalElemSize   = newStringSize + emptyElemSize;

    if (totalSize + totalElemSize > MAXSIZE)
    {
        cout << "Error, Stack Overflow!!" << endl;
    }
    else
    {

        elem *newElem      = (elem*)  (pool + totalSize);

        newElem->id           = nr;
        newElem->nameSize     = newStringSize;
        newElem->previousElemSize = lastElemSize;
        strcpy(&newElem->name, s);

        lastElemSize = totalElemSize;
        totalSize   += totalElemSize;
    }
}


inline void BigChunkStack::pop(char *s, int &nr)
{ // return item from the top of the stack and free it
    if (totalSize != 0)
    {
        totalSize       -= lastElemSize;
        elem *popped    = (elem*) (pool + totalSize);
        lastElemSize    = popped->previousElemSize;

        strcpy(s, &popped->name);
        nr      = popped->id;

    }
    else
    {
        cout << "Error, Stack Underflow!!"  << endl;
    }
}
```

The `BigChunkStack` class can be used in exactly the same manner as the `Stack` class in Listing 9.3. This means that for the user of the class, the dedicated memory management scheme of `BigChunkStack` is completely hidden, which is desirable. The dynamic behavior of the `BigChunkStack` is very different from that of the `Stack` class. At creation time, an instance of `BigChunkStack` will contain a block of memory which it calls the *pool* and which has the size `MAXSIZE`. This memory pool will be used to contain stack elements that are pushed onto the `BigChunkStack`. The pool will not fragment and, when an instance of `BigChunkStack` is destroyed, the pool will be returned to the OS in one piece. At first glance this technique might seem somewhat wasteful because of the large piece of memory that is in constant use. You should keep in mind, however, that the fragmented memory caused by the use of the `Stack` class will not be very useful after a while in any case. When a program has a runtime requirement that it should always be able to place a certain number of elements onto a stack, the usage of `BigChunkStack` will help guarantee this. This is especially interesting when a stack has a life span equal to, or close to, that of the program using it. This kind of MM system even makes it possible to calculate beforehand the minimal amount of memory that will be needed for a certain program to run correctly for an indefinite period of time.

A downside to the `BigChunkStack` is that the pool size must be known at compile time, or at least, with some minor changes to the code, at the time the `BigChunkStack` is created. For certain system requirements, this need not be a problem though, and it might even be advantageous. Later in this chapter, in the section "Resizable Data Structures," you will see how to make these kinds of implementations more dynamic. Chapter 12, "Optimizing IO" contains examples of combining allocation of large memory blocks with maximizing IO throughput. This chapter focuses on more MM theory.

Memory Management Theory

Volumes have been written on theories of memory management. The proposed techniques range from subtle variations on a theme to implementations with completely different underlying concepts. As this book does not have memory management as its main topic but rather looks at it from the viewpoint of performance and footprint, this section discusses some of the main memory management concepts from a practical angle.

When creating an MM, design decisions need to be made concerning the following functional areas:

- How to acquire and store initial memory to be managed
- How to select memory for allocation requests
- How to sort/merge released memory

How to Acquire and Store Initial Memory to Be Managed

In this chapter you have already seen two ways of storing memory to be managed by an MM: the freelist example used a dynamic list of free memory blocks which could be used to accommodate memory requests and the `BigChunkStack` used a large block of memory and broke it into smaller pieces to accommodate memory requests. Many variations on these concepts are of course possible. A combination of both concepts seems to be an ideal starting point for your MM. But whether your MM allocates all the memory it will use at the time of its initialization or claims more and more memory from the OS as it is needed, your MM will somehow have to keep track of the blocks of free memory that it can use. The remainder of this chapter refers to this list of blocks of free memory as the MM's *freelist*.

More will be said about memory block size considerations in the following section as this is really a topic in its own right.

How to Select Memory for Allocation Requests

After choosing schemes for storing free memory blocks and claiming initial memory for the manager, you are ready to decide how your MM will respond to memory allocation requests. When memory is requested from your MM, it will have to choose which block to use from those it manages. Here are someblock selection methods you might find interesting.

Best Fit

The Best Fit method entails searching for the smallest free block that is large enough to accommodate a certain memory request. The following example demonstrates the Best Fit method for a given MM with four memory blocks. The MM in this example is called on to accommodate two consecutive memory requests:

```
Initial Free Blocks:      A(160KB), B(70KB), C(99KB), D(120KB)

Request 1)
block size:        100KB
Best Fit:          D(120KB)

New Free Blocks:          A(160KB), B(70KB), C(99KB), D'(20KB)

Request 2)
block size:        130KB
Best Fit:          A(160KB)

New Free Blocks:          A'(30KB), B(70KB), C(99KB), D'(20KB)
```

At the start of the preceding example an MM has the free blocks of memory A through D. The sizes of the various blocks can be found after the block name between parentheses. The first request made to the example MM is for a block of 100KB. Only two blocks of the MM are actually large enough to accommodate this request: A(160KB) and D(120KB). The Best Fit method dictates that block D is used, as its size is closest to that of the requested memory block. After Request 1 has been dealt with, the MM contains a new block called D'. Block D' represents what is left of the original Block D after Request 1 has been serviced. The size of Block D' equals 120KB–100KB = 20KB.

The second request made to the example MM is for a block of 130KB. This time Block A is chosen, leaving a Block A' of 160KB–130KB = 30KB.

The idea behind the Best Fit method is that when a free block of exactly the right size can be found, it is selected and no further fragmentation is incurred. In all other cases, the amount of memory that is left over from a selected block is as small as possible. This means that in using the Best Fit method we ensure that large blocks of free memory are reserved as much as possible for large memory requests. This principle is demonstrated in the example; if Block A had been chosen to accommodate the first request, the MM would not have had a block large enough to accommodate the second request.

The danger with the Best Fit method is, of course, that the blocks left over after accommodating a memory request (like Blocks D' and A') are too small to be used again.

Worst Fit

Unsurprisingly, the Worst Fit method does the opposite of the Best Fit method. Worst Fit entails always using the largest free block available to accommodate a memory request. The following example demonstrates the Worst Fit method for an MM. The example MM has four memory blocks and it is called on to accommodate two consecutive memory requests:

```
Initial Free Blocks:      A(160KB), B(70KB), C(99KB), D(120KB)

Request 1)
block size:          70KB
Worst Fit:           A(160KB)

New Free Blocks:          A'(90KB), B(70KB), C(99KB), D(120KB)

Request 2)
block size:          40KB
Worst Fit:           D(120KB)

New Free Blocks:          A'(90KB), B(70KB), C(99KB), D'(80KB)
```

At the start of the preceding example the MM has free memory blocks A through D. Again the sizes of the various blocks can be found after the block name between parentheses. The first request made to the example MM is for a block of 70KB. The largest block available to the MMs is A(160KB). The Worst Fit method dictates that this block should be chosen. After

Request 1 has been dealt with, the MM has an Element A' that is 160KB–70KB or 90KB in size.

The second request made to the MM is for a block of 40KB. This time Block D is the largest block available, leaving a Block D' of 120KB–40KB or 80KB in size.

The idea behind the Worst Fit method is that when a request has been accommodated, the amount of memory that is left over from a selected block is as large as possible. This means that in using the Worst Fit method we try to ensure that leftover blocks are likely to be usable in the future.

The danger with the Worst Fit method is that after a while no block in the freelist will be large enough to accommodate a request for a large piece of memory.

First Fit

The First Fit method entails finding the first free block that is large enough to accommodate a certain memory request. This method allows memory requests to be dealt with expediently. As opposed to Best Fit and Worst Fit, not all the blocks managed by the MM need to be examined during block selection. What exactly happens as far as fragmentation is concerned depends on how the elements are ordered in the freelist.

How to Sort/Merge Released Memory

When a block of memory is released and thus returned to your MM, a reference to the released memory needs to be inserted somewhere in your MM's freelist. The method used to determine *where* to insert a released block into the freelist has a large impact on how your MM actually works. Consider an MM that orders the blocks of its freelist by size, with the largest block at the beginning of the list and the smallest at the end. When the First Fit method is used on a freelist ordered this way, the MM actually implements a Worst Fit algorithm because it will always select the largest available block. Similarly, when an MM orders the blocks of its freelist by size but with the smallest block first, the First Fit method actually translates into a Best Fit method. Clearly it pays to spend some time on the sorting mechanism to make sure your MM will perform as optimally as possible.

Other sorting methods follow:

- By memory address

  This method sorts the freelist entries on the value of the address of the first byte of each free block. Using this method is particularly interesting when you want to design an MM that is able to recombine fragmented memory back into larger blocks. Whenever a reference to a freshly released block is inserted in the freelist, a quick check can be done to determine whether the preceding and/or following block in the freelist connects to the new block. When this is the case, several freelist entries can be replaced by a new entry (with the address of the first byte of the first block and the size of the blocks combined).

- By release time

  This method keeps the released blocks in chronological order. The algorithm that implements this method is very straightforward: References to released blocks are always inserted at the beginning of the freelist, or perhaps always at the end of the freelist. By placing new blocks at the beginning of the freelist, the MM can be very fast when blocks of memory of the same size are allocated and deleted in quick succession.

In this section, you have seen several well-known techniques for MM implementation. No rule requires you to choose between these techniques. Depending on the requirements of your program, you may choose to mix several techniques together or create an entirely new technique that better suits your requirements. Another important thing to realize is that you can use as many, or as few, MMs in your programs as you see fit. You do not necessarily need to create one main MM to handle *all* memory requests. In fact, as you have seen in the `Freelist` and `BigChunkStack` examples, you could create a dedicated MM for every single class if that would help you. You might even decide to use OS memory management for most memory requests and write your own MMs only for specific (critical) classes.

In the summary of this chapter you can find a table with an overview of these methods.

Resizable Data Structures

The use of memory blocks and arrays (which are basically typed memory blocks) for data storage has several great advantages, such as quick and direct access and ease of implementation. Implementing arrays is a task which is fairly straightforward and far less error-prone and time-consuming than, say, using linked lists. The reason arrays are often put aside as valid programming solutions, though, is that their size seems to be too static in nature. Often array size is specified at compile time or it is determined at array-creation time, after which it does not change until the array is destroyed. Arrays are often declared as follows:

```
void MakeArrays(int size)
{
   char name[200];              // size determined at compile time.
   char *pName = new char[size]; // size determined at creation time.
   ~~
```

The following sections show how you can use arrays and memory blocks with dynamic sizes. This means you can keep the advantages of normal arrays and memory blocks and still be able to influence their size by enlarging or shrinking them when necessary.

Enlarging Arrays

This section shows how to increase the size of memory blocks. The `BigChunkStack` class from an earlier section of this chapter is taken as an example. You will remember that the `BigChunkStack` allocated a large block of memory during initialization. This block of memory was called a *pool* and objects that should be placed on the stack were copied into this pool. When the pool could not fit any more objects, an error was returned. This section shows you how you can expand the `BigChunkStack` with the ability to have its pool grow when it is in danger of filling up. The dynamic version of the `BigChunkStack` can be found in the companion file 09Source02.cpp on the Web site. In the rest of this section you will see what changes need to be made to the original `BigChunkStack`.

The first thing you have to do to make the `BigChunkStack` resizable is to change the implementation of the pool. In the original `BigChunkStack` the pool was declared as an array with a fixed size: `char pool[MAXSIZE]`. For a dynamic pool, you should declare the `pool` variable as a pointer and the `MAXSIZE` constant as a member variable. You can set initial values for both in the constructor:

```
class BigChunkStack
{
public:
    BigChunkStack()
    { totalSize = 0; MAXSIZE = 0;
      emptyElemSize = sizeof(elem); lastElemSize = 0;}
private:
    char    *pool;        // pointer instead of constant array.
    int     MAXSIZE;      // variable that will keep track of pool size.
```

Listing 9.5 shows the implementation of a new `BigChunkStack::push()` function that detects when the pool should grow.

LISTING 9.5 Resizing push Function for the `BigChunkStack`

```
inline void BigChunkStack::push(const char *s, const int nr)
{ // add new item to the top of the stack

    int newStringSize  = strlen(s) + 1;
    int totalElemSize  = newStringSize + emptyElemSize;

    while (totalSize + totalElemSize > MAXSIZE)
    {
        if (!grow())
        {
            cout << "Error, Stack Overflow!!" << endl;
            return;
        }
    }

    elem *newElem      = (elem*) (pool + totalSize);
```

9

LISTING 9.5 Continued

```
newElem->id          = nr;
newElem->nameSize    = newStringSize;
newElem->previousElemSize = lastElemSize;
strcpy(&newElem->name, s);

lastElemSize = totalElemSize;
totalSize   += totalElemSize;
}
```

The check that originally determined whether another object could be pushed onto the stack now makes sure the pool is always sufficiently large. It does this by repeatedly calling a grow() function to enlarge the pool while it is too small to contain the new data. The grow() function is where all the interesting work is done. Listing 9.6 shows the implementation of a BigChunkStack::grow() function that detects when the pool should grow.

LISTING 9.6 grow Function for the BigChunkStack

```
#define INITSIZE 1000

inline int BigChunkStack::grow()
// Create or Enlarge the pool size.
{
    if (MAXSIZE == 0)
    {
        // create.
        pool = (char*) malloc(INITSIZE);
        if (pool == NULL) return 0;

        MAXSIZE = INITSIZE;
        return 1;
    }
    else
    {
        // enlarge.
        MAXSIZE *= 2;

        char* tempPool = (char*) realloc(pool, MAXSIZE);
        if (tempPool == NULL) return 0;

        pool = tempPool;
        return 1;
    }
}
```

Basically, there are two situations in which the pool can grow. First, the pool can grow when there is no pool at all. This is the initialization of the pool in the `if` body of the `grow` function. The constant `INITSIZE` is used for the initial size. Any value could be chosen here; your choice of value will depend on the requirements of the stack.

Second, the pool can grow when the existing pool is too small to fit an object that is being pushed onto the stack. This is done by the reallocation in the `else` body of the `grow` function. Each time the pool needs to grow it doubles in size. Because reallocating memory blocks takes time, you do not want to do this too often.

The C++ function that is used to resize the pool is called `realloc`, which takes as arguments a pointer to the first byte of the block to be resized and an integer denoting the new desired size. When `realloc` is successful, it returns a pointer to the reallocated block. When there is not enough memory to perform the reallocation, a `NULL` pointer is returned and the block of data is left unchanged. This is why you will want to capture and test the returned pointer before initializing the pool variable with it. When the realloc is unsuccessful, you will not want to overwrite the existing pool pointer with it. Simply return an error and your program will still be able to pop elements from the stack later. For more information on the `realloc` call, consult your C++ documentation.

The changes made in this section to the `BigChunkStack` result in a stack that will grow when necessary. The following section shows additional changes that allow the stack to decrease in size when it becomes empty.

Shrinking Arrays

This section shows how to decrease the size of memory blocks. The `BigChunkStack` class is again taken as an example. The dynamic version of the `BigChunkStack` can be found in the companion file 09Source02.cpp on the Web site. In the rest of this section you will see what changes were made to the original `BigChunkStack` to allow it to shrink. The changes in this section and in the section "Enlarging Arrays" constitute all the changes to be made to the `BigChunkStack` to make it completely dynamic.

Listing 9.7 shows the implementation of a new `BigChunkStack::pop()` function that detects when the pool should shrink.

LISTING 9.7   Resizing `Pop()` Function for the `BigChunkStack`

```
inline void BigChunkStack::pop(char *s, int &nr)
{ // return item from the top of the stack and free it

    if (totalSize * 4 <= MAXSIZE)
```

LISTING 9.7   Continued

```
        shrink();

    if (totalSize != 0)
    {
        totalSize       -= lastElemSize;
        elem *popped    = (elem*) (pool + totalSize);
        lastElemSize    = popped->previousElemSize;

        strcpy(s, &popped->name);
        nr      = popped->id;

    }
    else
    {
        cout << "Error, Stack Underflow!!"  << endl;
    }
}
```

The check at the beginning of Listing 9.7 is the addition that allows the stack to shrink by call-ing the shrink() member function. The following rule is chosen for when the stack should shrink: The stack's pool will shrink when it is only 25% full. The shrink() function is where all the interesting work is done. Listing 9.8 shows a shrink function for the BigChunkStack.

LISTING 9.8   shrink Function for the BigChunkStack

```
inline void BigChunkStack::shrink()
// Shrink the pool size.
{
    if ((MAXSIZE/2) >= INITSIZE)
    {
        // shrink.
        char* tempPool = (char*) realloc(pool, MAXSIZE/2);
        if (tempPool == NULL) return ;

        MAXSIZE /= 2;
        pool = tempPool;
        return;
    }
}
```

The shrink function will decrease the pool by 50% as long as the resulting size is greater than or equal to the chosen INITSIZE. You will note that the realloc function is used again. realloc can be used to increase as well as decrease memory block sizes.

Summary

Memory is called *fragmented* when the blocks of memory that are not in use are interspersed with blocks of memory that are in use. Memory fragmentation occurs when programs use memory dynamically. When blocks of memory are being allocated and released dynamically, it is unlikely that this will be done in such a manner that released blocks of memory will again form continuous, larger memory blocks. Fragmentation has the following characteristics:

- Memory fragmentation is often hidden.
- Memory fragmentation gets worse over time.
- Memory fragmentation can slow down or even halt programs.
- Memory fragmentation can happen simply because you are trying to avoid it.

Memory managers (MMs) can be added to programs or systems to improve on the memory management scheme implemented by the target OS. Typical improvements are memory access and allocation speed, combating memory fragmentation, and sometimes even both. MMs can use different strategies for selecting a blocks of memory that should accommodate a memory request, as shown here:

Best Fit	Large blocks are preserved as much as possible to accommodate large requests.
Worst Fit	The remainder of a used block is as large as possible.
First Fit	A block is selected as expediently as possible.

Blocks of Data

IN THIS CHAPTER

Often, the programs you write will at some point need to perform actions on blocks of data. Think, for instance, of using numerical information for setting up graphics, or handling a textual database of client addresses. Your program might need to go through a large base of such addresses in order to produce a list of clients ordered by name, ZIP code, or age grouping. Perhaps you even need to generate specific subsets from a certain base of information, creating a list of clients with outstanding orders or bills, for instance. Of course, the larger the blocks of data are that your program needs to analyze, the more important become the algorithms it analyzes with. This chapter highlights the performance and footprint implications of various algorithms that are often used for just these kinds of actions, pointing out when and why slowdown can occur. It also introduces new techniques that may help you speed up your programs.

Throughout this chapter, pieces of example code are presented. The speed of these pieces of code is tested via a large data file named dbase.txt that can be found on the Web site. This data file contains 103,680 articles of a fictitious company; for each article, six attributes are specified. The total size of the data file is 4.8MB.

Note that this chapter focuses solely on using blocks of data. File IO and storage of data in memory are not part of this chapter; they are dealt with in Chapters 11, "Storage Structures," and 12, "Optimizing IO."

Comparing Blocks of Data

One action you are bound to need from time to time is that of comparing blocks of data. This may happen when you need to sort data, find some specific data element, or traverse a base of data. In the case of the example data file, which consists of textual article descriptions, this comparing of blocks of data basically translates into comparing strings. Note that strings are, in effect, nothing more than arrays of bytes, just like any other data block; the only difference is that strings are generally terminated by a null character. In this chapter, blocks of data will be treated as strings and text files as this makes the examples more readable.

Standard Pattern Matching

Comparing two patterns of data—or strings—in C++ is not that complicated because the C++ programming language contains a standard string implementation which can handle this. This string implementation is part of something called the Standard Template Library (STL) ; consult your compiler documentation for more information on STL. Comparing two standard C++ strings can be done as demonstrated in the following example:

```
#include <string>
#include <iostream>

using namespace std;
```

```
void main()
{
  string s1("This is string one.");
  string s2("This is string two.");

  if (s1 == s2)
  {
    // do something.
  }
}
```

The reason it is possible to compare two objects of the string class is that the == operator has been overloaded to perform just this action. In C, the piece of code would look like this:

```
#include <string.h>

void main()
{
  char s1[]= "This is string one.";
  char s2[]= "This is string two.";

  if (strcmp(s1,s2) == 0)
  {
    // do something.
  }
}
```

In order to test the merits of these two implementations, a program is used that loads and searches through the dbase.txt file, counting the number of *Small Table* articles in the colors yellow, black, silver, and magenta. The program can be found in the file 10Source01.cpp on the Web site. The article name and color are the first attributes of every article in the dbase.txt file, so a quick compare with the beginning of each line in the file will determine whether the article is to be counted or skipped. The timing mechanism of the program does not time the loading of the database, only the time that is spent in the search algorithms. You can examine the exact implementation of the program at your leisure; for now, it is important only to mention that this straightforward comparison between using the C++ string class and using char pointers proves the char pointer method to be much faster than the string method (two to five times faster, depending on the system used).

It seems that although the standard C++ string is very easy to use and offers a great many standard functions, it is not what you will want to use when you have to search through a large block of data.

10

BLOCKS OF DATA

Faster Pattern Matching

Without even changing the way in which you actually compare patterns (or strings), you can make your string comparisons faster in a lot of cases by using a macro that can skip the actual call to the strcmp function:

```
#define macro_strcmp(s1,s2) ((s1)[0]
➡!= (s2)[0] ? (s1)[0] - (s2)[0]:strcmp((s1), (s2)))

if (macro_strcmp(s1, s2) == 0)
{
    // do something
}
```

This macro is used to determine whether the first characters of both strings match. When the first characters are the same the strcmp function is called as you would normally do; when the first characters are not the same, however, the string will of course be different and strcmp is not called. This will save a lot of time for all strings of which the first character is different. Note that this even works for empty strings.

Only when different strings contain the same first character does this new method introduce extra overhead because of the extra check introduced by the macro. It depends on the type of strings in the database, therefore, whether or not this macro represents an improvement. For our example of finding *Small Table* articles in the dbase.txt file, this macro implementation is again faster (up to 34%). This is reflected in the results of the 10Source01.cpp program.

Another way to speed up string comparison is by treating the character arrays as integer arrays. On most systems an integer is four times larger than a character, and so four characters can be compared at the same time. When the strings have a length that is a multiple of the length of an integer, doing integer comparisons can greatly speed up your string comparison. Listing 10.1 shows what an integer string compare function can look like.

LISTING 10.1   Integer String Comparison

```
inline int int_strcmp(char *s1, char *s2, int len)
{
    if ((len & 0x03) != 0)
        return(macro_strcmp(s1, s2));

    for (int i =0; *(int*)&s1[i] == *(int*)&s2[i];)
    {
        i+=4;
        if (i >= len)
            return(true);   // match
    }
    return(false);
}
```

The int_strcmp function quickly checks whether the given string length is a multiple of four. If this is not the case, the previously discussed macro_strcmp function is called. For strings with a correct length, characters are compared in groups of four by casting the character pointers to integer pointers and thus reading integers from the string. The longer the compared strings are—and the more they look alike—the more benefits this int_strcmp function reaps compared to the previous implementations given in this chapter. For our example of finding *Small Table* articles in the dbase.txt file, this integer implementation is again faster (up to 50%). This is reflected in the results of the 10Source01.cpp program.

The reason why the string lengths have to be a multiple of the integer size for this function to work is that any other size will cause this function to compare beyond the length of a string. A string with a length of six, for instance, will be compared in two loop iterations. The first iteration compares the first four bytes, which is no problem. The second iteration compares the second four bytes, of which only two are part of the actual string. The third byte will be a null indicating the end of the string. The fourth byte, however, is not part of the string. Two strings of six characters that are identical could be found to be different just because of the value of these fourth bytes. The int_compare function can of course be altered to check for different string sizes but it is not very likely that it will still be faster in most string compare cases.

This may make you wonder whether the int_compare function is all that useful. It is, in fact, as databases often contain records with fixed field sizes anyway. By simply choosing a field size that is a multiple of the integer size, using the speedy int_strcmp becomes possible for those database records. This can be seen in the results of the 10Source01.cpp program.

Table 10.1 shows the complete results of the 10Source01.cpp program. Note that different systems may yield different absolute results, but the relations between the speeds of the various techniques should be fairly constant.

TABLE 10.1   Results of 10Source01.cpp

Compare C++ string	241
Compare strcmp	109
Memory compare	106
Compare macro	72
String 'n' compare	41
Compare ints	34

10

Note that the standard memory `compare` function `memcmp` basically yields the same results as the standard string compare `strcmp`. When you look at the source of 10Source01.cpp, you will also notice that `memcmp` needs to be told how many characters to compare. For straightforward string comparison, `strcmp` is, therefore, the better choice as it determines the string length without needing extra information—like a call to the `strlen` function, for instance. When comparing blocks of data that are not null terminated, you can, of course, use the `strncmp` variant, which does not necessarily need null terminators. Be advised, though, that string functions stop when they encounter a null byte!

Simple Pattern Search

Another action you are bound to need when handling blocks of data is that of finding a certain pattern of elements in a block of data. This can be compared to finding a substring in a string. Think, for instance, of using the Find function of a word processor to find occurrences of a word in a piece of text. This could, of course, be done by repeatedly calling `strncmp` to compare a search string against a piece of the text. Each call to `strncmp` would look at the same number of characters from the text, but each time starting at the next character in the text. Luckily, a standard function that does this already exists and it is called `strstr`. Usage could be as follows:

```
char *s1; // pointer to the text.
char s2[] = "substring to look for."
char *result;

if ((result = strstr(s1, s2)) != NULL)
{
    // do something
}
```

When string `s2` can be found in text `s1`, the function `strstr` returns a pointer to the first byte of the first occurrence. Null is returned when string `s2` cannot be found in text `s1`.

Faster Pattern Search

You can improve on standard string search mechanisms by not simply testing all possible substring combinations, but making informed decisions that allow you to skip ahead as much as possible. A whole range of algorithms have been derived from such a technique, which was developed by Boyer and Moore. This section presents a possible variation in order to demonstrate the basic principles. The exact algorithm variation that is best for a certain part of an application depends heavily on the data set it uses and the kind of search that is to be performed. The algorithm presented in this section can easily prove to be many times faster than the standard `strstr` function, but perhaps you can think of specific tweaks that improve it even more for the specific data set you want to use it on.

As with `strstr`, the basis of finding a search string in a block of text or a file is that of repeatedly comparing the search string against different substrings in the file. This time, however, you will use information gathered when a mismatch occurs to make an informed decision about where exactly the next substring should start. The remainder of this section refers to the string that is to be found as the *search string*, and the block of text it is to be found in as the *text file*.

At the heart of the algorithm is a loop that compares two strings: the search string and a substring of the text file. It does this character-for-character starting at the end of the strings and working its way back to the beginning of the strings:

```
j = len2;
while (textf[j] == searchstr[j] && --j >= 0) ;
```

When all the characters of both strings match, the algorithm is, of course, finished and it returns a pointer to the first character of the substring in the text file. When, however, a mismatch of characters is found, things become interesting:

```
if (j != -1)
{
     // Mismatch; align and check for text end.
}
else
{
     // Match; stop, return pointer.
}
```

A *lookup* character is taken from the text file. This is the first character following the substring which was just used in the comparison. When this lookup character can also be found in the search string, the search string is aligned with the text file in such a way that these two characters match up. Then comparison starts over. If, however, the lookup character is not part of the search string, the search string is aligned as follows: The first character of the search string is aligned with the character following the lookup character. Here is a textual example of how the search string *methin* is found in a text file containing the text *no thing as vague as something.*

```
  no thing as vague as something.
1 methin
2  methin
3         methin
4             methin
5                 methin
6                 methin
```

The very first comparison that is made is that of the search string *methin* being compared with the first six characters of the text file *no thi*. This is step 1.

As the comparison starts at the last character of each (sub)string, the letter *n* is compared with the letter *i*. These characters, of course, do not match, and so a lookup character is taken from the file. This is the first character in the file following the substring, in this case the letter *n* of the word *thing*. The letter *n* is also part of the search string and so the search string is aligned with its rightmost *n* (which is in fact its only *n*) corresponding with the lookup character. We arrive at step 2.

Comparison starts again and this time a whole range of characters match, four in total. Not all of the search string matches though, and the first mismatch is the letter *e* of the search string which does not match up with a space in the text file. Time for another alignment, it seems. The lookup this time is the letter *g* of the word *thing* in the text file. The search string does not contain a letter *g* and so it is aligned with its first character just past the lookup character. This way, we arrive at step 3.

Now things start to speed up. In this comparison, the *n* of the substring is compared with the *a* of the word *vague* in the text file. Again alignment can take place after the lookup character (another *g*), sending us to step 4. In step 5 the same happens again, this time with the letter *s* as a lookup character.

The lookup character that brings us from step 5 to step 6 is the letter *n* of the word *something* in the text file. The search string contains a letter *n* and so it is aligned accordingly. This time the search string matches the substring of the text file completely. We have a winner!

Note that a simple moving `strncmp` would have needed 23 steps whereas this algorithm needs only six.

The implementation of this concept comes in two parts. One part is the actual search algorithm, the other is an initiating function which creates a table that is consulted by the search algorithm in order to determine where the next substring should start. Listing 10.2 shows an implementation of a search routine; it takes a pointer to the text file and the length of the text file as input (the search string itself is processed by the initiating function as you will see later):

LISTING 10.2   Fast Pattern Match Search Function

```
char *search(const char *textf, int len)
{
    // Check if searchstr is longer than textf or zero length.
    if (search_len > len || search_len == 0)
        return NULL;

    unsigned char * end = (unsigned char*) textf + len;
    int len2 = search_len -1;
```

LISTING 10.2   Continued

```
    int j;

    for(;;)
    {
        // main loop for comparing strings.
        j = len2;
        while (textf[j] == searchstr[j] && --j >= 0) ;

        if (j != -1)
        {
            // Mismatch; align and check for end of textf.
            unsigned char* skipindex = (unsigned char*) textf + search_len;
            if (skipindex >= end)
                return NULL;   // string not in textf.

            textf += skips[*skipindex];
        }
        else
        {
            // Match found.
            return (char*) textf;
        }
    }
    return NULL;
}
```

The main parts of this function have already been explained. Note, however, that there is an if at the beginning of the function to determine whether any search is needed at all. After this follow two calculations which prepare variables so they do not need to be recalculated during the main loop. The only other new bit consists of the four lines of code to be executed at the mismatch. These lines of code find the lookup character and use it to determine the alignment with a new substring. For this alignment the array *skips* is used. It contains the exact number of characters to skip for each possible lookup character. The skip value for a given lookup character is as follows: For every character that is *not* part of the search string, the skip value is equal to the number of characters in the search string plus one. For every character that *is* part of the search string, the skip value is its position in the search string counted from the end of the string. For our example search string *methin*, the *skips* array will therefore have the following values:

```
    m = 6
    e = 5
    t = 4
    h = 3
    i = 2
```

10

BLOCKS OF DATA

```
n = 1
Every other character = 7
```

This means that for each different search string that you want to find, you will have to make one call to a function that will create this array of skip values for you. Listing 10.3 shows an implementation of such a function: It takes a pointer to the search string as an input parameter.

LISTING 10.3   Fast Pattern Search Initiation Function

```c
#include <string.h>
unsigned char skips[256];    // possible nr of look-ups.
unsigned char search_len;    // search string length.
char * searchstr;            // actual search string.

void init(const char *str)
{
    search_len = strlen(str);
    int len2 = search_len + 1;

    // For chars not in searchstr.
    for (int i = 0; i < 256;i++)
        skips[i] = len2;    //length + 1.

    // For chars in searchstr, with double chars only
    // right most survives.
    for ( i = 0; i < search_len; i++)
        skips[str[i]] = search_len - i;   // pos back to front.

    searchstr = (char*) str;
}
```

Note that two loops are utilized to create the `skips` array. One loop sets the skip values for the characters that are not in the search string (in fact, it simply sets the whole array to this default value). The other loop sets specific values for the characters that are part of the search string. Because this second loop traverses the search string from front to back, something special happens to characters that occur in the search string more than once. Only the rightmost occurrence of such a character is remembered in the *skips* array. It is only possible to remember a single occurrence of each character because remembering each occurrence of a character, and using it, would simply cause too much overhead. The rightmost occurrence of a character is chosen as a survivor as it allows greater skips. Here now is an example of the use of the search algorithm:

```c
char textfile[] = "no thing as vague as something.";

void main (void)
{
```

```
    init("methin");
    char *place = search(textfile, strlen(textfile));
}
```

Note that a search routine such as this one is not particularly suitable for simply trying to determine whether two strings are equal, as was the subject of previous sections. The reason for this is that a searching algorithm introduces some overhead before getting to the actual string compare work. This Fast Strings search does not, however, stop on encountering a null byte. This means it can be used without problem on any kind of (non-string) data set.

The nature of the text file and the search string determine how effective search string algorithms are. Dependencies are, for instance, the length of the search string, the length of the text file, the number of unique characters in the search string, and how often these characters appear in the text file. Generally it can be said, though, that the longer the search string is, and the less often its characters appear in the text file, the faster the fast search algorithm will be.

The complete source of the Fast String search can be found in the companion file: 10Source02.cpp, which compares searching a string with strstr to the Fast String search and a case-insensitive Fast String search (which is explained in the next section). As was noted at the beginning of this section, you can improve on this basic Fast String search by analyzing the data set you want to use it on. For instance, for text files of which the length is known—because it is fixed or perhaps because memory has just been allocated for it—no length calculation is needed in the call to the search function.

Case-Insensitive Fast String Search

When a pattern search is performed for strings of characters, often a match needs to be found regardless of the case of the characters in the search string or the text file. This is called a case-insensitive search. With a few minor changes the fast search string presented in this section can be transformed into such a case-insensitive search. To be able to do this kind of search quickly, you need two more data structures. The first new data structure will store a copy of the search string, containing only small characters. With this copy you can speed up the search considerably because you have fewer cases to test against: only small search string characters against lowercase or uppercase text file characters. You can of course dynamically allocate the exact amount of memory needed for this copy, but this will take time. If you can spare the footprint you may opt to use a static array. However, remember that the size of this array effectively determines the maximum size of the search string. Therefore it is important to choose the size of this array sensibly. In Listing 10.4, this array is called searchstr. The second new data structure will contain information on where in the search string characters of the alphabet occur. This structure also helps speed up the search but its main function is to guard against an obvious error; trying to match a nonalphabetic search string character against its *capital* in the text file. As you know, only alphabetic characters have a corresponding capital letter. This data structure is in effect a Boolean array and can be mapped onto anything from a bit array to an integer array. The choice here again is speed versus performance. Note that the chosen structure should be able to hold a value for each character in the search string; this means that its length should correspond to that chosen for the static search string array. In the code sample to follow this second data structure is a simple byte array called alfa.

Now let's look at the changes to be made to the Fast String search functions. First there is the init function, which was in charge of creating the skips array. It will now also initialize the searchstr array and the alfa array. Furthermore, the skips array will contain skip values for lowercase as well as uppercase letters found in the search string. An example:

```
Search string: methin

skips array: 6 5 4 3 2 1 6 5 4 3 2 1    7
alfa array:  1 1 1 1 1 1 1 1 1 1 1 1    0
             M E T H I N m e t h i n    other chars
```

Listing 10.4 shows an example of an init function which can be used for a case-insensitive Fast String search.

LISTING 10.4 Case-Insensitive Pattern Search Initialization Function

```c
unsigned char searchstr[256];    // Max pattern length is 256.
unsigned char alfa[256];         // Remember where alphabet chars are located.
unsigned char skipsInsens[256];  // Skips array.
unsigned char patlenInsens;      // Length of search pattern.


// Init function.
void initInsens(const char *str)
{
    int len1 = 0;

    // Get length and make 'smalls' copy.
    unsigned char c = str[len1];
    while ( c != '\0')
    {
        alfa[len1] = 0;
        if (c >= 'A' && c <= 'Z')
        {
            searchstr[len1] = c + 0x20;
            alfa[len1] = 1;
        }
        else
        {
```

LISTING 10.4 Continued

```
            searchstr[len1] = c;
            if (c >= 'a' && c <= 'z')
                alfa[len1] = 1;
        }
        c = str[++len1];
    }

    int len2 = len1 + 1;

    // For chars not in pattern.
    for (int i = 0; i < 255; i++)
        skipsInsens[i] = len2;   //length + 1.

    // For chars in pattern.
    //   with double chars only right most survives.
    for ( i = 0; i < len1; i++)
    {
        skipsInsens[searchstr[i]] = len1 - i;
        if (alfa[i]) skipsInsens[searchstr[i]-0x20] = len1 - i;
    }

    patlenInsens = len1;
}
```

The changes to the `search` function are minor, apart from having to use the new names for the search string, the search string length, and the skips array (if you did actually decide to use new names as was done in this section), but the check on the character match needs to be changed from

```
while (textf[j] == searchstr[j] && --j >= 0) ;
```

to

```
while (
    ((textf[j] == searchstr[j]) ||
    ((alfa[j]) && (textf[j] == (char) (searchstr[j]-0x20))))
    && --j >= 0) ;
```

What this new check actually does is first check whether a character of the search string matches a character in the text file. If it does, the function continues as it normally would. If, however, a character does not match and it is an alphabetic character, another check is done with an uppercase version of the search string character. So for a mismatch of a nonalphabetic character—for example '%'—we get the following dialog:

```
Does '%' match? No, stop comparing.
```

And for a mismatch of an alphabet character—for example 'a'—we get the following dialog:

```
Does 'a' match? No. Does 'A' match? No, stop comparing.
```

The complete implementation of the case-insensitive search string function can be found in the file 10Source02.cpp, which compares searching a string with `strstr` to the Fast String search and the case-insensitive Fast String search.

The Theory of Sorting Data

Apart from comparing blocks of data, you will often find that you need to sort a particular set of data. In a base of sorted data, you can locate elements faster and it becomes easier to present output in a certain logical format. Think, for instance, of representing the same information in different contexts: a list of employees ordered by day of birth for a birthday card list, the same list of employees ordered by salary for cost analysis, and so on. It is easier (and faster) for a program to group data according to a certain criterion—for example, an unsorted telephone directory.

In the previous sections, you have already read about a basic mechanism used in sorting—namely, matching patterns of data. Sorting is in effect ordering data on the basis of a comparison. The element—or part of the element—that is used in this comparison is called the *key*. When a database of employee records is sorted on employee name, the employee name is the sorting key. When the database is then sorted using employee age, the age is the sorting key. This section discusses sorting theory further. Before we get down to the actual sorting algorithms, though, there will be some general theory on sorting.

Algorithm Issues

The Good, the Bad, and the Average

In comparing sorting algorithms, it is important not only to look at the worst-case performance but also at the best-case and the average-case. Average case is, of course, the one you will run into most of the time; best case is what you will want to demo to a potential client. Worst case and average case can be very different; they can even differ in orders of magnitude, as you will see later with the quick sort algorithm. Still this does not necessarily mean that you will discard an algorithm based solely on worst-case characteristics. Worst case might happen very seldom and may even be predictable or acceptable. Let's say on average a certain sorting algorithm takes two seconds to sort the office's financial data; it may be acceptable for this to take up to five minutes once or twice a month. A smart employee will let this inconvenience coincide with a caffeine break. You may even try to detect possible worst-case scenarios inside the sorting algorithm—as the section on sorting techniques shows—but to get this detection completely watertight will of course make your algorithm impossibly slow. (It would mean checking all the data.)

Algorithm Footprints

It is important to realize that the runtime footprint of a sorting algorithm is often more than the space that the actual code of the sorting algorithm takes up. One reason for this is that some sorting algorithms are what is called *in-place*, and others are not. A sorting algorithm is in-place when the data set stays the same size (or a little over that size) while it is being sorted. A sorting algorithm which is not in-place will need more space for the data set when it is sorting. For small databases this is unlikely to be a problem but for large bases this can seriously constrain the maximum database size. This is because a percentage of the base size in memory needs to be reserved for sorting purposes. Another reason why the runtime sorting algorithm footprint can be larger than that of the code is the needed stack frame. When a sorting algorithm uses recursion (see Chapter 8, "Functions") the runtime footprint can suddenly boom during sorting.

Algorithm Stability

Another characteristic of sorting algorithms is something called stability. A sorting algorithm is called stable when it leaves elements with identical keys in the same order during sorting. This means that when an unsorted database contains two employees with the same name, these employees will emerge in the sorted database in the same order when employee name is the sorting key. Although this stability might seem obvious, not many sorting algorithms guarantee this. Of course, it depends on the requirements of your program whether stability is necessary or not.

Algorithm Simplicity

The final sorting algorithm characteristic of this section is the complexity of the implementation itself. So far you have read only about the mathematical complexity, but this does not have to correspond directly to the complexity of the software that implements the sorting algorithm. Algorithms which are relatively easy to implement have the advantage that development and maintenance time is low and chances of bugs are fewer. These advantages can translate directly into saving money on development. When it is acceptable for a certain sorting part of a program to be slow, the choice can be made for an algorithm that is easy to implement and maintain instead of a brilliantly fast algorithm that only the implementer understands on the day that he writes the code. In general, of course, the fastest sorting algorithms do tend to be the more complex ones to implement, as you will see in the section "Sorting Techniques."

Sorting Techniques

This section explains the theory behind some of the most popular sorting techniques used today. Each subsection highlights a specific sorting technique, telling you about its specific characteristics and giving an example of how you could implement the technique. You can use or modify these examples to suit your needs . At the end of the chapter an overview is given of all sorting techniques discussed so you can quickly see which technique is useful for which situation.

In order to keep the theoretical narrative of this section as close to the point as possible, arrays of integers are used as examples of bases to be sorted. This way, the overhead of other implementation issues is minimized. Throughout the text, references are made to the *array* as thebase of data to be sorted; the value of each element to be sorted is also its sorting key as all elements are integers. Sorting techniques can, of course, be used to sort more complex elements, using one of their fields as a key. Examples of this are given in the sources of this chapter.

Insertion Sort

Insertion sort is a very basic sorting algorithm which is easy to understand and implement. Insertion sort looks at each element of the array and checks whether its value is smaller than that of the previous element. When this is the case, the element has to be moved to some place earlier in the array. In order to find the right place for the element, insertion sort moves back through the array until it encounters an element which is smaller. The element to be moved is placed *after* this smaller element. All elements between the old and the new place of the moved element are moved one place up. The following example demonstrates this:

```
Unsorted array: 30 20 40 10
```

```
First check:
30    40 10      20 < 30, so search backwards for a place to insert 20
   30 40 10      30 is moved forward and the front of the array is reached
20 30 40 10      20 placed at the front of the array

Second check:
20 30 40 10      40 > 30, nothing to do.

Third check:
20 30 40         10 < 40, so search backwards for a place to insert 10
   20 30 40      40, 30 and 20 are moved forward
10 20 30 40      10 is placed at the front of the array
```

Note that the first array element can initially be considered sorted. Only when the second element is compared to the first can a decision about the place of either be made. Listing 10.5 shows an example of an implementation of insertion sort.

LISTING 10.5   Insertion Sort

```c
void InsertionSort(long *data, long n)
{
    long i, j, item;
```

LISTING 10.5 Continued

```
// i divides the array into a sorted region, x<i
// and an unsorted region, x >= i.

for(i=1;i<n;i++)
{
    // Select the item at the beginning of the as yet unsorted section.
    item = data[i];

    // If this element is greater than item, move it up one.
    for(j=i; (j > 0) && (data[j-1] > item); j--)
        data[j] = data[j-1];

    // Stopped when data[j-1] <= item, so put item at position j.
    data[j] = item;
}
}
```

You can see in the sorting example that insertion sort is an $O(n^2)$ algorithm; in a worst-case scenario each element will cause all the elements before it to be moved once; $n*(n-1)$ is basically $n*n$, which is n^2. For insertion sort, the average case is also $O(n^2)$.

The pros of insertion sort are

- Simple implementation
- High efficiency for small amounts of data (virtually no overhead)
- Small runtime footprint (in-place)
- Stable algorithm (original order of identical elements is preserved)

The con of insertion sort is

- Low efficiency for normal to large amounts of data

Because of its small runtime footprint and high efficiency for small data sets, insertion sort is ideal for augmenting other sorting algorithms. After a size check, an overhead-heavy sorting algorithm can decide to invoke insertion sort for a data set which is too small to justify overhead. By doing so the last drop of performance can be squeezed out of a sorting algorithm.

Bubble Sort

Bubble sort is another fairly straightforward sorting algorithm. Bubble sort compares the first two elements of the array, switches their places when they are in the wrong order, and then moves up one position in the array to compare the following two elements. It does this repeatedly until it has reached the end of the array, and then it goes back to the beginning of the array and starts over. This whole process is repeated until bubble sort can pass over the entire array without switching any elements. With bubble sort the elements bubble step by step to the place they are supposed to be. The following example demonstrates bubble sort:

```
Unsorted array: 30 10 40 20


First iteration:
10 30 40 20      10 < 30, so switch these elements.
10 30 40 20      40 > 30, so leave second tuple.
10 30 20 40      20 < 40, so switch these elements

Second iteration:
10 30 20 40      30 > 10, so leave these elements
10 20 30 40      20 < 30, so switch these elements
10 20 30 40      20 < 30 and 30 < 40 so leave these elements.
```

Listing 10.6 shows an implementation of bubble sort.

LISTING 10.6   Bubble Sort

```cpp
void BubbleSort(unsigned long data[], unsigned long n)
{
    // Sort array data[] of n-items
    unsigned long i, j;
    bool changes = true;

    // Make max n passes through the array or stop when done.
    for(i=0;(i<n) && (changes == true);i++)
    {
        changes = false;
        for(j=1;j<(n-i);j++)
        {
            // If items are out of order --> exchange them.
            if( data[j-1]>data[j] )
            {
                long dummy = data[j-1];   // SWAP TWO ITEMS
                data[j-1] = data[j];
                data[j] = dummy;
                changes = true;
            }
        }
    }
}
```

This implementation consists of two loops. The inner loop runs through the data array and switches elements when needed. The outer loop controls the number of times the inner loop traverses the array. Note the double stop condition; in a worst-case scenario the inner loop is executed as many times as there are elements in the array. The outer loop can be preempted, however, when an iteration over the data array proves that the array is sorted—that is, no more elements were switched.

The pros of bubble sort are

- Simple implementation
- High efficiency of memory usage (in place)
- Stable algorithm

The con of bubble sort is

- Low efficiency—O(n^2)

Without further optimizations, bubble sort is slower than insertion sort. It is presented in this chapter because of its easy implementation and its great popularity.

Shell Sort

Shell sort, invented by Donald L. Shell, is still fairly easy to implement. It is, however, much faster than the previous sorting techniques when larger bases of data are sorted. Shell sort is similar to insertion sort with the difference that it moves data over larger, and variable, spacings. This is good because, in general, elements of an unsorted array are found more than one place removed from where they should be. As you saw in the section "Insertion Sort," insertion sort uses a spacing of 1. This means that two successive elements are compared and, if needed, switched in place. With shell sort you could choose a spacing of 2, for instance. In that case, elements 1 and 3 are compared, instead of elements 1 and 2. After this, elements 4 and 2 are compared, instead of elements 2 and 3. Shell sort is usually used with a different spacing for each time the algorithm iterates the array. The spacing is initially chosen as *large* and becomes smaller with each iteration until the final iteration through the array is done with a spacing of 1 (this is a normal insertion sort). The idea behind this is that fewer iterations are needed to completely sort the array. The following example demonstrates a shell sort iteration with a spacing of 2, followed by an iteration with a spacing of 1:

```
Unsorted array: 40 70 20 30 60

First iteration with spacing = 2.
40 70 20 30 60          40 > 20, so switch
20 70 40 30 60          70 > 30, so switch
20 30 40 70 60          40 < 60, no switch

Second iteration with spacing = 1.
20 30 40 60 70          20, 30, 40 are ok, 70 > 60, so these are switched.
```

Getting Our Hands Dirty

Choosing the spacings for your shell sort algorithm is crucial to its performance. Luckily, a lot of research has already been done on different spacing strategies. The following spacing guidelines were proposed by Donald E. Knuth in his book *The Art of Computer Programming*:

> Starting with a spacing of 1, a following spacing is calculated as follows: three times the previous spacing plus one.

This implies a fixed spacing range which is as follows: 1, $(3*1+1) = 4$, $(3*4+1) = 13$, $(3*13+1) = 40$, $(3*40+1) = 121$, and so on. Knuth further proposes you choose as a starting spacing from this list the spacing which is two orders below the first spacing that is higher than the number of elements you want to sort. That may sound complicated but it's not that bad. The following example demonstrates:

```
Spacings list:          1, 4, 13, 40, 121, ..
Number of elements(n):  100

First spacing > n:      121
Starting spacing:       13
```

Here, 121 is the first spacing in the spacings list which is higher than the number of elements to sort (n = 100). So, as a starting space you choose the spacing which is found two elements below 121 in the spacings list. This a spacing of 13.

A shell sort of 100 elements will use the following order of spacings: 13, 4, 1.

Similarly, a shell sort of 122 elements will use the following order of spacings: 40, 13, 4, 1.

Listing 10.7 shows an implementation of shell sort, using Knuth's spacing advice.

LISTING 10.7 Shell Sort

```
void ShellSort(unsigned long data[], long lb, long ub)
{
    long n, i, j, t, h;

    // Calculate largest stepsize.
    n = ub - lb + 1;
    h = 1;
    if (n < 14)
        h = 1;
    else
    {
        while (h < n)
        h = 3*h + 1;
        h /= 3;
        h /= 3;
```

LISTING 10.7   Continued

```
    }

    while (h > 0)
    {
        // sort-by-insertion with stepsize of h.
        for (i = lb + h; i <= ub; i++)
        {
            t = data[i];
            for (j = i-h; j >= lb && (data[j] > t); j -= h)
                data[j+h] = data[j];
            data[j+h] = t;
        }

        // calculate next stepsize.
        h /= 3;
    }
}
```

The implementation starts with an `if..else` construct which determines the initial spacing, based on the concepts you have just seen. After this, a `while` loop handles the number of array iterations. Note the calculation of the new spacing at the end of the `while`: `h /=3`. The `for` loop inside the `while` takes care of a single array iteration, sorting the array in a way similar to insertion sort.

The average case sorting time for shell sort with Knuth spacing is $O(n^1.25)$. The worst-case sorting time is $O(n^1.5)$. This may seem like an arbitrary difference, but this is not really the case. For 100 elements, the difference is already 316 : 1000.

The pros of shell sort are

- Simple to implement and still quite fast.
- In-place (efficiency).

The con of shell sort is

- Still there are faster methods.

An important characteristic of shell sort is that its worst-case performance is better than most more advanced sorting methods (like quick sort, as you will see in a later section). For this reason, shell sort is popular for life-critical systems where unexpected delays of $O(n^2)$ can be dangerous.

There are sorting methods that have a better worst-case performance than shell sort; refer to Table 10.2 for an overview on sorting method characteristics.

10

BLOCKS OF DATA

Heap Sort

As the name suggests, heap sort makes use of a structure called a *heap*. Before we define exactly what a heap is, here is a quick recap of tree terminology: A *tree* is a data structure in which elements are related to each other in *parent* and *child* relationships. Parents are called *nodes*. Each child has at most one parent. Each parent can have several children but at most one parent. There is one parent that has no parents of its own; it is called the *root*. A child that is not a parent itself is called a *leaf*. Figure 10.1 shows a simple tree structure.

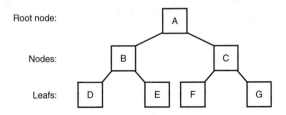

FIGURE 10.1

A tree structure.

In Figure 10.1, the leaf F has a parent called C which in turn is a child of the root node A.

Each node in a tree is, in fact, the root of a subtree. This is why nodes are sometimes referred to as subtrees. The tree in the previous example has two subtrees; the subtree with root B and the subtree with root C.

A tree is called binary and balanced when it adheres to the following constraints: The children are distributed evenly over the tree with each node having exactly two children. The only possible exception to this is the last node of the tree; this node can have a single child when there are not enough children to go around. Only the lowest nodes in the tree can have leaves as children. The tree in Figure 10.1 is thus a balanced binary tree. A balanced binary tree is said to have the *heap* property when each node has a value that is larger than that of its children; it can, of course, be equal to one of its children. Figure 10.2 shows some examples of different kinds of trees.

FIGURE 10.2

Different types of trees.

In the beginning of this section on sorting we promised you that all examples would sort arrays. In order to store a heap in an array, a mapping of the two data types has to be made.

This mapping will of course also dictate how heap elements can be found in the array. The following two sections address these issues. Note that throughout this section the small letter *n* is used to indicate the number of elements in a given data structure.

Mapping a Heap on an Array

You can map a heap onto an array by simply *reading* it like a piece of text—from left to right, and top to bottom. Figure 10.3 shows this.

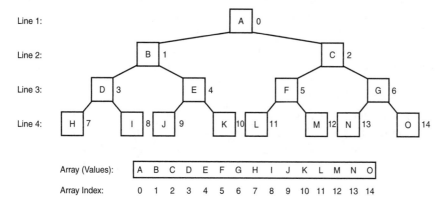

FIGURE 10.3
Heap-to-array mapping.

The top part of Figure 10.3 shows a heap structure which contains the letters A through O. The lower part of Figure 10.3 shows the array that will represent the heap. In order to get from the heap to the array, you *read* the heap and place its elements in the array in the order of reading: The first line in the heap picture consists of a single letter, the letter A. It is placed at the beginning of the array. The second line in the heap picture contains the letters B and C. They are placed in the following two slots of the array and so on. For extra clarity, the eventual array indexes accompany the elements in both pictures, so A will be stored in array[0], and O will be stored in array[14].

> **NOTE**
>
> Technically the tree in the previous example is not a heap because the integer value of A is *lower* than that of B and C instead of higher. This setup is chosen, however, because mapping from the tree to the array is easier to understand this way.

Array Indexing

Navigating the heap is made easy by the mapping chosen earlier in the chapter.

Here are some important access points:

Total number of nodes in the heap is n / 2, and in the example, 15 / 2 = 7. *Note that the number is rounded downwards, 7.5 becoming 7.*

The last node in the array is (n / 2) –1, and in the example, (15 / 2) – 1 = 6; array[6] = G.

For any node *array[x]*, the leaves of that node are found at *array[2x+1]* and *array[2x+2]*. In the example array[6] = G, its leaves are array[13] = N and array[14] = O.

To use a heap in a sorting algorithm, two different kinds of functions need to be performed. First of all, the initial tree needs to be transformed into a heap. This means moving around elements of the array until each node of the tree has a value higher than that of its (two) leaves. Secondly, the heap needs to be transformed into a sorted array. The following two sections address these issues.

Making an Initial Heap

Listing 10.8 shows the first half of what will become a HeapSort function. It processes an array of integers, called data. It addresses this array as if it represents a balanced binary tree which may or may not yet have the heap property. The code snippet reorders the array elements of data so that each node has a value that is larger than that of its children, effectively creating a heap.

LISTING 10.8   Heap Sort, Part I

```
int i, j, j2, k;
int tmp;

// Outerloop: considers all nodes, starting at the last one and
//   working back to the root.
for(k = (n>>1) - 1; k >= 0; k--)
{
    // k points to the node under evaluation.
    // j2+1 and j2+2 point at the children of k.
    tmp = data[k];

    // Innerloop: for each changed node, recursively check the
    //   child node which was responsible for the change.
    for(j = k; (j<<1) <= n-2; j = i)
    {
        // find the largest child of node k.
        j2 = j <<1;
        if (j2+2 > n-1) // only one child
            i = j2+1;
        else
        {
            if (data[j2+1] < data[j2+2])
```

LISTING 10.8   Continued

```
                i = j2+2;
        else
                i = j2+1;
        }

        // i now points to the child with the highest value.
        if (tmp < data[i])
            data[j] = data[i]; // promote child
        else
            break;
    }
    data[j] = tmp;
}
```

How does Listing 10.8 create a heap? Basically, it looks at each node of the tree and makes it a heap; this means switching the largest child of a node with the node itself whenever the node is not the largest value of the three. The algorithm starts at the last node of the tree and works its way back to the root. This means, for the example heap, the following nodes are initially evaluated: G, F, E, D. These are the nodes in the last *line* of the heap—that is, nodes with leaves as children. The next node to be evaluated is node C. The children of C are, of course, nodes themselves. When a change is made to node C, one of the subtrees of C needs to be reevaluated. For instance, initially C has the children F and G. G is the highest of the three so elements G and C are switched. Subtree F is unaffected by this but the subtree that was G (and now is C) needs to be reevaluated. This needs to be done recursively, of course. This is exactly what the inner loop of the previous code snippet does; for each node, it checks for changes and recursively checks each subnode responsible for the change. The outer loop simply backtracks through the array from the last node up to the root. When the algorithm finally arrives at the root node, the array represents a heap. Now all that remains is sorting that heap.

Sorting a Heap

Listing 10.9 shows the second half of what will become a HeapSort function. It sorts an array of integers, called data. It addresses this array as if it represents a heap.

LISTING 10.9   Heap Sort, Part II

```
// remove roots continuously
for(k=n-1; k>0; k--)
{
    // k points to the (sorted) back of the array.
    //  switch the root with the element at the back.
    tmp = data[k];
    data[k] = data[0];
```

10

LISTING 10.9 Continued

```
// make the array into a heap again.
for(j = 0; (j<<1) <= k-2; j = i)
{
    j2 = j<<1;
    if ( j2+2 > k-1 )      // only one child
        i = j2+1;
    else
    {
        if ( data[j2+1] < data[j2+2] )
            i = j2+2;
        else
            i = j2+1;
    }

    // i now points to the child with the highest value.
    if (tmp < data[i])
        data[j] = data[i];      // promote child
    else
        break;
}
data[j]  = tmp;
}
```

How does Listing 10.9 sort a heap? It takes the root node of the heap, which is the largest number in the array, and switches it with the last element in the array; this is the final leaf child of the final node. The ex-root element is now exactly where it needs to be. However, the *new* heap needs to be reevaluated. This is done in the same way as was done in the inner loop of the code snippet that made the initial heap. When the re-valuation of the heap has been done, the root element is again taken and switched with the final leaf of the final node. The sorted part of the array thus grows from the back of the array to the front.

Pros and Cons of Heap Sort

Heap sort is an $O(n \log_2 n)$ algorithm (for best and worst case!), which means it is the fastest algorithm we have seen so far. Furthermore, its overhead is quite small, which means it can be used also for small amounts of data.

The pros of heap sort are

- High efficiency for average and worst case
- Small runtime footprint (in-place)

The cons of heap sort are

- Unstable algorithm
- More complex algorithm than the previous sorting methods discussed

In the companion file 10source03.cpp, a complete HeapSort function can be found which is usable as a template. All that is missing from the snippets in this section to create a complete HeapSort() function is the function header:

```
void HeapSort(int *data, int n)
{
    // add Part I: Listing 10.8.

    // add Part II:  Listing 10.9.
}
```

Quick Sort

Quick sort, invented by C. A. R. Hoare, is an $O(n^2)$. It is less complex to implement than heap sort, which is why it can be slightly faster; however, worst-case performance is $O(n^2)$. Precautions can be taken to make worst-case performance as unlikely as possible. Because of its high speed, quick sort has been added to the standard C library. Its name in the library is qsort(). When calling qsort you need to provide your own compare function which qsort will use to determine the larger of two array elements as it sorts through your data. This makes it possible to use the standard implementation for a wide variety of types. The compare function must, of course, conform to the rules specified for arguments and the return value, or qsort will not work. Listing 10.10 shows an example of the use of qsort with a self-made compare function that allows qsort to sort arrays of longs.

LISTING 10.10 Using the Standard QSort

```
int compare( const void *arg1, const void *arg2 )
{
/* Return value:
    < 0 elem1 less than elem2
    0 elem1 == elem2
    > 0 elem1 greater than elem2
*/
    return (*(long*) arg1 -  *(long*)arg2);
}

void main()
{
    qsort((void *)longArray, (size_t) n, sizeof(long),  compare);
}
```

In this example, the first qsort argument is longArray, which is the array of longs that is to be sorted. The second argument is n, which is the number of elements in the array. The third argument is the size of each array element, which is calculated with the statement sizeof(long). The final argument is a pointer to the compare function. Note that the compare function receives two pointers to array elements. Because you, as a user of the qsort function, know which type or array elements you are sorting, you can do a cast to that type in the compare routine. The valid range of return values is included as a comment in the example.

When you want the use a quick sort for only a specific type of data structure, it can be wise to implement your own version of the algorithm. At the very least, you will be able to eliminate the call to the compare function by directly inserting the compare code into the quick sort routine itself. You may be able to do more, depending on you data set. Here is the theory behind quick sort.

The quick sort algorithm sorts a data array in two phases: the partition phase and the sort phase. In the partition phase, the data array is divided into two around what is called a pivot element. The other array elements are *pivoted* around this pivot element. This means that all the elements which are smaller than the pivot are put together in one part of the array, and all the elements which are larger than the pivot are placed on the other side of the pivot. Here is an example:

```
Initial array:  1 7 3 9 6 4 8 2 5
Pivot:          array[4] = 6

Pivoting:
1 7 3 9 6 4 8 2 5      7>6 and 5<6, switch
1 5 3 9 6 4 8 2 7      9>6 and 2<6, switch
1 5 3 2 6 4 8 9 7      4<6, switch
1 5 3 2 4 6 8 9 7
```

Starting from the two outermost boundaries of the array (the first and the last elements), elements are compared with the pivot value. Values which are larger than the pivot and are on its left side are switched with elements which are smaller than the pivot on the right side. Note that the number of mismatches on the left side does not have to coincide with the number of mismatches on the right side. Array evaluation simply continues from both sides until they meet in the middle.

How far this first partition step actually helps you along the way depends on the value of the pivot element which is chosen. The maximum gains are had when the pivot element just happens to be the median of all values in the array. In the preceding example, the element in the middle of the array was chosen but any other element would also have worked as it is the *value* of the pivot that counts and not its position in the array. There is a danger in choosing the first or the last element in an array as the pivot element, however. When you use quick sort on an array which is already sorted, taking the first or last element as a pivot creates the largest overhead.

After the partition phase has been completed, the sort phase commences. The sort phase consists of two recursive calls to the quick sort function itself. The first call will execute another quick sort on the left half of the partitioned array, and the second call will execute another quick sort on the right half of the array. This way, each half of the array is pivoted once more around a new pivot, after which two more recursive calls can be made. Recursion stops when a quick sort invocation receives an array with size 1. It becomes clear now why choosing the first (or last) element of a sorted array as a pivot creates an unfortunate situation; each recursive call will split the original array into a single element and the rest of the array. This means there will be as many recursive calls as there are elements in the array, resulting in a worst case scenario of $O(n^2)$. Here is a functional description of the quick sort algorithm:

```
int Partition (int data[], int n)
{
    // Select a pivot element.

    // re-order data[0] till data[n-1] until the following is true:

    //   data[0] till data[pivot-1] <= data[pivot] and
    //   data[pivot+1] till data[n-1] >= data[pivot]

    return pivot; // position of pivot element AFTER re-ordering.
}


void QuickSort(int data[], int n)
{
    if (n > 1)
    {
        int pivot = Partition(data, n);

        if (n < 3) return;

        QuickSort(data, pivot);
        QuickSort(data + pivot + 1, n - pivot - 1);
    }
}
```

Note that actual sorting can be speeded up by selecting a good pivot value. However, remember that the more complicated you make the method of determining the pivot, the slower the partitioning phase will be, unless, of course, you have specific information on the array you want to sort. Note also the two if statements. The first if statement stops execution for arrays with one element or fewer; there is just no sorting to do with fewer than two elements. The second if statement stops on an array of two elements or fewer. This is possible because after partitioning an array of two elements, no more sorting needs to be done because the two elements will be in the correct order. There is another optimization in this example. Many quick sort implementations used today take three parameters: the data array and an upper and lower bound variable to identify which part of the array is to be sorted. By passing an updated array beginning, and the total number of elements that are left in the part of the array to sort, one parameter has been eliminated. This is interesting because calls to quick sort are made recursively and the less information each recursion places on stack, the smaller the runtime footprint will be. This brings us to another optimization, which is slightly more complicated. The two recursive calls that quick sort makes to itself can be translated into one recursive call and one iteration. Functionally the body of the quick sort function would then look like this:

```
void QuickSort(int data[], int n)
{
    while(n > 1)
    {
        int pivot = Partition(data, n);

        if (n < 3) return;

        // call quick sort on the second part.
        QuickSort(data + pivot + 1, n - pivot - 1);

        // All that remains to be sorted is first part,
        //   adapt n and restart.
        n = pivot; // n is upperbound + 1!
    }
}
```

Of course the `Partition` functionality does not have to be placed in a separate routine. By placing it in the quick sort itself, another function call is eliminated. Also, you can tweak which part of the partitioned array you select for the recursive call and which part for the iteration. Listing 10.11 shows a quick sort function which takes all the mentioned optimizations into account.

LISTING 10.11   Fast Quick Sort

```
template <class T> inline void FQuickSort(T *data, long n)
{
    T pivot, tempElem;
    long left, right, tempIndex;

    while(n > 1)
    {
```

LISTING 10.11 Continued

```
    right = n-1;
    left = 1;

    // switch the pivot with the first array element.
    tempIndex = right / 2;
    pivot = data[tempIndex];
    data[tempIndex] = data[0];

    // Partition the array.
    while (1)
    {
       while (pivot > data[left] && left < right) left++;
       while (pivot <= data[right] && right >= left) right--;
       if (left >= right) break;

       // Switch two array elements.
       tempElem = data[left];
       data[left] = data[right];
       data[right] = tempElem;
       right--; left++;
    }
    // switch pivot back to where it belongs.
    data[0] = data[right];
    data[right] = pivot;

    // Sort phase.
    if (n < 3) return;

    tempIndex = n - right - 1;
    if (right > tempIndex)
    {
       // first part is largest.
       FQuickSort(data + right + 1, n - right - 1);
       n = right; // n is upperbound + 1!
    }
    else
    {
       // second part is largest.
       FQuickSort(data, right);
       data += right + 1;
       n = tempIndex;
    }
  }
}
```

The quick sort implementation of Listing 10.11 is presented as a template so it can be called for arrays of different types. Calling examples of this are given after a brief walkthrough.

There are only two new items introduced in the FQuickSort function. First of all, the pivot is chosen as the middle element in the array. To make the partition routine less complex, the pivot is switched with the first array element before partitioning. Second, the largest of the partitioned array parts is sent into iteration, the smallest into recursion.

As promised, here is an example of the usage of this quick sort implementation:

```
int   integerArray[] = {100, 1001, 24, 317 , 314, 2000, 2009, 7009};
short shortArray[]    = {10, 20, 11, 317 , 314, 510, 12, 709};

FQuickSort(integerArray, 8);
FQuickSort(shortArray, 8);
```

The advantage of quick sort is

- High efficiency for average case

The cons of quick sort are

- Very low efficiency for worst case
- Large runtime footprint
- Unstable algorithm

Quick sort averages on O(nlog2 n) with a worst case of O(n^2). Note that although quick sort does the sorting of its data in-place, it is not, in fact, an in-place algorithm as its stack usage can run up pretty high on large data sets.

As promised, the accompanying sources on the Web site contain sorting examples which sort more than just arrays of integers, and comparisons are made between sorting with a quick sort, a radix sort, and the standard qsort:

| 10source04.cpp | Sorts arrays pointers to strings |
| 10source05.cpp | Sorts records by using operator overloading |

At the end of the following section, more will be said about these sources.

Radix Sort

Radix sort takes a whole different approach to sorting. Radix sort no longer compares sortable items with each other; the essence of radix sort is that it sorts according to the value of subelements. For instance, when the elements to sort are of type integer, radix sort will iterate the array four times, once for each byte of an integer. During the first iteration, it sorts the elements of the array according to the value of the least significant byte, and it ends up sorting elements according to the value of the most significant byte during the fourth iteration. Here is a numeric example:

```
Original    Iteration Iteration   Iteration Iteration
array:          I        II          III        IV

1005          2204      2204        1005       1005
2204          1005      1005        2037       1508
2037          2037      1508        2204       2037
1508          1508      2037        1508       2204
```

The first column of the preceding example shows a random array. The second column shows what the array looks like after the first iteration. During this first iteration, the numbers are ordered according to the value of the least significant digit. Radix sort thus focuses on the following values during the first iteration: 5, 4, 7, 8. It places them in the order 4, 5, 7, 8. The second iteration looks only at the following digit, recognizing the values 0, 0, 3, 0. The third iteration recognizes the values 0, 0, 2, 5 and the fourth iteration recognizes the values 1, 2, 2, 1. As this example demonstrates, the number of iterations that radix sort need to make in order to sort an array of elements depends not on the number of elements to be sorted, but on the size of a single element. This means that radix sort is an $O(m*n)$ algorithm—where m is the number of subelements. Sorting a data type of two bytes can be done in two iterations.

A radix sort implementation needs enough space for a second array. This is because radix loop iterations copy all the elements from one array to the other, placing the elements at a different position in the second array. However, a following iteration will copy all the elements back to the first array, so only two arrays are ever needed. But how does radix sort know where in the second array to place the copied elements? In order to do this, it needs to divide the new array into sections. There should be a section for every possible value of the subelement which it focuses on.

In Figure 10.4, the array elements consist of two subelements: the first and second digit. Two iterations are needed to sort this kind of element. The first iteration will focus only on the least-significant digit. Before this iteration starts, the occurrences of each value of the least-significant digit are counted. The results are two occurrences of the value 0, two occurrences of the value 1, and a single occurrence of the value 6. With this information the destination array can be divided into subsections. An index is created for each subsection, pointing to the first available space in that subsection. Now the source array is iterated over and each source value is copied to the appropriate subsection in the destination array. Note that when a value is copied to a subsection, the index of that subsection must be increased by 1. This way an index will always point to the next available space.

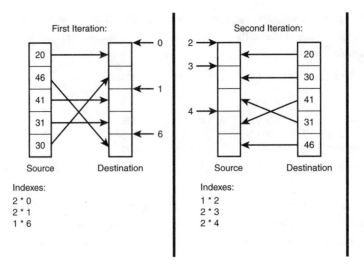

FIGURE 10.4

Radix sort for two subelements.

The second iteration will focus only on the most significant digit. It finds the following occurrences of that digit: a single occurrence of the value 2, two occurrences of value 3, and another two occurrences of value 4. Three subsection indexes are set accordingly and the elements are copied back to the original array (which has become the destination for this iteration).

Note that radix sort must always traverse the source array from the least-significant digit or element to the most-significant digit or element, which ensures that the ordering created by a previous iteration is maintained. For example, in the first iteration of the preceding example, the values {46, 41} are placed in the order {41, 46} in relation to each other. In the second iteration, these values come together in the same subsection. If this second iteration had started at the back of the destination array, these values would have been switched again, because the value 46 would have been found and copied before the value 41 would be found. This would cause an unsorted output. This is also where endian-ness starts to play a role. On Intel machines, which use little-endian byte order, the number 0x01020304 is placed in memory as follows: 0x04030201. On big-endian machines, such as 68xx architectures and MIPS, this number is placed in memory as: 0x01020304. Simply put, this means that finding the least and most significant bytes may have to be done differently on different machines. With the cpu_info() function found in the booktools, you can determine the endian-ness of a target machine. Note that endian-ness only plays a role for base types. For strings, for instance, the endian-ness of a target machine is of no consequence because strings are placed in memory byte for byte. Listing 10.12 shows an implementation of radix sort.

Listing 10.12   Radix Sort, Part I

```
template <class T>
inline void radix(int byte, unsigned long n, T *source, T *dest)
{
    unsigned long count[256], i, c, s=0;
    unsigned char *q;
    int size = sizeof(T);

    // Create array of sub section indexes.
    memset(&count[0], 0x0, 256*sizeof(unsigned long));

    // Count occurrence of every byte value in T
    q = (unsigned char *)source;
    for (i = 0; i < n; i++)
    {
        count[q[byte]]++;
        q+=size;
    }

    // Create indexes from counters.
    for (i = 0; i < 256; i++)
    {
        c = count[i];
        count[i] = s;
        s += c;
    }

    // Copy elements from the source array to the destination array.
    q = (unsigned char *)source;
    for (i = 0; i < n; i++)
    {
        dest[count[q[byte]]++] = *(T*)q;
        q+=size;
    }
}
```

This implementation is presented as a template so it can be called for arrays of different types. Calling examples of this are given after a brief walkthrough.

Note that because computers work easier with bytes than with digits 0–9, each iteration will look at a single byte of an array element. There will, of course, be at most 256 indexes, one for each value of a byte. The array count is used to store the number of occurrences of each subelement value. The memset command sets the initial values of this array to 0. After the occurrences of each byte value have been counted, indexes must be created. The value of a

10

Blocks of Data

subsection index is the sum of all preceding counts. The final loop in this implementation copies array elements from the source to the destination array. You will notice that this implementation does, in fact, only a single loop iteration; it receives the position of the subelement to focus on through the argument byte. Thus the function radix() must be called once for each subelement in an array. The other arguments that this function receives are n, denoting the number of elements in the array; source, which is the source array; and dest, which is the destination array. Listing 10.13 shows a function that will call radix() for every subelement of an array.

LISTING 10.13   Radix Sort, Part II

```
#define L_ENDIAN // or don't define L_ENDIAN.

template <class T> void RadixSort (T *data, unsigned long n)
{
    int i, elemsize = sizeof(T);
    T *temp = (T*)malloc (n * elemsize);

    if (temp != NULL)
    {
#ifdef L_ENDIAN
        for (i=0; i < elemsize-1; i+=2)
        {
            radix(i, n, data, temp);
            radix(i+1, n, temp, data);
        }
        if (elemsize & 1)    // odd elemsize  -> one more to go?
        {
            radix(elemsize-1, n, data, temp);
            memcpy(data, temp, n * elemsize);
        }
#else
        for (i = elemsize-1; i > 0; i-=2)
        {
            radix(i, n, data, temp);
            radix(i-1, n, temp, data);
        }
        if (elemsize & 1)    // odd elemsize  -> one more to go?
        {
            radix(0, n, data, temp);
            memcpy(data, temp, n * elemsize);
        }
```

LISTING 10.13 Continued

```
#endif
      free (temp);
   }
}
```

As promised, here is an example of the usage of this radix sort implementation:

```
int   integerArray[] = {100, 1001, 24, 317 , 314, 2000, 2009, 7009};
short shortArray[]    = {10, 20, 11, 317 , 314, 510, 12, 709};

RadixSort(integerArray, 8);
RadixSort(shortArray, 8);
```

As was mentioned before, radix sort is an O(m*n) algorithm. The number of elements in an array determines how long an iteration will take, but the number of subelements determines how many iterations are needed.

The pros of radix sort are

- High efficiency for average-size data elements
- Fairly easy to implement

The cons of radix sort are

- Low efficiency for large data elements
- Large runtime footprint
- Unstable algorithm

For data types of which the size is a multiple of two bytes, radix sort could be tweaked to look at a word per iteration instead of a byte.

Because sorting time for radix sort is a function of the key length—O(m*n)—and for quick sort it is a function of the number of elements—O(n log2 n)—it would seem that radix sort would be faster than quick sort when m < log2 n. However, this is too simply stated as both methods have a different kind of overhead. The real pivot at which implementations of both sorting techniques overtake each other can be determined by doing speed tests with different element lengths. The following two files that can be found on the Web site do this for different string lengths:

| 10source04.cpp | Sorts an array of pointers to strings |
| 10source05.cpp | Sorts records using operator overloading |

You should note that for a sufficiently large amount of records and a sufficiently small key length, radix sort is faster than quick sort.

Merge Sort

Merge sort is not really a sorting algorithm; rather, it is an algorithm that *merges* different sorted bases together. Its obvious use is that of merging two previously separate databases of the same type together. It can, however, also be used to sort a database that does not fit into memory in its entirety. This means that merge sort can help overcome serious footprint issues.

In order to sort a database that does not fit into memory, you first have to divide it up into smaller chunks that *can* be fit into memory. Let's say you keep your (un)sorted data on some kind of external disk. Each chunk needs to be loaded from the disk, sorted (using whatever algorithm you deem best), and stored back on the disk. Now you have a collection of sorted chunks. This is where merge sort comes into the picture. Merge sort takes two or more of these sorted chunks and merges them into a single chunk, which is also sorted. Merge sort keeps merging chunks of sorted data until a single, sorted output is created.

A single merge has to reserve memory on the disk for its output file. This output file will be as large as the sum of the sizes of the selected chunks that will be merged. The space that is available on the disk thus determines which, and how many, chunks to select for a single merge step. The merging itself consists of taking the first elements of each of the selected chunks and placing the smallest of those in the output file. This is done repeatedly until all elements of the selected chunks have been placed in the output file.

At this point, the selected chunks can be deleted, creating space on the disk. This space can be used for the following merge step. Figure 10.5 shows a possible two-step merging of selected chunks.

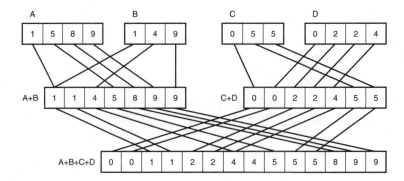

FIGURE 10.5

Two-step merge sort.

In Figure 10.5, there are four sorted chunks that need to be merged into a single database (or output file): A, B, C, and D. The first merge creates intermediate output files containing all elements of A+B and C+D. The second merge creates a single output file containing all elements of A+B+C+D.

Summary

Table 10.2 summarizes the characteristics of the sorting methods discussed in this chapter.

TABLE 10.2 Sorting Method Characteristics

Sorting Method	Average	Worst Case	Stable	In Place	Remark
Insertion	O(n^2)	O(n^2)	Yes	Yes	Good for few items and teaching purposes
Bubble	O(n^2)	O(n^2)	Yes	Yes	Good for teaching purposes and easily maintainable code
Shell	O(n^1.25)	O(n^1.5)	No	Yes	Good for general purpose and time-critical systems
Heap sort	O(nlog2 n)	O(nlog2 n)	No	Yes	Best for time-critical systems and large lists
Quick sort	O(nlog2 n)	O(n^2)	No	No	Best for many strings
Radix sort	O(m*n)	O(m*n)	No	No	Perfect for large lists with numbers

Note that often interesting results can be gained by combining sorting algorithms. Think, for instance, of a quick sort implementation that calls insertion sort when it receives an array with a small number of elements or a sorting algorithm that uses radix sort for small keys and quick sort for longer keys. The best mix-and-match for you to use depends, of course, on the data set you are using and the way in which you want to use it. The best advice here is to experiment.

Storage Structures

IN THIS CHAPTER

Previous chapters discussed how to set up efficient structures for storing pieces of related data and the different techniques used for sorting data efficiently. This chapter discusses how you can manage collections of data structures. It looks at the performance and footprint characteristics of several structuring techniques and gives examples of when and how to use each structure. Ready-to-use implementations are added.

Arrays

One of the most straightforward data structures is the array. Using one-dimensional arrays for storing static data sets or data sets with a predictable size causes few problems. And it is footprint-efficient too; no extra memory is needed for storing pointers to other elements of the data set and fragmentation does not occur during the addition and deletion of elements. Using arrays for dynamic data sets is a different matter, however, as you have already seen in Chapter 9, "Efficient Memory Management." This section, therefore, looks at how efficient arrays actually are when it comes to inserting, deleting, searching, traversing, and sorting data sets.

The file 11Source01.cpp that can be found on the Web site compares the performance of arrays against that of other data structures. There is a section at the end of this chapter that presents the timing results of these tests.

Inserting

Adding elements to arrays can be tricky at times. Basically, there are two situations in which to add elements to an array: when there is still enough space left in the array and when there is not enough space left in the array. The following sections take a closer look at performance and footprint implications of these two situations.

Inserting Elements into an Array That Is Not Full

When an array is not full yet, all elements found after the place where the new element is to be inserted must be moved up one position. In the worst case, the new element must be placed at the front of the array (array[0]) and all other elements need to be moved. This results in an O(n) operation. In the best case, the new element must be placed at the back of the array resulting in an O(1) operation. This proves that adding sorted elements to an array is wildly efficient. Furthermore, when elements are read from a sorted storage—a database file, for instance—the whole file can be read as a single block and placed into memory. Chapter 12, "Optimizing IO," which deals with efficient IO usage, will come back to this.

Inserting Elements into an Array That Is Full

When you need to add an element to an array that is full, you are often out of luck. It is often not possible for you to reserve more memory at the back of an existing block or array. This means that to increase the number of elements that will fit in the array, a new array probably needs to be allocated. All the elements from the old array need to be copied to this new array, and the new element itself needs to be added to the new array also—at least an O(n) operation. This is a lot of work and uses quite a lot of memory, because for a short time both the old and the new array exist simultaneously. When this is not possible because of footprint constraints, it means that parts of the original array need to be transferred to some external storage and back again in order to successfully create the new array. It seems unlikely that you will want to do this for each element that needs to be added to a full array so, in practice, a full array will be extended with a number of empty spaces. An example of this was given in Chapter 10, "Blocks of Data." It is worth thinking about whether or not you can predict the number of elements that will be—or are likely to be—added.

Deleting

Deleting elements from an array is very similar to inserting elements, as far as performance and footprint issues are concerned. Keeping a sorted array without any *holes* in it involves moving all the elements after the deleted element down a space in the array. In the worst case, this is again an O(n) operation; in the best case, it is an O(1) operation. Resizing the array to take up less memory as it shrinks may again involve a costly copy action. An idea here may be to mark items as deleted and postpone actual removal of elements until a good number of elements can be removed in one go.

Searching

A great advantage of arrays is that they are random access. No extra pointers or indexes, or even traversing, is necessary when you know the number of the element you want (a = array[5];). This is an O(1) operation. When you need to find out if a particular element is part of an array, you have a worst-case searching time of O(n) when the array is not sorted. This is because you simply must look at the elements one at a time; when you are out of luck, the element you are looking for is either not in the array or it just happens to be the last element of the array that you check. For sorted arrays, searching is a much happier business. You could opt to use a binary search to quickly locate an element. With a binary search, you recursively check the value of the search element against a value that lies between two boundaries inside the array. In a single check, the search value is checked against the value of the element in the middle of the array. When the search value is greater than the value in the middle, a binary search is started on the second half of the array. When the search value is smaller than the value in the middle, a binary search is started on the first half of the array. Here is an example:

```
Search element: 453.
Array:          001 003 005 007 011 099 207 305 407 453 599 670 700 803 999
n:              15
```

Step 1: Compare 453 against the value of the middle element (which is array[n/2] = 305). 453 > 305, so do another binary search on the second half of the array. For this new binary search, the array to focus on is a subset of the original: the lower boundary (lb) = 8, the upper boundary (ub) is 15, and n' = 14 − 8 + 1 = 7.

Step 2: Compare 453 against the value of the middle element (array[((ub-lb+1)/2)+lb] = 670). 453 < 670, so do another binary search on the first half of this new array. For this new binary search, the array to focus on is a subset of the previous: the lower boundary = 8, the upper boundary is 10, and n" = 10 − 8 + 1 = 3.

Step 3: Compare 453 against the value of the middle element (array[((ub-lb+1)/2)+lb] = 453). 453 = 453—game, set, and match.

Listing 11.1 shows an implementation of a binary search algorithm.

LISTING 11.1 Binary Search Algorithm

```
long binsearch(int item, int data[], long lb, long ub)
{
   while(1)
   {
      long n = ub-lb;   // n = number of elements - 1

      // When there are 1 or 2 elements left to check.
      if (n <= 1)
         if (item == data[lb])
            return lb;
         else if (item == data[ub])
            return ub;
         else
            return -1;

      // Where there are more than 2 elements left to check.
      long middle = ((n+1)/2) + lb;
      int mItem = data[middle];

      if (item == mItem)
         return middle;

      if(item < mItem)
         ub = middle-1;
      else
         lb = middle+1;
   }
}
```

This binsearch function is utilized in the file 11Source01.cpp that can be found on the Web site.

`binsearch()` takes as input parameters the item to search for (item), a pointer to the first element in the array (data), the index of the first element (lb), and the index of the last element (ub). Usage is as follows:

```
int array[] = {1,2,5};
long      n = 3;
int    item = 2

long a = binsearch(item, array, 0, n-1);
```

Finding an array element using a binary sort is an O(log2 n) operation. It is very similar to searching a balanced binary tree, as you will see later on.

Traversing

Traversing an array is pretty straightforward. An incrementing counter as array index will do the job nicely (`array[i++]`). Furthermore, arrays can be traversed in both directions (forward and backward) without special functionality. It does not matter on which array element you start and traversing can easily wrap from the end of an array back to the front: (`i++; i %= n;`).

Sorting

Arrays can be sorted very efficiently, as you learned in Chapter 10.

Linked Lists

Another fairly straightforward storage structure is the linked list. A linked list is in fact a set of data elements that are chained together by pointers. Each element contains a pointer to the next element in the list, or a NULL pointer in case there are no further elements in the list. Figure 11.1 shows a linked list.

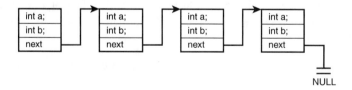

FIGURE 11.1
A linked list.

How you link list elements together is of course entirely up to you. One type of linked list that is often used is the double linked list, in which elements contain pointers to the next list element as well as to the previous element. The advantage of this is that you can navigate through the list in both directions given a pointer to any of the elements. Figure 11.2 shows a double linked list.

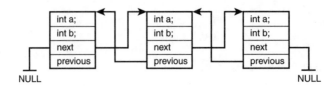

FIGURE 11.2
A double linked list.

A skip list is another list of linked elements which contains additional information that allows you to skip some elements while traversing. Think, for instance, of a list of alphabetically ordered names. Instead of using only a single pointer to the next element, you could create a skip list by adding to each element a pointer to the first element of the next letter in the alphabet:

```
struct SkiplistNode
{
    char          * name;
    SkiplistNode  * nextName;
    SkiplistNode  * nextLetter;
};
```

Exactly when and what you skip will differ per skip list implementation. Figure 11.3 shows a skip list containing alphabetically ordered names. Each list element points to its successor. In addition to this, each first element of a particular letter points to the first element of the following letter. This makes it possible, for instance, to quickly find all names beginning with a certain letter by first *skipping* to the correct letter and then traversing elements from there on.

Skip lists do not have to be limited to one additional pointer per element, of course. You could decide to add another pointer to some elements to point to letters in a different alphabet, for example.

The advantage of lists compared to arrays is that you can more easily add elements to and remove them from a list than an array (given that the array may at some time become full).

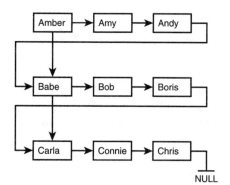

FIGURE 11.3
A skip list.

The file 11Source01.cpp that can be found on the Web site compares the performance of linked lists against that of other data structures. There is a section at the end of this chapter that presents the timing results of these tests.

Inserting

Inserting an element in a linked list consists of updating the next/previous pointers of the element to insert, the element to insert before, and the element to insert after. Special care has to be taken when inserting into an empty list and when inserting before the first element or after the last element. Nevertheless, the actual inserting action is not dependent on the length of the list and is therefore an O(1) operation. When, however, the place to insert an element still has to be found, some searching needs to be done beforehand. For this, see the section "Searching."

Deleting

Deleting an element from a linked list consists of updating the next/previous pointers of the element before the deleted element, the element after the deleted element, and perhaps (when the element is not destroyed but simply removed from the list), also the deleted element itself. Special care has to be taken when deleting the last element from a list, deleting an element at the back of the list, and deleting the first element of a list. Deleting is also an O(1) operation. When, however, the element to delete still has to be found, some searching needs to be done beforehand. For this, see the following section, "Searching."

Searching

Searching through a linked list is not that exciting. In the case of a single linked list, you have no choice but to take a pointer to an element, and from that point check each element one by one, moving to the next element on a mismatch. This is an O(n) operation because in a worst-case scenario you start at the beginning of the linked list and end up checking each element till you reach the end. When a linked list is sorted and you have more than one element pointer to start from, you can jump into the list at a more optimal point. You determine which pointer points to the element furthest in the list—but not past the key you are searching on—and start with that element. Basically what you have done here is create a sort of skip list using element pointers. Worst-case operation is now dependent on the number of search points and how well they are placed. With a double linked list and a pointer to the middle list element, searching is reduced to an O(n/2) operation on a sorted list when you can determine with certainty in which direction to start searching.

Traversing

Traversing a linked list is a matter of following the next pointers of the elements. In a double linked list, two directions of traversing are possible. In a skip list, fast traversing the list is possible because parts of the list that are not interesting at the moment can be skipped while traversing.

Sorting

Although the dynamic use of linked lists is less complex than that of arrays, the opposite is true for sorting. Sorting is especially problematic with single linked lists. This is because access to the elements is no longer random but has to be done through other elements. Sorting directly on the linked elements is therefore far from efficient. The sorting functions of the previous chapter can be used for linked lists when either a) the linked list is a class that overloads the operators [ ], =, <=, ==, and so on, or b) the sorting functions are updated to use member functions of the list class in order to access and manipulate elements. Listing 11.2 shows the different kinds of element access for sorting via operator overloading or class method adoption.

LISTING 11.2   Element Access for Sorting

```
~
// Element access example for arrays
//    or linked lists with operator overloading.
if ( data[i] < data[i+1]
{
  temp      = data[i+1];
  data[i+1] = data[i];
  data[i]   = temp;
}
~
~
// Element access example for linked lists using list methods for access.
if ( list1.GetElem(i)->key < list1.GetElem(i+1)->key)
```

LISTING 11.2   Continued

```
{
  list1. SwapElems(i, i+1);
}
~
```

Though the example that uses list methods for access may look shorter and thus more efficient, you should not forget that each call to a list function is in itself an O(n) operation! And it makes no difference whether the function called is an operator or some other method (GetElem() versus []). To refrain from having to search the list each time you need to access an element, you could create an array containing a pointer to each list element. This is the only way to speed up access. During sorting you access the list elements through the array of pointers for element evaluation, and then you sort the pointers based on that element evaluation. Only when the pointers are sorted do you traverse the linked list one last time to set the elements in the right order. However, this means you change the footprint of the data storage during sorting. Having said all this, if sorting directly on list elements is necessary, an insertion sort or merge sort is probably advisable. See Chapter 10.

Hash Tables

The previous paragraphs showed that arrays and linked lists each have their own strengths and weaknesses. The array provides fast access to its elements but is difficult to extend; the linked list is easy to extend but does not provide very fast access to its elements. For bases of data with a large number of elements, you of course want the best of both worlds. The hash table provides a means to bring this about. By combining the implementations of arrays and lists, a hash table that is set up well is both fast to access and easy to extend.

Hash tables come in as many shapes and sizes as implementers and designers can imagine, but the basic premise is graphically explained in Figure 11.4.

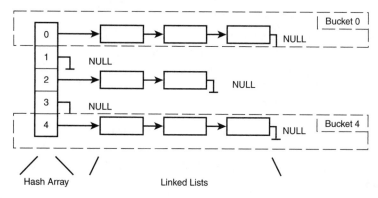

FIGURE 11.4

Hash table example.

The hash table depicted in Figure 11.4 is basically an array of linked lists. As with the skip list from the previous section, the hash table helps you by ensuring that you no longer have to traverse a complete list to find an element. This is because the elements are stored in several smaller lists. A hash table is therefore a sort of *skip array*. Each list maintained by the array of the hash table is called a *bucket*. A bucket is thus identified by a single (hash) array element. In Figure 11.4 the hash table contains five buckets numbered 0–4. In order to determine which bucket could contain the element you are looking for, you need to have specific information on how the array orders its lists. As with sorting, the place where elements are stored in a hash table is determined by one of the fields of that element. This field is called the *key*. Elements containing employee data could, for instance, be stored according to Social Security number or name. The function that maps key values of elements to buckets (or indexes of the hash table array) is called the hash function. Here is an example of a simple hash function:

```
unsigned int hash(int keyvalue)
{
    return (key % HASH_ARRAY_SIZE);
}
```

This hash function divides the key value by the size of the hashing array and uses the remainder as an index. Note that when the size of the hash table is a power of two, the costly modulo % operator can be replaced by a simple bitwise mask. For example, when hash table size is 128, the statement % tableSize can be replaced by &&0x7F. This way only bucket values ranging from 0–127 are in fact returned. Table 11.1 gives an overview of the most important hash table terminology.

TABLE 11.1   Hash Table Terminology

Term	Definition
Key	That part of the element to store, by which the elements of the database will be sorted, searched, and so on (also called hash key).
Bucket	A single position in the hash array, behind which another structure may lie to contain the elements of that bucket.
Hash Function	A function that maps a key value to a bucket.
Perfect Hash Function	A hash function that maps each unique key value to a unique integer

It is not hard to imagine that the quality of the hash function directly determines the quality of the hash table. When a hash function maps too few or too many key values to a single bucket, the hash table will become very inefficient. The following two figures present extreme examples of what could happen. Figure 11.5 shows what happens when too few elements are mapped to a single bucket.

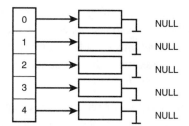

FIGURE 11.5
All buckets are used but contain only a single element.

When a hash function maps each key value to a separate bucket (perfect hash function), all buckets will eventually be in use but will contain only a single database element. What you have now is in effect an inefficient array. Each array slot contains a pointer to a single element. This means that memory (footprint) is used unwisely and element access is done through an extra indirection. But the good thing is that it's resizable! Figure 11.6 shows what happens when too many elements are mapped to a single bucket.

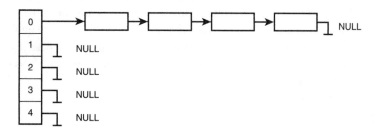

FIGURE 11.6
One bucket is used, containing all elements.

When a hash function maps each key value to the same bucket, only one bucket is used and it contains a list of all the database elements. What you have now is in effect a linked list with the added overhead created by an (almost empty) array.

It is clear that an ideal hash table would look far more balanced. In order to create a balanced hash table, the hash function needs to be able to divide the data elements evenly over the available buckets. Remember, however, that the more complicated this function is, the slower it will be. Hash functions are discussed in more detail in a following section.

Of course, hash table characteristics themselves also play an important part in what a hash table will look like when it is in use. Think, for instance, of the number of buckets used. With too few buckets, the lists that contain the bucket elements will become sufficiently large to slow down element access once more. Analysis of the data you will store should help you determine the desired bucket values. Another thing to consider is how you want to store elements within a bucket. The simplest way is to just append new elements to the end of the list of a bucket. With sufficient buckets (and thus short lists per bucket) this may prove to be very practical. However, as list sizes increase, it may be a good idea to think about storing the elements inside a bucket in an ordered fashion.

At the beginning of this section it was noted that hash tables can come in many shapes and sizes. Basically, the data set you want to store will determine the optimal hash table implementation. An array of lists is a much-used mechanism, but there is no reason why a bucket cannot contain a simpler or even more complex data structure. Think of a bucket containing a data tree or yet another hash table. This second level hash table might even use a different hash function.

The file 11source01.cpp that can be found on the Web site compares the performance of hash tables against that of other data structures. There is a section at the end of this chapter that presents the timing results of these tests.

Inserting

Inserting elements into a hash table that is set up according to the example in this section can be a very fast operation (O(1)). This operation consists of determining the correct bucket (via the hash function) and adding the element to the linked list of that bucket. When the linked list of the bucket is ordered, the operation can take longer because the correct place for insertion needs to be determined. In the worst case, this is an O(L) operation, in which L is the number of elements already in the bucket.

Deleting

Deleting an element from a hash table that is set up according to the example in this section is also an O(L) operation (worst case), in which L is the number of elements in the bucket from which an element will be deleted. This is because, whether or not the list is ordered, the element to be deleted has to be found.

Searching

Searching for an element in a hash table that is set up according to the example in this section can be very fast. Searching ranges from an O(1) operation (best case) to an O(L) operation (worst case), in which L is the maximum number of elements in a bucket.

Traversing

Traversing a hash table that is set up according to the example in this section can be quite easy when all the possible key values are known. In that case, the hash function can be called for ascending key values, thus finding the buckets. Within the buckets, the elements can be traversed in the same manner as with any linked list. However, when all possible key values are not known, there is little left to do but traverse the available buckets in some order—ascending, for instance.

Sorting

Sorting hash tables is not generally done. The hash function is used in order to make a mapping from key value to bucket. Doing any external sorting on this mapping means that elements can no longer be found via the hash function. However, few hash functions also dictate the order of elements within a bucket. As stated before, it can prove to be a good idea to keep the elements in the buckets in some kind of predetermined order. The sorting mechanism that can be used is dependent on the structure that is used for the buckets. For a hash table that is set up according to the example in this section, the sorting implications for buckets are the same as those specified in the section on sorting linked lists.

Hash Functions

In the previous section, you saw that finding elements in a hash table is fastest when you use a perfect hash function. This function guarantees that each possible key value will be mapped to a unique bucket number. This implies that each bucket contains at most a single element, and your hash table is in effect an array in which you can use the key value as an index. However, perfect hash functions are not always easy to find. When more than one key value is mapped to a bucket number by a certain hash function, this is called a *collision*. When the hash function cannot satisfactorily be rewritten into a perfect hash function, you have two options for dealing with collisions:

1. Allow more than one element to be placed in a bucket.

   This option was demonstrated in the previous section, where each bucket basically consisted of a linked list. The number of elements that can be placed in such a bucket is limited only by memory. Using linked lists to represent buckets is called *chaining*, because the elements in a bucket are chained together. Other structures are of course also possible, such as trees, arrays, or even further hashing tables.

2. Do a fix on the collision.

   It is also possible to try to fix collisions. In doing this you repeatedly look for a new bucket until an empty one is found. The important thing to realize here is that the steps to find an empty bucket must be repeatable. You must be able to find an element in the hash table using the same steps that were taken to store it initially. Collisions can of course be fixed in numerous ways. Table 11.2 contains popular collision fixes.

TABLE 11.2 Popular Hash Table Collision Fixes

Fix	What You Do
Linear probe	Do a linear search starting at the collision bucket until you find an empty bucket.
Rehashing	Perform another hashing, with a different hash function, perhaps even on a different key of the element.
Overflow area	Reserve a separate area for colliding keys. This could be a second hash table, perhaps with its own hash function.

Requirements for hash functions are clearly pretty strict. If a hash function is not a perfect hash function, it at least has to be perfect in combination with other strategies (option 2) or it should allow a good average distribution of elements over available buckets (option 1). In both cases though, the hash function you use for your hash table is dependent on the kind and amount of data you expect, and the nature of the key that is used. This section shows some sample hash functions for different data types. Listing 11.3 shows a simple hash function for string keys.

LISTING 11.3 Simple Hash Function for String Keys

```
// Hashing Strings
int Hash(char* str, int tableSize)
{
   int h = 0;
   while (*str != '\0')
      h += *str++;

   return h % tableSize;
}
```

The hash function in Listing 11.3 simply adds the character values of a string and uses the modulo operator to ensure the range of the returned bucket index is the same as the range of the available buckets. This hashing function does not take into account the position of characters, therefore anagrams will be sent to the same bucket. If this is undesirable, a distinction can easily be made by, for instance, multiplying each character by its position or adding a value to a character that depends on its position. Of course, you can also decide to write a hash function that uses two or more fields of your own data types. Listing 11.4 shows a hash function for a user-defined date key.

LISTING 11.4 Hash Function for User-Defined Date Keys

```
// Hashing Dates
struct date
```

LISTING 11.4   Continued

```c
{
    int    year;
    char   day;
    char   month;
};

int Hash(date *d, int tableSize)
{
    if (tableSize <= 12)
        return (int) (d->month % tableSize);
    if (tableSize <= 31)
        return (int) (d->day % tableSize);

    return (((d->year << 9) +
             (d->month << 5) +
             (d->day))
             % tableSize);

}
```

The hash function in Listing 11.4 uses a number of the fields of a data type, dependent on the number of available buckets. When this *date* type is used with a hash table of 12 buckets or less, the month is used as a bucket index, taking into account again the number of available buckets. If this type is used with a hash table of 31 buckets or less, the day is used as a bucket index. For larger numbers of buckets a combination of year, day, and month is used as a bucket index. With this example date type it is not hard to imagine that a hash function can be refined using analytical information on the expected data. If, for instance, a hash table is used to store insurance information using claim dates, you might expect a large number of elements to be added around the month of December. Similarly, the months June and July might generally have less than their fair share of claims. A good hash function could take these kinds of known characteristics into account by spreading the load of December over several buckets and/or combining the load of the June and July buckets.

Another way to determine a key that is based on a numeric value is the multiplication method. Instead of using division, as was done in the first sample hash function, multiplication is used. In the multiplication method, the hash function determines the bucket by multiplying the key with a constant and then taking the most significant bits of that outcome. Again, this is simplest when the hash table size—and therefore the range of the buckets—is a power of two. This is because you can take a fixed number of bits from the multiplication outcome. You do this by shifting the outcome to the right over the number of least significant bits that you want to drop:

```c
hash = (key * c) >> nr_of_bits_to_skip;
```

For instance, when the key is an 8-bit value, and the constant c has the value of 128, the maximum value of the expression (key $*$ c) will be 255 $*$ 128 = 32640. This value can be represented by a 15-bit number (2^{15} = 32768). When the hash table size is 256 buckets, you want a bucket index that is 8 bits in size; therefore, the `nr_of_bits_to_skip` is then 15 − 8 = 7. This means that by doing seven bitwise shifts to the left, you end up with the eight most significant bits of the multiplication outcome as your bucket index. Similarly, when the hash table size is only 128 buckets, the `nr_of_bits_to_skip` equals 15 − 7 = 8. This is because the bucket index must range from 0–127, which can be captured in a 7-bit answer. There is one problem left, however, which is determining the optimal value of the constant c. You can run tests on a representative data set to determine the value of c that gives you a desirable spread of elements over buckets. Knuth (in his book *The Art of Computer Programming*) suggests using the following value for c:

```
range_of_the_key * R.
```

in which the `range_of_the_key` is 256 for an 8-bit key and so on and R is $((5^0,5)–1)/2)$.

Here are some example calculations for multiplication hash functions using Knuth's suggested constants:

```
Example 1:
Key size       : 8 bits
Hash table size: 256 buckets

hash = (key * 158) >> 7;


Example 2:
Key size       : 16 bits
Hash table size: 128 buckets

hash = (key * 40503) >> (32 - 7);
```

Binary Trees

Binary trees, sometimes called binary search trees (bst), are popular storage structures. You can search through trees much faster than through linked lists. A well-balanced tree can be searched as efficiently as a sorted array: O(n log2 n). This is because tree searching has the same properties as a binary search algorithm for an array—see the `binsearch` function in the section on arrays. However, the overhead per stored element is higher with trees than with a single linked list. A binary tree has references to (at most) two child nodes so, just like with double linked lists, two pointer fields need to be added to each stored element. As with linked lists, the elements of a tree are stored in memory separately, causing the same danger of memory fragmentation. Still, the advantages of binary trees have earned them a place in the standard toolset of every programmer. What binary trees look like and how they can be used was introduced in Chapter 10 in the section on heaps. This section looks at the positive and negative characteristics of binary trees.

The file 11Source01.cpp that can be found on the Web site compares the performance of balanced and unbalanced trees against that of other data structures. There is a section at the end of this chapter that presents the timing results of these tests.

Inserting

The function used for inserting elements into a binary tree in effect also takes care of sorting the tree. This is because the placement of each element in the tree has to adhere to the rules of the internal tree structure. The structure of a tree is only valid when each child on the left of its parent has a key value that is equal to or lower than the key value of the parent, and each child on the right of its parent has a key value that is larger than that of its parent. Sadly, it is still possible to create a very inefficient tree even when your insert function observes the structuring rules perfectly. The following example will demonstrate this.

Assume we have an empty tree in which we want to insert the following set of values: 50, 25, 80, 32, 81, 12, 63. The first element, 50, is added and becomes the root. The second element, 25, is lower than 50 and placed left of the root. The third element, 80, is higher than the root and placed on its right. This goes on until all elements have been added and a tree is created as shown in Figure 11.7.

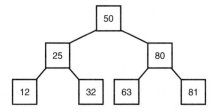

FIGURE 11.7
A tree fed with random ordered data.

When we add the same elements to an empty tree but in sorted order, we get an entirely different picture. The first element, 12, is added as the root. The second element, 25, is higher than the root and is placed to its right. The third element, 32, is higher than the root and higher than the child of the root and is placed on the right of the child of the root. The fourth element, 50, is higher again than the last element inserted and is placed to its right. This goes on until all elements have been added and a treei is created as shown in Figure 11.8.

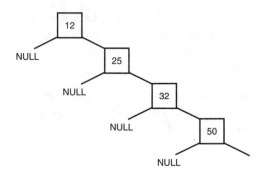

FIGURE 11.8

A tree fed with ordered data.

The storage structures of Figure 11.7 and Figure 11.8 have a valid tree structure. However, the structure in Figure 11.8 is totally unbalanced and is actually nothing more than a single linked list with the added overhead of a NULL pointer for each element. The efficiency of the unbalanced tree is reduced to that of a linked list also. Instead of O(n log2 n), tree access is now an O(n) operation. This means that if searching or adding an element to a balanced binary tree with 50,000 elements takes 50 ms, for instance, that same operation can take up to two minutes for an unbalanced tree. So, the better a tree is balanced, the more efficient it will be. So the order in which elements are fed to a binary tree actually influences its efficiency. It is of course possible to write a function that can be used to periodically attempt to balance the tree, but executing such a function will be very time-consuming and will most likely result in O(n*n) behavior. (See Chapter 5, "Measuring Time and Complexity.") A later section, "Red/Black Trees," shows an example of a tree modified for balanced inserting and deleting.

Deleting

Deleting elements from a binary tree can be more involved than inserting elements. When the element to delete is a leaf, it can be removed without much difficulty. When the element to delete has only one child, that child can simply replace the deleted element. However, the element to delete can also have two children, each of which is a possible root of a subtree. These subtrees must be reintegrated into the remaining tree after the parent element is deleted. The most straightforward way of doing this is by simply feeding the elements of the subtrees back into the tree using the insert function of the tree. This can be time-consuming, however, and needs to be done with care because feeding elements to a tree in a sorted order can result in a very slow tree structure. Another way to reintegrate subtrees that are left over after a delete action is to find the in-order successor of the deleted element and have it take the place of the deleted element. An *in-order successor* is explained in the section on traversing trees. Figure 11.9 demonstrates this deletion strategy.

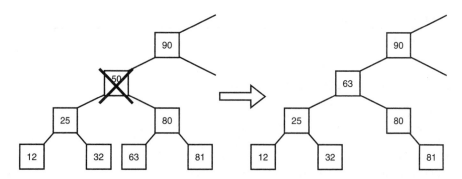

FIGURE 11.9

Deleting an element from a binary tree.

In Figure 11.9, the element with key value 50 is deleted. The delete action creates two sub-trees: one headed by the key value 25 and another headed by the key value 80. The in-order successor of key value 50 is key value 63. It can by found by traversing the subtree of the right child of the deleted element. As you will recall, in-order traversal first moves down a (sub)tree by passing along the left child of each node it encounters. When no further nodes can be found to the left, the in-order successor is reached. This in-order successor is moved to replace the deleted element, creating a valid tree structure once more. Yet again, as with inserting elements into a tree, the balance of the tree can be upset, causing slower subsequent search results. In order to keep trees nicely balanced, a modification to the standard structure is needed. A later section, "Red/Black Trees," shows an example of a tree modified for balanced inserting and deleting.

Searching

The speed with which your algorithm can search a tree is very much dependent on the *shape* of the tree. This is because the height of the tree (number of nodes between root and leaf) determines the number of search steps your algorithm may have to take before finding an item or deciding that an item is not present in the tree. A balanced binary tree will have left and right branches for all nodes that do not contain leafs. This means that each step of your search-ing algorithm will choose a branch based on comparison of the item key with the node key. Listing 11.5 gives an example of a simple search algorithm for finding a node in a binary tree based on the value of its key.

LISTING 11.5   Searching for a Node in a Binary Tree

```
TreeNode *Tree::GetNode(TreeNode *current, char *key)
{
```

LISTING 11.5   Continued

```
    if (current == NULL)
        return(NULL);

    int result = strcmp(current->key, key);

    if (result == 0)
        return(current);

    if (result < 0)
        return(GetNode(current->left, id));
    else
        return(GetNode(current->right,  id));
}
```

As with a binary search, in the best case each test will split the data set to search in half. Searching a balanced binary tree is then an $O(\log 2\ n)$ operation. However, not all trees are balanced. A worst-case setup of an unbalanced tree is a tree in which each node has only one child, making it impossible to choose between branches during a search. This type of tree is nothing more than a linked list, and searching it is therefore an $O(n)$ operation. Generally speaking, building a tree with randomly received data will produce a more or less balanced tree; however, when elements are added to a tree in sorted order, a linked list will be the result. This implies that in order to obtain good searching times ($O(\log 2\ n)$), more work needs to be done during the inserting (and also sorting and deleting) operations on trees in order to keep the structure balanced. Sadly, the standard tree structure does not lend itself well to easy balancing during these operations. Because the tree structure itself can do so much for your searching times, it is a valid effort to think of updates to ensure better performance for these kinds of operations. Later sections represent different kinds of trees that take this into account.

Sorting

Doing external sorting on a binary tree structure should not be necessary because tree properties exist only due to the relations between the elements within the tree. The tree setup is therefore already sorted, and the sorted order is maintained during addition (and deletion) of elements. An unsorted tree would be a collection of elements with seemingly random connections. Finding an element in that kind of tree would mean traversing all elements, resulting in an $O(n)$ operation. This in fact implies that you are dealing with linked list properties with the additional overhead of useless links.

Traversing Fundamentals

There are three different ways of traversing binary trees: Pre-order, In-order, and Post-order.

Pre-order

Pre-order traverse means visit the root, traverse left subtree of the root, traverse right subtree of the root. Listing 11.6 shows an implementation of a pre-order function that traverses a tree to print information from each node.

LISTING 11.6   Pre-order Traverse Function for a Binary Tree

```
void Tree::PreorderTraverse(TreeNode *current)
{
    if(current != NULL)
    {
        current->info.PrintInfo();
        PreorderTraverse(current->left);
        PreorderTraverse(current->right);
    }
}
```

The order in which the keys of the balanced tree at the beginning of this section would appear through the traverse function of Listing 11.6 is 50, 25, 12, 32, 80, 63, 81.

In-order

In-order traverse means traverse left subtree of the root, visit the root, traverse right subtree of the root. Listing 11.7 shows an implementation of an in-order function that traverses a tree to print information from each node.

LISTING 11.7   In-order Traverse Function for a Binary Tree

```
void Tree::InorderTraverse(TreeNode *current)
{
    if(current != NULL)
    {
        InorderTraverse(current->left);
        current->info.PrintInfo();
        InorderTraverse(current->right);
    }
}
```

The order in which the keys of the balanced tree at the beginning of this section would appear through the traverse function of Listing 11.7 is 12, 25, 32, 50, 63, 80, 81.

Post-order

Post-order traverse means traverse left subtree of the root, traverse right subtree of the root, visit the root. Listing 11.8 shows an implementation of a post-order function that traverses a tree to print information from each node.

LISTING 11.8   Post-order Traverse Function for a Binary Tree

```
void Tree::PostorderTraverse(TreeNode *current)
{
    if(current != NULL)
    {
        PostorderTraverse(current->left);
        PostorderTraverse(current->right);
        current->info.PrintInfo();
    }
}
```

The order in which the keys of the balanced tree at the beginning of this section would appear through the traverse function of Listing 11.8 is 12, 22, 25, 63, 81, 80, 50.

Traversal Continued

Looking at the order in which the example keys pop from the different traverse methods, you can see that in-order traversal comes across all tree elements in sorted order. However, recursion is needed to visit all elements, which means that the amount of stack used (see Chapter 8) increases with the depth of the tree. Not only can this cause memory problems when traversing large bases of data, it is also performance-inefficient as function call after function call is made. Luckily, it is possible to rewrite the traversal routine into an iterative function; however, changes to the standard tree structure are needed. The changes consist of replacing the null pointers of the leaf nodes with something useful. For instance, the left child pointer of a leaf node is made to point at the node's in-order predecessor, and the right child pointer is made to point at the node's in-order successor. Figure 11.10 shows what this would make the balanced tree from the beginning of this section look like.

The added references are depicted in Figure 11.10 by curved arrows. Note that two NULL pointers still remain. These denote the first and last elements of the tree. This kind of binary tree is called a *threaded* tree. By following the links of a threaded tree, a traversal function can access the tree as if it were a linked list, while other operations (such as a search) still retain the positive characteristics of the tree structure. For each link to a child, however, some extra administration is needed. A traversal routine has to know whether a child link is a normal link or a link to a threaded successor/predecessor. Also, creating the threaded links slows down the insert and delete operations, so there is some overhead to consider when using threaded trees. Listing 11.9 shows what an in-order traversal function for a threaded binary tree can look like.

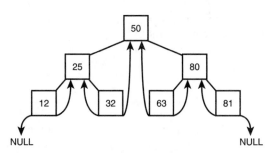

FIGURE 11.10

A threaded binary tree.

LISTING 11.9   In-order Traverse Function for a Threaded Binary Tree

```
void InorderTraverse(TreeNode *current)
{
    while (current != NULL)
    {
        if (current->ltype == 1 && current->left != NULL)
        {
            // Normal link to left child.
            current = current->left;
        }
        else
        {
            // Nothing on the left so process current node.
            current->info.PrintInfo();

            if (current->rtype == 1)
            {
                // Normal link to right child or last element.
                current = current->right;
            }
            else
            {
                // Right child threads to successor.
                // Keep following threaded links till right is normal.
                do
                {
                    current = current->right;
```

LISTING 11.9   Continued

```
                        current->info.PrintInfo();
                }
                while (current->rtype == 0);
                current = current->right;
        }
      }
    }
}
```

In addition to the member variables `left` and `right`, the nodes of the threaded tree in Listing 11.9 have two new member variables `ltype` and `rtype`. These variables denote the type of connection pointed to by `left` and `right`. When `left` points to a threaded link, `ltype` will be 0; when `left` points to a normal child on its left, `ltype` will be 1. The same is true for `rtype` and `right`.

Red/Black Trees

Red/Black trees, introduced by R. Bayer, are binary search trees that adhere to a few extra structuring rules, and that have a few extra properties in each node. These new rules and properties make it easier to keep the tree structure balanced when inserting and deleting elements. The extra properties found in the nodes of a Red/Black tree are

1. A pointer to the parent of the node.
2. A code indicating the color of the node.

In a Red/Black tree, the color code of each node is either *red* or *black*. The extra structuring rules that Red/Black trees adhere to are

1. If a node is red, its children have to be black.
2. Each leaf is a NIL node and is black.
3. The path in the tree from the root to any leaf contains the same number of black nodes.

A NIL node will be a special sentinel node used to indicate an empty leaf.

When insert and delete operations observe these structural rules, the tree remains well balanced. The number of black nodes between a leaf of the tree and its root is called the *black-height* of the tree. Looking at the structuring rules closely, you can determine that any path from a leaf to the root can never be more than twice the length of any other leaf-to-root path. This is because the minimum path contains only black nodes (number of nodes equals black-height), and the maximum path contains a red node between each black node (number of nodes equals black-height multiplied by 2).

The following sections explain how the new properties and rules are put to use in order to maintain a well-balanced tree.

Inserting Theory

In order to insert an element into a Red/Black tree, the tree is traversed to find an appropriate insertion point. An element is always inserted in the place of a leaf node. The newly inserted node is given the color red, and it will have two black leaf nodes (which are, according to structuring rule 2, in fact NIL nodes). Because of this, structuring rules 2 and 3 still hold after inserting a new element. And if the parent of the inserted element happens to be black, the operation is completed. However, structuring rule 1 will be violated when the parent happens to be a red node—according to rule 1 a red parent is only allowed to have black children. This means that after inserting an element, the tree structure may need to be rebalanced.

Two tools are used in rebalancing the tree structure. The first is simply changing the color of a node, the second is rotating nodes around in the structure. The remainder of this section will show that there are actually two situations in which a rebalancing of the tree structure is needed: one when the parent of the new element is red and its *uncle* is black, and the other when both the parent and the uncle of the element are red.

Rebalancing a Red/Black Tree for a Red Parent and a Black Uncle

Figure 11.11 shows one of the two situations in which the tree structure needs to be rebalanced after insertion of an element.

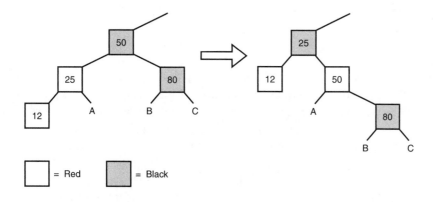

FIGURE 11.11

Inserting with a red parent and a black uncle.

In the left half of Figure 11.11, part of a Red/Black tree is shown, containing the following elements: 50 (Black), 25 (Red), 80 (Black). The element 12 is inserted (Red). The parent of element 12 will be element 25. For reference sake, element 80 will be called the *uncle* of element 12. The Red/Red parent-child link of elements 12 and 25 is a violation of rule 1 and needs to be rebalanced. The rebalancing is shown in the right half of Figure 11.11. The rebalancing consists of elements 50 and 25 changing place and color. In effect, element 50 becomes the right child of the element that used to be its left child. After this rotation of elements, the Red/Black tree structure is valid again; the top of the changed tree (element 25) is black, so the color of its parent does not matter. Also, the black-height of the tree is unchanged. The tree structure is valid.

Rebalancing a Red/Black Tree for a Red Parent and a Red Uncle

However, it is also possible that the uncle of a newly inserted element is red instead of black. Figure 11.12 shows what happens in that case.

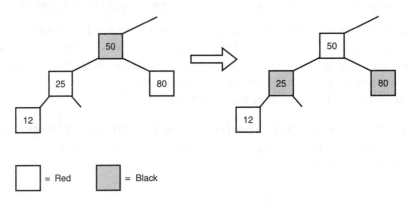

FIGURE 11.12

Inserting with a red parent and a red uncle.

In the left half of Figure 11.12, part of a Red/Black tree is shown containing the following elements: 50 (Black), 25 (Red), 80 (Red). The element 12 is inserted (Red). The parent of element 12 will be element 25; the uncle is element 80. In rebalancing the Red/Red parent-child link of elements 12 and 25, retyping can be used. The parent (25) will be colored black, removing the illegal Red/Red parent-child link. But now a new violation is created; the number of black nodes between the leaf and the root is increased. The *grandparent* of the new element (50) therefore has to be retyped also. In doing this, element 50 has become a red node with a red child (80). This child is retyped also. This brings us to the right half of Figure 11.12. Note that no further changes need to be made to the subtree represented by element 80. Element 80 is black and can thus contain both red and black children, and the black-height is maintained because element 50 is now red.

Inserting Practice

These two techniques—rotation and retyping—may both be needed in this second situation because the rebalancing is not finished yet. Further changes may be needed above element 50 in Figure 11.12, because it may have a red parent. This can cause another Red/Red parent-child violation. So, in effect, retyping can propagate all the way up to the root of the tree. Sometime during this rebalancing, a rotation may also be needed; for example, when a black node is turned to red while having a black uncle. Luckily, as you have seen in this section, after a rotation the tree structure is valid and the rebalancing can stop. Listing 11.10 rebalances a Red/Black tree after an insert.

LISTING 11.10   Rebalancing a Red/Black Tree After Inserting a New Left Element

```
template <class T >
void RedBlackTree<T>::InsertRebalance(Node <T>*newNode)
{
    Node <T>*tempNode;

    // Continue checking up to the root, as long as the parent is RED.
    while (newNode != root && newNode->parent->color == RED)
    {
        if (newNode->parent == newNode->parent->parent->left)
        {
            tempNode = newNode->parent->parent->right;
            if (tempNode->color == BLACK)
            {
                if (newNode == newNode->parent->right)
                {
                    newNode = newNode->parent;
                    RotateLeft(newNode);
                }
                newNode->parent->parent->color = RED;
                newNode->parent->color = BLACK;
                RotateRight(newNode->parent->parent);
            }
            else
            {
                tempNode->color = BLACK;
                newNode->parent->color = BLACK;
                newNode->parent->parent->color = RED;
                newNode = newNode->parent->parent;
            }
        }
```

This template function can be found in the file 11Source02.cpp that can be found on the Web site. Note also that this is actually only half of the solution. In Figure 11.12 the new elements were inserted to the left of their parents. However, it is also possible that an element needs to be inserted to the right of a parent. In that case, the implementation code has to be mirrored: left becomes right and right becomes left. This can be seen in the second half of the InsertRebalance function. Listing 11.11 shows this mirroring code.

LISTING 11.11   Rebalancing a Red/Black Tree After Inserting a New Right Element

```
        else
        {
            tempNode = newNode->parent->parent->left;
            if (tempNode->color == BLACK)
            {
                if (newNode == newNode->parent->left)
                {
                    newNode = newNode->parent;
                    RotateRight(newNode);
                }
                newNode->parent->parent->color = RED;
                newNode->parent->color = BLACK;
                RotateLeft(newNode->parent->parent);
            }
            else
            {
                newNode->parent->parent->color = RED;
                newNode->parent->color = BLACK;
                tempNode->color = BLACK;
                newNode = newNode->parent->parent;
            }
        }
    }
    root->color = BLACK;
}
```

As you can see in the diagrams in this section, insertion is an $O(\log 2\ n) + O(h)$ operation. This is because the search for the place to insert is a binary search ($O(\log 2\ n)$), and the rebalancing is either a rotation that is not dependent on the number of elements in the tree ($O(1)$) or a retyping that can propagate all the way to the root of the tree ($O(h)$), where h = tree height.

Deleting

Deleting an element from a Red/Black tree starts the same way as with a normal binary tree. After this, a balancing action may be needed, which is very similar to the one used after inserting an element. As you might expect, deleting a red node from a Red/Black tree does not cause any violations. Looking at how elements are deleted from a normal binary tree, the following cases of violations can be identified when deleting an element from a Red/Black tree:

1. A black parent with two leaf nodes is deleted.

   The element is removed and replaced by a black leaf. The path between this leaf and the root now contains a number of black nodes that is one lower than the black-height of other leaf-to-root paths. This is a violation of structuring rule 3. The resulting leaf is in a state that is referred to as *Double Black*, meaning that it is off balance because a black node is missing.

2. A black parent with a single child (and one leaf node) is deleted.

   The only child replaces its deleted parent, keeping its original color. A black node has now disappeared from the path between the child and the root of the tree. This is a violation of rule 3. When the child itself is red, it can be colored black and the violation disappears; if it was already black, it becomes Double Black and the violation remains.

3. A black parent with two children is deleted.

   The parent is replaced by its in-order successor. If this successor is red, rule 3 is violated due to the disappearance of a black node from the path to the root. If this successor is black, rule 3 is violated due to the fact that the original children of the in-order successor miss a black node in the path to the root.

The violations need to be removed once again using the two techniques explained in the section on inserting: rotation and retyping. An implementation of the rebalancing delete operation can be found in the file 11Source02.cpp that can be found on the Web site.

Searching

Searching a Red/Black tree is no different from searching any other balanced binary search tree. The changes made to transform a normal binary tree into a Red/Black tree only affect the ability to balance the structure after insert and delete operations. Searching a balanced binary tree is then an O(log2 n) operation

Sorting

Sorting Red/Black trees, just like sorting any binary tree, is not very useful. The tree structure is sorted by the way elements are inserted into the tree.

Traversing

Traversing a Red/Black tree is no different from traversing any other binary search tree.

Summary

This section summarizes the chapter by discussing the test results of the files 11Source01.cpp and 11Source02.cpp. Note that timing values may differ somewhat between systems but the relationships between values in a table should be fairly constant.

The first test done by 11Source01.cpp is placing initial data into the various data structures. Table 11.3 shows the results of 11Source01.cpp for placing initial data into various structures.

TABLE 11.3   Timing Results Storing Initial Data in Storage Structures
Filling Data Structures

Array	List	Hash	UnbalTree	BalTree
60	100	60	102710	60

Arrays are the fastest structures here. Note that in the 11Source01.cpp file the array is treated as a non-dynamic structure; that is, no reallocation of the structure is done to accommodate new elements. Memory is allocated once and only field values are set during the filling of the array. This stands in contrast to the other structures where a new element *must* be created each time data is added to the structure.

The next test done by the 11Source01.cpp file is searching for an element with a certain key value. Table 11.4 shows the results of 11Source01.cpp for searching for elements in various structures.

TABLE 11.4   Timing Results Searching Elements in Storage Structures
Looking Up the First and Last 250 Entries

Array1	Array2	Array3	List	Hash	UnbalTree	BalTree
0	0	540	3630	0	3570	0

Note that three different timing values are included for arrays. Array1 reflects the time needed to find a specific element when its key can be used directly to access the element. Array2 reflects the time needed to find a specific element from a sorted array using a binary search algorithm. Array3 reflects the time needed to find a specific element in an unsorted array. This means simply traversing the array from the beginning until the correct key value is found or the end of the array is reached. You may find it interesting to play around a bit with the number of buckets used by the hash table. You can do this by changing the value of the HASHTABLESIZE definition. You should find that when the number of buckets decreases, and thus the list size per bucket increases, performance of the hash table becomes less and less efficient.

The first test done by 11Source02.cpp is timing the filling of a normal tree against a Red/Black tree:

Tree	RBtree
220	270

We see that the filling of the Red/Black tree is slightly slower. This has everything to do with the additional administration we have to do and the fact that filling the normal tree is done in such a way that it always results in a perfect tree.

The next test done by 11Source02.cpp is looking up and checking all entries:

Tree	RBTree
110	110

As expected, the lookup of an element is as fast in a Red/Black tree as in a normal (balanced tree). But since the Red/Black tree is guaranteed to always be balanced, good lookup times are therefore guaranteed. This cannot be said of a normal tree, where lookup times increase when the shape of the tree becomes more and more unbalanced!

The last test done by 11Source02.cpp is removing all entries one by one:

Tree	RBtree
49870	110

Deleting nodes shows a tremendous time difference between a normal tree and a Red/Black tree. The reason for this is that the normal tree doesn't have a rebalancing mechanism and entire subtrees of nodes that are removed need to be reinserted, which is very time-consuming. Because the Red/Black tree does have a delete and rebalance mechanism, no such problems occur.

In conclusion, we can say the following about the data storage structures discussed in this chapter:

Arrays

An array is the best structure for static data because it has no overhead and there is no danger of fragmentation within the bounds of the array. Dynamic data can be more complicated as data needs to be copied. This can also mean that a larger footprint is needed.

Lists

A list is a good structure for storing small data sets with a highly dynamic nature. It has more overhead per element than the array, and fragmentation is a danger. However, dynamically adding and deleting elements is fast and does not require extra footprint beyond the memory needed for storing elements. Searching for an element can be quite time-consuming, depending on the type of list (double- or single-linked).

Hash Tables

A hash table is a good structure for larger sets of data for which a unique or distributing key function (hash function) can be designed. The hash table implementation can make use of as many or as few other data structures as necessary. Depending on this, the overhead per element can be as small as that of the array or as large as other structures combined.

Binary Trees

A binary tree is a good structure for larger amounts of highly dynamic data, as long as the tree structure can remain relatively balanced. This means data must be added and deleted in an unsorted order. The binary tree has more overhead per element than the list and becomes as inefficient as the list when it is unbalanced.

Red/Black Trees

A Red/Black tree is a good structure for larger amounts of highly dynamic data. The Red/Black tree has more overhead per element than a normal binary tree but stays balanced independent of the order in which elements are added and deleted. Danger for memory fragmentation is as high as with the other structures—excluding the array—and inserting and deleting elements will be slower than with a normal binary tree. For larger amounts of data, this time is won back in faster traversal (because good balance is guaranteed) and searching.

Optimizing IO

IN THIS CHAPTER

As a C++ implementer you have access to the standard C functions for performing IO as well as the new streaming classes introduced by C++. It is not always obvious, however, what the differences between these techniques are—apart from their notation—and whether there are performance penalties involved in using a certain technique. This chapter looks at the pros and cons of each technique and notes where to use each.

Efficient Screen Output

This section looks at the different basic techniques that can be used for performing screen output.

The different techniques are discussed in separate sections and the "Test Results" subsection later in this section does an execution speed comparison of the techniques.

Using `printf()`

The `printf()` function can be used to write a string to the standard output stream (`stdout`). The string that is passed to `printf()` can contain complex formatting information that makes `printf()` a handy tool for doing conversions from binary variable values to strings. `printf()`, in fact, allows you to combine strings with automatically converted variables into a single output string. `printf()` was already part of C, but can still be used in C++. This is how you write an array *input* of N strings to screen using `printf()`:

```
for(int i = 0; i < N ; i++)
{
    printf("Test %s \n",input[i]);
}
```

The "Test Results" section evaluates the speed of a `printf()` function compared to the other screen writing techniques.

Using `puts()` and `putchar()`

The `puts()` function writes a string to the standard output stream (`stdout`). The terminating zero character of the string is replaced by a newline character. This is how you write an array *input* of N strings to screen using `puts()`:

```
strcpy(tmp, "Test ");
for(int i = 0; i < N ; i++)
{
    strcpy(&tmp[5], (char*)input[i]);
    puts(tmp);
}
```

Note that, unlike with `printf()`, it is impossible to give extra arguments and formatting to `puts()`. This is why a `strcpy()` is used to add the prefix *Test*. Another way to solve the prefix problem would be to use two separate calls to `puts()`:

```
for(int i = 0; i < N ; i++)
{
    puts("Test ");
    puts((char*)input[i]);
}
```

The output of each `puts()` invocation will, however, appear on a separate output line.

The `putc()` and `putchar()` functions both write single characters to an output stream. `putchar()` writes to `stdout`, but `putc()` can be told to write to an alternative output stream. `putchar(c)` is therefore identical to `putc(c, stdout)`. Listing 12.1 shows how you can write an array *input* of N strings to screen using `putchar()`.

LISTING 12.1 Writing Arrays of Strings to Screen with `putchar()`

```
char c;
int j = 0;
char Test[] = "Test ";

for(int i = 0; i < N ; i++)
{
    while ((c = Test[j++]) != '\0')
    putchar(c);

    j = 0;
    while ((c = input[i][j++]) != '\0')
        putchar(c);
    putchar(13);  // write '\n.
    putchar(10);
    j = 0;
}
```

Both `putc()` and `putchar()` are implemented as functions as well as macros. The macro definitions take precedent. For using `putchar()` always as a function you have to undefine the macro. To undefine the `putchar()` macro, place the following line of code in your source file before `putchar()` is used:

```
#undef putchar
```

When you want to use `putchar()` as a function only for a certain call, force the function invocation by using `putchar()` as follows:

```
(putchar)(c)
```

Using `puts()` and `putc()` is certainly more laborious than, for instance, using `printf()`. `puts()`, however is a very fast output technique. The "Test Results" section evaluates its speed compared to the other screen-writing techniques.

Using cout

Apart from the standard C functions for screen output, C++ programmers also have access to the streaming classes provided by that language. Table 12.1 shows the different streams which are available in C++.

TABLE 12.1 C++ Streams

cin	Standard input stream (`istream` class), default connected to keyboard.
cout	Standard output stream (`ostream` class), default connected to screen.
cerr	Standard output stream for errors (`ostream` class), default connected to screen.
clog	Buffered version of `cerr` (`ostream` class), default connected to screen.

The difference between `cerr` and `clog` is that `cerr` messages are processed immediately and `clog` messages are buffered. Messages that should appear onscreen as soon as possible should, therefore, be sent to `cerr`. If a message is not supposed to slow down program execution too much, `clog` should be used. This section demonstrates the use of `cout` so it can be compared to the other screen output functions.

The `cout` class can only be used in C++. It is as powerful as the `printf()` function in that it can also be used to convert binary values into strings and combine these values with normal strings into a single output string. The syntax of `cout` is very different from that of `printf()`, however. This is how you write an array *input* of N strings to screen using `cout`:

```
for(int i = 0; i < N ; i++)
{
    cout << "Test " << input[i] << '\n';
}
```

Using cout like this does not write a string to screen immediately, however; the text appears only when the output buffer is flushed. Flushing the output buffer can be done by adding `<< endl` or `<< flush` to the output stream. This is how you write an array *input* of N strings to screen using `cout` and flushing the buffer after every write action:

```
for(int i = 0; i < N ; i++)
{
    cout << "Test " << input[i] << endl;
}
```

Test Results

This section compares the speed of the different techniques for writing text strings to the screen. Table 12.2 presents the timing results generated by the program in the accompanying file 12Source01.cpp.

TABLE 12.2 Timing Results Screen Output Techniques

Technique	Time (ms)
cout + endl or flush	500
cout + \n	380
printf()	440
puts + copy	400
puts twice	540
putchar macro	610
putchar function	670

Note that file output can also be achieved with the function described for screen output. This can be done by redirecting program output with the > sign. In order to write the test result of this section file, type the following DOS command:

```
12Souce01 > outputfile.txt
```

Note also that stdio and iostream have independent buffering, meaning that

```
printf ("A string printed using printf\n");
cout << "testing cout" << endl;
```

might output:

```
A string printed testing cout
using printf
```

Therefore, is it better to choose stdio or iostream. If you really need both, you should explicitly flush before switching.

Efficient Binary File IO

This section looks at the different basic techniques that can be used for manipulating binary files. The different techniques are discussed in separate sections. A "Test Results" subsection at the end of this section does an execution speed comparison of the techniques.

Using FILE Functions

The FILE functions can be used to read to and write from standard IO. These functions were already part of C but can still be used in C++. Table 12.3 shows the various FILE functions.

TABLE 12.3   FILE Functions

fopen	Open a file for reading/write of text/binary content
fclose	Close an opened file
fread	Read a block of data from an opened file
fwrite	Write a block of data to an opened file
fprintf	Print to an opened file (text)
fscanf	Read variable values from an opened file (text)

Listing 12.2 shows how FILE functions can be used to read data from one binary file and write it to another.

LISTING 12.2   Using FILE Functions to Read and Write Binary Files

```
#define BLOCKSIZE     4096
#define ITEMSIZE      1

FILE *inp, *outp;
long  numRead, numWritten;
int   errorCode = 0;

if ((inp = fopen(inputFilename, "rb")) != NULL)
{

  if ((outp = fopen(outputFilename, "wb")) != NULL)
  {
        while (!feof(inp))
        {
                numRead = fread(buf, ITEMSIZE,  BLOCKSIZE, inp);
                numWritten = fwrite(buf, ITEMSIZE, numRead, outp);
        }
        fclose(outp);
  }
  else
        printf("Error Opening File %s\n", outputFilename);

fclose(inp);
}
else
  printf("Error Opening File %s\n", inputFilename);
```

As was noted in Table 12.3, the `fread()` and `fwrite()` functions can be used to transfer blocks of bytes. These functions use two arguments to determine the block size. The first is the item size, denoting the size in bytes of the items in the file. The second is the number of items to be read or written. Item size multiplied by number of items equals the number of bytes transferred. In Listing 12.2, an item size of 1 was chosen because bytes are to be written and read. The number of items, therefore, effectively determines the block size. Choosing a small block size of course means extra overhead because more `fread()` and `fwrite()` calls are needed to transfer a file. Choosing a large block size means less overhead but a larger footprint in memory. The "Test Results" subsection lists an execution speed comparison between different binary file techniques by varying block sizes.

Random Access

Of course, you will not always access files sequentially as was done in the previous listings. When you know how a file is built up—because it contains database records, for instance—you will want to access specific records directly without having to load the file into memory from its very beginning. What is needed is random access. You want to tell the file system exactly which block of bytes to load. As you have seen in the previous listings, a file is identified and manipulated through a pointer to a FILE object. This FILE object contains information on the file. It keeps, among other attributes, a pointer to the current position in the file. It is because of this attribute that it is possible to call, for instance, `fread()` several times, with each call giving you the next block from the file. This is because the current position in the file is increased after each call with the number of bytes read from the file. Luckily, you can influence this current position directly through the `fseek()` function. `fseek()` places the new current position of a file at an offset from the start, the end, or the current position of a file:

```
int fseek(FILE *filepointer, long offset, int base);
```

`fseek()` returns 0 when it executes successfully. Table 12.4 shows the different definitions that can be used for the third argument, `base`.

TABLE 12.4 Positioning Keys for `fseek`

SEEK_CURR	Current position in the file
SEEK_END	End of the file
SEEK_SET	Beginning of the file

Listing 12.3 demonstrates random file access using `fseek()` to load every tenth record of a file containing 100,000 records.

12

OPTIMIZING IO

LISTING 12.3   Random Access with Standard IO

```
FILE *db;
Record Rec;    // defined elsewhere.

if ((db = fopen(dbFilename, "r+b")) != NULL)
{
   for (unsigned long i = 0; i < 500000; i+=10)
   {
      fseek(db, i*sizeof(Record), SEEK_SET);    // seek record # i
      fread(&Rec, sizeof(Record), 1, db);

      strcpy(Rec.name, "CHANGED 1");
      Rec.number = 99999;

      fseek(db, i*sizeof(Record), SEEK_SET);    // seek record # i
      fwrite(&Rec, sizeof(Record), 1, db);
   }
   fclose(db);
}
else
   printf("Error Opening File %s\n", dbFilename);
```

In the "Test Results" section, FILE random access is compared to stream random access.

Using Streams

The classes ifstream and ofstream can be used to read and write to and from files in C++. And of course C++ would not be C++ if it did not try to make life easier by deriving different classes from these two. Table 12.5 shows the different classes that can be used to perform file input as well as output.

TABLE 12.5   C++ File IO Streaming Classes

fstream	File stream class for input and output
stdiostream	File stream for standard IO files

Table 12.6 shows the functions available on the C++ IO streams.

TABLE 12.6   Functions Available on the C++ IO Streams

open	Open a stream
close	Close a stream
setmode	Set the mode of a stream (see open function)
setbuf	Set size of the buffer for a stream

TABLE 12.6   Continued

get	Read from an input stream
put	Write to an output stream
getline	Read a line from an input stream (useful in text mode)
read	Read a block of bytes from an input stream (useful for binary mode)
write	Write a block of bytes to an output stream (useful in binary mode)
gcount	Return the exact number of bytes read during the previous (unformatted) input
pcount	Return the exact number of bytes written during the previous (unformatted) output
seekg	Set current file position in an input stream
seekp	Set current file position in an output stream
tellg	Return current position in an input stream
tellp	Return current position in an output stream

Table 12.7 shows the functions associated with IO streams which can be used to assess the status of a stream.

TABLE 12.7   Status Functions Available on the C++ IO Streams

rdstate	Returns current IO status (possible returns: goodbit | failbit | badbit | hardfail)
good	Returns != 0 when there is no error
eof	Returns != 0 when the end of the file is reached
fail	Returns a value != 0 when there is an error, use rdstate to determine error
bad	Returns a value != 0 when there is an error, use rdstate to determine error
clear	Resets the error bits

Now look at how a C++ programmer can use a stream class to perform the same read/write behavior as was done in the section "Using FILE Functions." Listing 12.4 shows how stream functions can be used to read data from one binary file and write it to another.

LISTING 12.4   Using stream Functions to Read and Write Binary Files

```
unsigned char ch;

ifstream inputStream(inputFilename,  ios::in | ios::binary);

if (inputStream)
{
```

LISTING 12.4   Continued

```
    ofstream outputStream(outputFilename, ios::out | ios::binary);

    if (outputStream)
    {
        while(inputStream.get(ch))
            outputStream.put(ch);

        outputStream.close();
    }
    else
        cout << "Error Opening File " << outputFilename << endl;

    inputStream.close();
}
else
    cout << "Error Opening File " << inputFilename << endl;
```

Note that some useful flags can be found in Listing 12.4, which can be used when opening a stream. The flags are defined in C++ and can be used to force a certain behavior; `ios::binary`, for instance, opens a stream in binary mode. For a full list of flags consult language or compiler documentation.

Listing 12.4 actually reads and writes single characters from and to files. This is equivalent to using a block size of 1 for the functions discussed in the section "Using `FILE` Functions." Reading and writing can be done faster by choosing larger blocks of data to transfer, as you will see in Listing 12.5. Compare this with Listing 12.4 to compare speed between different techniques. The results of this test can be found in the later section "Test Results."

LISTING 12.5   Using Stream Functions with a Larger Block Size

```
#define BLOCKSIZE          4096

ifstream inputStream(inputFilename, ios::in | ios::binary);

if (inputStream)
{
   ofstream outputStream(outputFilename, ios::out | ios::binary);

  if (outputStream)
  {
    while(!inputStream.eof())
    {
      inputStream.read((unsigned char *)&buf, BLOCKSIZE);
```

LISTING 12.5 Continued

```
        outputStream.write((unsigned char *)&buf, inputStream.gcount());
      }
      outputStream.close();
    }
    else
      cout << "Error Opening File " << outputFilename << endl;

    inputStream.close();
  }
  else
    cout << "Error Opening File " << inputFilename << endl;
```

Apart from using a certain block size, it is also possible to define a buffer for a stream. Writing to a buffer can be faster because output is flushed only when the buffer becomes full. In effect, a buffer is used to combine several smaller write or read actions into a single large action. Listing 12.6 shows how buffers can be added to streams to *collect* read and write actions.

LISTING 12.6   Reading and Writing a File Using `ifstream` and `ofstream` with Buffers

```
#define BLOCKSIZE            4096
#define STREAMBUFSIZE    8192
unsigned char streambuf1[STREAMBUFSIZE];
unsigned char streambuf2[STREAMBUFSIZE];

ifstream inputStream;

inputStream.setbuf((char *)&streambuf1, STREAMBUFSIZE);
inputStream.open(inputFilename, ios::in | ios::binary);

if (inputStream)
{
 ofstream outputStream;

 outputStream.setbuf((char *)&streambuf2, STREAMBUFSIZE);
 outputStream.open(outputFilename, ios::out | ios::binary);

 if (outputStream)
 {
    while(!inputStream.eof())
    {
      inputStream.read((unsigned char *)&buf, BLOCKSIZE);
      outputStream.write((unsigned char *)&buf, inputStream.gcount());
    }
```

LISTING 12.6   Continued

```
    outputStream.close();
}
else
    cout << "Error Opening File " << outputFilename << endl;

inputStream.close();
}
else
    cout << "Error Opening File " << inputFilename << endl;
```

You will find a speed comparison between different stream accesses and traditional FILE functions in the "Test Results" section later on in this chapter.

Random Access

As was the case with the FILE functions, streams also allow you to access files randomly. In the introduction to this section, you saw the two stream methods that allow you to do this: seekg() and seekp(). seekg() is used to manipulate the current pointer for input from the file (g = get), and seekp() is used to manipulate the current pointer for output to the file (p = put). Both seekg() and seekp() can be called with either one or two arguments. When one argument is given, this is seen as the offset from the beginning of the file; when two arguments are given, the second argument denotes the base of the offset. Values for this base can be found in Table 12.8.

TABLE 12.8   Positioning Keys for seekp/seekg

ios:curr	Current position in the file
ios::end	End of the file
ios::beg	Beginning of the file

Listing 12.7 demonstrates random file access using seekp() and seekg() to load every tenth record of a file containing 100,000 records.

LISTING 12.7   Random Access with Streams

```
fstream dbStream;
Record Rec;

dbStream.open(dbFilename, ios::in | ios::out | ios::binary);

if (dbStream.good())
{
    for (unsigned long i = 0; i < 500000; i+=10)
```

LISTING 12.7   Continued

```
    {
        dbStream.seekg(i*sizeof(Record));
        dbStream.read((unsigned char *)&Rec, sizeof(Rec));

        strcpy(Rec.name, "CHANGED 2");
        Rec.number = 99999;

        dbStream.seekp(i*sizeof(Record));
        dbStream.write((unsigned char *)&Rec, sizeof(Rec));
    }
    dbStream.close();
}
else
    cout << "Error Opening File " << dbFilename << endl;
```

In the "Test Results" section, `stream` random access is compared to `FILE` random access.

Test Results

This section compares the speed of the different techniques for transferring data to and from binary files. The program in the file 12Source02.cpp that can be found on the Web site can be used to perform these timing tests.

Read/Write Results

The program reads its input from a file `test.bin`, which you should place in directory `c:\tmp\`. The test works best when you use a file of at least 65KB, as a block size of 65KB is used in one of the tests. The program writes its output into the file `c:\tmp\test.out`, which it will create itself. Of course it is also possible to use different paths and filenames, just be sure to adjust the `inputFilename` string in `main()` accordingly.

Table 12.9 presents the timing results generated by the program in the file 12Source02.cpp for reading and writing binary files.

TABLE 12.9   Timing Results for Reading and Writing Binary Files

Technique	Block Size	Time
StdIO	1	4120
StdIO	4096	260
StdIO	65536	110
StreamIO	1	1540
StreamIO	4096	380
StreamIO	BUFFERED	220

The first three rows of Table 12.9 show the results for the FILE functions using different block sizes (1, 4,096, and 65,536 bytes). Rows 4 and 5 show the results for the stream class with different block sizes (1 and 4,096) and row 6 shows the results for the stream class using buffered IO.

Random Access Results

For the random-access test, the program in the file 12Source02.cpp creates a file called test.db in the directory c:\tmp\. Of course, it is also possible to use a different path and/or filename, just be sure to adjust the dbFilename string in main() accordingly.

Table 12.10 presents the timing results generated by this program.

TABLE 12.10   Timing Results for Random Access Binary Files

Records	Stdio	Streams
100000	970	770
500000	6771	5310
1000000	22080	10990

In Table 12.10, you not only see that streams seem to be faster in random access than standard IO, but their advantage increases as more records are read. The reason for this is that the fstream class—which is used in this test—gets a buffer attached to it by default. This means that some IO requests will read from this buffer instead of from the file when the required data happens to be buffered. The standard IO functions cannot easily use a larger block size to retrieve more than a single block from the file because the blocks are no longer found sequentially. Once again this proves that it is crucial to think carefully about what kind of buffer and block size to use.

Efficient Text File IO

File access for text files is done through the same functions (and classes) as file access for binary files. You determine whether to treat a file as a text file or as a binary file through a flag when opening the file. The difference between files that are opened as text files and those which are opened as binary files lies in whether or not the accessing functions interpret Carriage Return (CR) and Line Feed (LF) codes found in the file data. A binary file is seen as one long string of byte values, whereas a text file is seen as a collection of strings separated by CR and/or LF codes. Generally, programmers open and create text files only when they are to contain actual character data (such as that defined by ASCII or Unicode). Giving CR and LF codes a special meaning allows you to specify further functionality, which can be handy when working with files that will contain text. It is very easy, for instance, to write functionality that searches for a certain line number in a text file or counts the number of lines in a file. This section looks into the different uses of text files in programming and supplies ready-to-use text file functionality, which can speed up text file access in programming.

Why Text Files?

You might wonder why it could still be a good idea to use text files in situations when binary files can store the same data more efficiently. Not only is it possible to omit CR/LF codes from binary files, but storing byte values as text strings can take up two or three times as much space—a single byte with the numerical value 255 is represented in text by a string of, for instance, two hexadecimal characters ('F', 'F') or three decimal characters ('2', '5', '5'). Moreover, compression can be used in binary files. (A compressed text file cannot really be called a text file anymore.) However, text files still have their place, even when we are talking about storing data. Proof of this is, for instance, the fact that many configuration files used under UNIX and Windows are still text files. Even Internet pages, described in HTML, are basically text files with predetermined formatting, not to mention the fact that your compiler uses text files (called source files) as input. The section looks at different uses of text files.

Text Files as Configuration Files

The most important reason for choosing text files as configuration files is that they can be read and changed by users without the use of special tools or programs. The program or process that is being configured does not even need to be started; any simple text editor will do the job. This can be a real lifesaver when a program is unable to start properly because of a faulty configuration! It also saves development time because programmers no longer have to write and test functionality to take the user's configuration input from a user interface environment and translate it to (or from) an actual binary configuration file. Another advantage is the fact that human-readable configuration files can perhaps be reconstructed by users when they become corrupted, and different versions of the files can be created through simple copy and paste actions. These configuration files can even be faxed to wherever this kind of support is needed.

Text Files as Data Storage

It is not always necessary to write a complete database management system in order to store data on file. In Chapter 10, "Blocks of Data," you saw how a text file can be used as a database. Again the advantages apply, as given in the section "Text Files as Configuration Files." Another advantage is that this kind of database file can easily be shared across platforms.

When using text files as data storage you effectively have two choices of implementation. You can use either fixed-length records, in which a certain record can be found by multiplying its number by the number of bytes contained in a record, or variable-length records (records containing variable-length fields), in which you appoint special characters as field separators. The following examples show different choices of implementation for a database that contains records with the following fields: item type, item color, item material, and item order number.

```
// Impl 1:Using fixed length records:
stool          red          wood       125600
chair          blue         iron       128000
rocking chair  aquamarine   cast iron  130000

// Impl 2:Using variable length fields with field separators:
stool#red#wood#125600
chair#blue#iron#128000
rocking chair#aquamarine#cast iron#130000

// Impl 3:Using field and record separators:
stool#red#wood#125600@chair#blue#iron#128000@rocking chair#aquamarine#
➥cast iron#130000
```

When you are using length records you pay a footprint penalty because each record in the database, regardless of its content, is the same size. This size is determined by the largest possible value of each field. The upside to this implementation is that searching through the database is fast (O(1)) because you can use direct access. The first byte of record 15 is found at position 15 times the record size in bytes. The opposite is true for variable length records. Each record is made to fit exactly its content, and so footprint is less of an issue. However, access to the records needs to be sequential (O(n)), basically by counting the field separators. The implementation that is best for a given situation depends on the footprint requirements and the type of access which will be used most often.

When using text files as data storage, simple text functions can be used to manipulate the database records. Listing 12.8 shows a function that can be used to retrieve the value of a certain field from a text database which has been loaded into memory.

LISTING 12.8   Getting a Field from a String

```c
char *GetField(char *s, char c, int n, char *fld)
{
    int i=0, j=0, lens = strlen(s);

    if (n < 1)
        return (NULL);

    if (n > 1)  // Not the first field
    {
        i = GetOccurrence(s, c, n-1);
        if (i == -1)
            return(NULL);
        else
            i++;
    }
```

LISTING 12.8 Continued

```c
    j = GetOccurrence(s, c, n);
    if (j == -1)
        j = lens;

    if ( (j <= i) || (i > (int)lens) || (j > (int)lens) )
        return(NULL);

    // the part between i and j _is_ the field
    strncpy(fld, &s[i], j-i);
    fld[j-i] ='\0';
    return(fld);
}
```

The function in Listing 12.8 takes four arguments: a pointer to the loaded database (s), a character that is used as a field separator (c), the number of the field to be found (n), and a pointer to a buffer into which the field is to be copied (fld). The function assumes that there is no field separator before the first field and after the last, and it can be called as follows:

```c
GetField(s, '#', 4, tmp);
```

This call will attempt to find the fourth field in the database and copy its value in the tmp (fields are separated by a '#' character).

But GetField() does not do all the work on its own; it makes use of a function called GetOccurrence() to find the next occurrence of a field separator. Listing 12.9 shows an implementation of GetOccurrence().

LISTING 12.9 Finding a Character in a String

```c
int GetOccurrence(char *s, char c, int n)
{ // Return the position of the Nth occurrence of character c in s
  // Return -1 if not found
  int i, j=0;

    for (i=0; i < (int)strlen(s); i++)
    {
        if (s[i] == c)
        {
            j++;
            if (j >= n)
                return(i);
        }
    }
    return(-1);
}
```

Of course Listings 12.8 and 12.9 just show one way of finding fields. You can opt to write a `GetRecord()` function, for instance, which takes as an input argument the number of fields per record so it can locate a specific record in a database.

The `TextFile` Class

As you saw in the section "Efficient Binary File IO," in order to achieve fast file access it is important to use intelligent buffering. You also read in the introduction to this section that binary files and text files are basically the same thing, apart from how CR and LF are interpreted by the access functions. This means that the theory introduced in "Efficient Binary File IO" can also be used for text files, as long as CR and LF are treated correctly. This is good news because when you decide to use text files as data storage or configuration files, you still want fast access, even when the files become large. This section introduces a new class which does just that. It is called `TextFile` and can be found in the files 12Source03.cpp and 12Source03.h on the Web site.

The `TextFile` class essentially performs buffered binary file IO. This means that each file access will read a block of binary data from a file to a buffer, or write a block of binary data from a buffer to a file. Meanwhile, the user of the class can access the buffered data without incurring disc access overhead for each access. Basically this is what you already saw in the section "Efficient Binary File IO"; however, because the `TextFile` class knows that it is actually treating text files, it gives you some very handy functionality; it allows you to treat the buffer as a collection of lines of text—remember, a line in a text file is terminated by a combination of CR and LF (under UNIX, just LF). This means that you keep reading lines from the `TextFile` class as you need them, whereas *it* takes care of disc access and buffering. The same is also true for writing to a file.

Because the theory behind the `TextFile` class can be found in the section "Efficient Binary File IO," this section only gives a description of the `TextFile` interface and examples of how to use it. Table 12.11 contains the interface description of the `TextFile` class.

TABLE 12.11   `TextFile` Interface

Function:	`TextFile()`
Type:	Constructor
Remarks:	The constructor initiates member variables.
Function:	`~TextFile()`
Type:	Destructor
Remarks:	The destructor calls the close function.

TABLE 12.11   Continued

Function:	`open()`
Type:	Public member function.
Argument 1:	char*, pointer to a user-managed filename string. This string can contain path elements such as drive and directory names.
Argument 2:	char (optional), either 'r' for an input file to read from, or 'w' for an output file to write to. The default value for argument 2 = 'r'.
Return value:	int, 0 when the file could not be opened.
Remarks:	Opens the specified file for the specified action.
Function:	`close()`
Type:	Public member function.
Remarks:	Closes the current file if it is still open. When the file is opened for writing, the buffer is flushed to file if it is not yet empty.
Function:	`getline()`
Type:	Public member function.
Argument 1:	char*, pointer to a user-managed buffer which receives the next line from the file.
Return value:	int, 0 when the end of the file is reached.
	-1 when no file is opened or the file is opened for writing.
	n when successful, n denotes number of characters in the buffer including terminating zero.
Remarks:	Reads the next linefrom the file into the user-managed buffer, unless the file is not opened for reading or the end of the file is reached.
Function:	`putline()`
Type:	Public member function.
Argument 1:	char*, pointer to a user-managed buffer which contains the next line to be written to file.
Argument 2:	int (optional), format to be used for line termination; options are CR, LF, CRLF, LFCR; by default this argument is set to CRLF.
Return value:	int
Remarks:	int, 0 when there is an error while writing to the file.
	-1 when no file is opened or the file is opened for reading.
	1 when successful.

12

OPTIMIZING IO

You can use the `TextFile` class via normal instantiation, as the following example demonstrates:

```
char tmp[255];                 // dependent on how long you make your file lines.
TextFile file;

if(file.open("test.txt") == 0)  // open default = 'for reading'.
    return;

while (file.getline(tmp) > 0)    // read all the lines.
{
```

And of course it is also possible to use it via inheritance, as the following example demonstrates:

```
class MyFileClass : public TextFile
{
    MyFileClass():TextFile(){}
    MyOpen(char *s)
    {
        // do something;
        open(s);    // call to TextFile::open();
```

Searching Text Files

How efficiently you search through text files depends on two things: first, how efficiently you load data from the file, and, second, how efficiently you search through the loaded data. Both subjects have already been covered in this book. You have a very good basis for efficient text file searching when you combine the Fast Pattern Search introduced in Chapter 10 with the enhanced file IO made available through the `TextFile` class introduced in the previous section. The following example shows how you can combine these two concepts:

```
char tmp[255], *c;
int n;

init(SearchString);                   // init function for the search.
while ((n = file.getline(tmp)) > 0)    // read all the lines.
{
    if ((c = search(tmp, n)) != NULL) // search a line.
        break;
```

Doing a case-insensitive search for the `SearchString()` is accomplished by calling the case-insensitive versions of the fast pattern match functions (see Chapter 10). A more complicated and generic way of searching through text files is the topic of the following section.

Searching Using Wildcards

Searching with the aid of wildcards is used when a match is needed for a generic pattern instead of an exact string. This mechanism is often used in command-line interfaces such as DOS. A wildcard search to reveal all text files in a certain directory can be initiated, for instance, with the following command:

```
dir *.txt
```

The '*' indicates that any number of characters (even 0) and any kind of character can appear in that position. In this case it means that any string ending in '.txt' will match. Another special character that can be used in wildcards is '?', indicating that any (single) character can be placed in that position—sort of like a joker in a card game. The command

```
dir picture?.bmp
```

matches all files with the name 'picture' followed by one more character and ending with '.bmp'. Possible matches are picture1.bmp, picture2.bmp, pictureA.bmp, but not picture10.bmp or picture.bmp.

It is likely that you might want to perform such a wildcard match on a text file or a text string in some of your programs at some point. Think, for instance, of finding function names in a source file using the search pattern "*(*)". Listings 12.10 and 12.11 show a function that can be used for wildcard matching. Table 12.12 explains its interface.

TABLE 12.12 The CompareStr() Arguments

Variable	Explanation
Argument 1	char*, a pointer to the string to compare with.
Argument 2	char*, a pointer to a string specifying the search string—possibly containing wildcard characters.
Argument 3	bool, Boolean indicating whether a case-sensitive search (0) or a case-insensitive search (1) is wanted.
Argument 4	bool, Boolean indicating whether argument 1 might contain additional characters after the pattern.
Return value	bool, indicating whether argument 1 and argument 2 match according to wildcard rules. (0 = no match. 1 = match.)

LISTING 12.10 Pattern Matching Using Wildcards, Part 1

```
#define anychars      '*'
#define anysinglechar '?'
```

LISTING 12.10 Continued

```
int CompareStr(char *s, char *pattern, bool ignoreCase, bool allowTrailing)
{
    long l, m, n = 0L;
    long lens = strlen(s), lenpattern = strlen(pattern);

    for (l=0, m=0; (l < lenpattern) && (m < lens); l++, m++)
    { // walk the pattern and compare it to the string
        if (pattern[l] != anychars)    // normal character or '?'  ?
        {
            if (pattern[l] != anysinglechar)
            {
                if (ignoreCase == true)
                {
                    if (toupper(pattern[l]) != toupper(s[m]))
                        return(false);
                }
                else
                    if (pattern[l] != s[m])
                        return(false); // Character MISMATCH
            } // else NO prove that we don't match
        }
        else // We've got an expandable WILDCARD (*), Lets have a closer look!!
        {
        l++;
            for (n = m; (n < lens) ; n++)  // try to find a working combination
                if (CompareStr(&s[n], &pattern[l], ignoreCase, allowTrailing))
                    return(true);       // found == full match -> communicate
                                        // to callers
            return(false);      // couldn't find a working combination
        }
    }
}
```

The function CompareStr() walks through the string and the pattern, trying to match up the characters. As long as no wildcard characters are detected in the pattern, it does a normal character compare. However, as soon as a wildcard is detected something special has to happen. The '?' character (anysinglechar) is easy enough to deal with; it matches with any character in the string so no compare is actually needed. The '*' character (anychars) is more complicated. When a '*' is detected, a match must be found between the rest of the pattern after the '*' character and some part of the string. In order to do this, CompareStr() calls itself recursively, but each time starting with a different part of the string.

But this is not the end of the function, for at this point there are three possible situations:

- The end of both the string and the pattern has been reached. There is nothing left to compare and no mismatch occurred, which means the pattern matches the string.

- The end of the string has been reached but there are still characters left in the pattern. In this case, the string and the pattern match only if the remaining characters in the pattern are all '*'.

- The end of the pattern has been reached but there are still characters left in the string. In this case the string and the pattern match only if the last character of the pattern is a '*'.

Listing 12.11 shows the code which takes care of these three cases.

LISTING 12.11 Pattern Matching Using Wildcards, Part 2

```
    if (1 < lenpattern) // Trailing *'s are OK too!
    {
        for (n = 1; n < lenpattern; n++)
        if (pattern[n] != anychars)
                return(false);
    }
    else
    {
        if (pattern[l-1] != anychars)
        {
            if ((m < lens) && (allowTrailing == false))
                return(false);
        }
    }
    return(true);   // If we're still here, we've found a match!!
}
```

The CompareStr() function can also be found in the file 12Source04.cpp on the Web site.

A very simple way to do a pattern search on a larger string (or a text file loaded into memory), is shown in Listing 12.12.

LISTING 12.12 Using CompareStr() to Do a Pattern Match on a Text File

```
char *resultArray[MAXRESULTS];
int  index = 0, n = 0;

while (n < lengthOfFile && index < MAXRESULTS)
{
    if (CompareStr(&file[n], pattern, 1, 1))      // Case Insensitive,
                                                  // allow trailing.
        resultArray[index++] = &file[n];
    n++;
}
```

Summary

Different techniques can be used for writing text strings to screen. Table 12.2 showed the results of a speed comparison between the techniques.

These results were generated with a program which can be found in the file 12Source01.cpp.

There are also different techniques for reading and writing binary files. Table 12.9 showed the results of a speed comparison between C- and C++-style techniques using different buffer sizes.

These results were generated with a program which can be found in the file 12Source02.cpp.

This chapter also showed different ways of speeding up text file access by using intelligent parsing functions and loading text as binary blocks. Examples of this are given in the functions and classes in the files 12Source02.cpp, 12Source03.cpp, 12Source03.h, and 12Source04.cpp.

Optimizing Your Code Further

CHAPTER

13

IN THIS CHAPTER

This chapter gives examples of further areas in which performance and footprint optimizations can be made. This is done not so much by examining source code, as was done in previous chapters, but by taking a step back and looking at the problem domain (the arithmetic background) and the environment in which the source code is to operate (OS and tasks).

Arithmetic Operations

Most programs at some point perform arithmetic operations. This can be as simple as small addition or multiplication, or as complex as three-dimensional volume calculations. Whatever the case may be, often arithmetic operations can be broken down into several smaller, simpler steps involving a series of basic calculations and conversions. These steps are ideal candidates for optimization because they are generally used repeatedly on large amounts of data, and most contain looped or recursive functionality. The many optimization techniques discussed in this book are well suited for arithmetic optimization. Think for instance of rewriting recursive routines into iterative routines, using loop unrolling, creating tables of predetermined values and optimizing mathematical equations. Because arithmetic operations are an important area for optimization, which in practice often gets overlooked or executed in a far from optimal form, the following sections give tips and examples on how to use optimization techniques specifically for arithmetic operations.

Using Bit Operators for Arithmetic Operations

Interesting optimizations can be made by looking at bit representations of byte values. The example in Listing 13.1 demonstrates this. Often during a calculation it is important to know whether a number is a multiple of another number—that is, whether it can be divided by another number without any remainder. For this, the % operator (modulo operator) is often used as shown in Listing 13.1.

LISTING 13.1   Counting Multiples

```
int i, k;
long j, count = 0;

for (k = 0 ; k < DATALEN; k++)
    for (i = 1; i <= 256; i <<= 1)
    {
        if ((data[k] % i) == 0)
            count++;
    }
```

The example in Listing 13.1 checks each byte in a data block whether it is a multiple of 1, 2, 4, 8,…128. Because this example checks for very specific (but certainly often occurring) numbers, it can be optimized with a fast and simple bitwise check, as shown in Listing 13.2.

LISTING 13.2 Bitwise Counting Multiples

```
int i, k;
long j, count = 0;

for (k = 0; k < DATALEN; k++)
    for (i = 1; i <= 256; i <<= 1)
    {
        if ((data[k] & (i-1)) == 0)
            count++;
    }
```

The example in Listing 13.2 avoids the use of the time-consuming % operator by making use of the knowledge that when a number is a multiple of x, all the bits representing x-1 are not set. This means, for instance, that a number is a multiple of eight when its first three bits are not set (the binary representation of eight is 1000, the binary representation of seven is 0111). The result of using a bitwise & instead of the % operator is that the example routine becomes up to five times faster. A program that demonstrates this can be found in the file 13Source01.cpp on the Web site.

More examples of bit operator use can be found in the listings of the following sections.

Identifying Static Parts in Calculations and Conversions

Part of optimizing is making sure that no double work is done. Information which is static, and therefore does not change between different usages of a certain piece of code, can be precalculated at program startup or perhaps even at compile time. This means time is won whenever this information is used. This can be done for intermediate or even end results of calculations. Refer to Chapters 7, "Basic Programming Statements," and 11, "Storage Structures," for more details on using recalculated values. The following sections show examples of calculations that contain, perhaps unexpectedly, static parts, and how they can be optimized.

Determining the Number of Bits Set in a Data Block

A routine that determines the parity of a data block is a good example of a calculation containing static parts. The parity of a data block depends on the number of bits in that block that are set (a bit is set when it has the value 1). For instance, the number of bits set in a byte with value 9 is 2. (The binary representation of 9 is 1001).

The most straightforward way to determine the number of bits set in a data block is to check the bits of every byte in the block and increase a counter for every bit that is set. Listing 13.3 shows an example of how this could be implemented.

LISTING 13.3   Using Two for Loops to Count Set Bits in a Data Block

```
int i, k;
long count = 0;

for (k = 0 ; k < DATALEN; k++)
    for (i = 1; i <= 256; i <<= 1)
    {
        if (data[k] & i)
            count++;
    }
```

Upon loop termination the variable count in Listing 13.3 will contain the number of set bits in data block data. Notice that a logical and is used together with mask i to determine whether or not a particular bit is set.

This function can be sped up significantly when the inner for loop is eliminated. Unrolling this loop will take care of that (refer to Chapter 7 for more details on loop optimization). Listing 13.4 shows a bit-counting function that uses only a single loop.

LISTING 13.4   Using One for Loop to Count Set Bits in a Data Block

```
int k;
long count = 0;

for (k = 0; k < DATALEN; k++)
{
    count +=((data[k] & 128) >> 7) +
            ((data[k] &  64) >> 6) +
            ((data[k] &  32) >> 5) +
            ((data[k] &  16) >> 4) +
            ((data[k] &   8) >> 3) +
            ((data[k] &   4) >> 2) +
            ((data[k] &   2) >> 1) +
            ((data[k] &   1));
}
```

As with Listing 13.3, the variable count in Listing 13.4 will contain the number of set bits in data block data upon loop termination. Notice that the inner loop of Listing 13.3 has been transformed into eight fixed logical ands. The results of these and operations are shifted with the >> operator, so each bit that is set increments count only by one.

Counting set bits with the code in Listing 13.4 is up to five times faster than counting set bits with the code in Listing 13.3. It seems this loop unrolling is a valuable calculation optimization here; it allows you to process five times as much data per second while collecting parity information. But this code can be made faster still. When you analyze the problem domain carefully you will see that static data information is gathered dynamically. The static data is the number of bits set in a byte with a certain value. For instance, a byte with the value 1 will always have only a single bit set (the binary representation of 1 is 0001). Similarly, each byte with the value 5 has two bits set (the binary representation of 5 is 0101). It is possible, therefore, to create a predetermined list containing the number of bits set for each value a byte can have. This list contains 256 values and can be used as shown in Listing 13.5.

LISTING 13.5   Using a Lookup Table to Count Set Bits in a Data Block

```
//                        0 1 2 3 4 5 6 7 8
unsigned char lookupTable[] = {0,1,1,2,1,2,2,3,1..

int i, k;
long count = 0;
for (i = 0; i < DATALEN; i++)
{
    count+=lookupTable[data[i]];
}
```

In Listing 13.5, each byte of the data block is used as an index in the lookupTable in order to determine the number of bits set for its value. For instance, a data byte with the value 8 will cause the number 1 to be retrieved from the lookup table (the binary representation of 8 is 1000). The code in Listing 13.5 is up to be four times faster than that of Listing 13.4. The file 13Source01.cpp contains a program that compares the speeds of the bit count solutions presented in Listings 13.3, 13.4, and 13.5. Table 13.1 shows the results of this program.

TABLE 13.1   Results of Counting the Number of Bits Set in a Block of 8192 Bytes

Listing	Time
Two loops (13.1)	6210
One loop (13.2)	1160
No loop (13.3)	320

The final solution put forward in Listing 13.5 is up to twenty times faster than the first solution put forward in Listing 13.3. Clearly it pays to spend some time determining static parts of calculations and how to handle these. A remaining question is whether or not the static allocation of a 256-byte array can be justified by the performance won. This is true for most systems (even most memory-tight embedded systems). Notice, however, that transforming the solution of Listing 13.4 into a macro and using it a few times in a source file will already take up more than 256 bytes.

Converting Byte Values to ASCII

Often programs need to convert binary data into text strings for output. As you may expect, conversions contain a high level of static information. A conversion often used by programmers is that of binary data into hexadecimal text strings. Listing 13.6 shows the kind of conversion functionality that is often used for this purpose.

LISTING 13.6 Standard Conversion of Byte Values to Hex String

```
inline void Nibble2Ascii(int nibble, char &c)
{
    if (nibble < 10)
        c = (char)(0x30 + nibble);
    else
        c = (0x37 + nibble);
}

void HexStr1(char *s, int val)
{
    Nibble2Ascii(val >> 4, s[0]);
    Nibble2Ascii(val %16, s[1]);
    s[2] = 0x0;
}
```

When you look for static information in binary-to-hex string conversions, you will notice that the text representation of each nibble is predetermined and does not have to be calculated at all. Once again a simple array with predetermined answers will do nicely. Listing 13.7 demonstrates a conversion routine that is more than twice as fast as that of Listing 13.6.

LISTING 13.7 Optimized Conversion of Byte Values to Hex String

```
char   HexString[] = {"0123456789ABCDEF"};

void HexStr2(char *s, int val)
{
```

LISTING 13.7   Continued

```
    s[0] = HexString[val >> 4];
    s[1] = HexString[val & 0xf];
    s[2] = '\0';
}
```

The same can be done for conversions of byte values to decimal strings. It is of course possible to convert each byte individually using a standard C/C++ function:

```
// Convert byte j to decimal.
char s[4];
itoa( j, s, 10 );
```

But when large blocks of bytes need to be converted or when conversion is performed often, you may opt to build a two-dimensional array to store all the possible answers and simply select a pointer to the correct answer string on conversion.

```
char decLookup[256][4];    // fill this at some point.
~
// Convert byte j to decimal.
s = decLookup[j];
```

This way each byte value is converted only once and after this each following conversion is suddenly over forty times faster. Footprint considerations here are whether to make a static array of values in a source file—in which case the runtime footprint as well as the storage footprint increases with the size of the table (refer to Chapter 1, "Optimizing: What Is It All About?" for more details on footprint terminology)—or to create the array dynamically during runtime. When you choose the second option do not be fooled into thinking that the footprint of the table can be optimized by using 256 pointers to variable length strings in order to save some bytes on the first 99 entries. As it is, the table is 4*256 bytes large, which is also the size of an array of pointers.

The file 13Source01.cpp on the Web site contains a program that compares conversion speeds of several conversion methods. It also shows how standard C/C++ functions like `toupper()` and `tolower()` can be optimized in a similar way.

Optimizing Mathematical Equations

When calculations contain no static parts to optimize, think about optimizing the mathematical equations instead. This can yield very good results. The following example demonstrates this. Let's say you need to determine the sum of a range of numbers that increase with a given step size. Examples of such ranges are 0,2,4,6,8 (step size = 2) and 5,10,15,20 (step size = 5). The most straightforward way to do this is to add all the numbers one by one. Listing 13.8 shows an example of how this could be implemented.

LISTING 13.8 Standard Determination of the Sum of a Range

```
int k;
long count = 0;
for (k = 0 ; k < DATALEN; k++)
      count+= data[k];
```

Again, however, the few things known about the data can be used to create a better algorithm. The information you have is the length of the data block and the range, which contains numbers that increase with a given step size. Given this, the following mathematical function can be derived for the sum:

```
                  (n * s (n - 1))
sum = n * b +  ---------------
                         2
```

```
b = begin value
s = step value
n = nr of data elements
```

Listing 13.9 shows how this formula can be implemented to determine the sum of the range.

LISTING 13.9 Determining the Sum of a Range of Numbers that Increase with a Given Step Size

```
step = (data[1]-data[0]);

count = DATALEN * data[0] +
      ((DATALEN * step * (DATALEN-1))  >> 1);
```

The variable step in Listing 13.9 is only needed when you want to use a non-fixed step size that is dynamically determined by looking at the range itself.

Note that the advantage here is that determining the sum went from an O(n) algorithm (Listing 13.8) to an O(1) algorithm (Listing 13.9)—refer to Chapter 5, "Measuring Time and Complexity," for more details. This means that the amount of time needed to determine the sum is not related to the size of the data block for Listing 13.9. It will not surprise you that this solution is therefore thousands of times faster. The file 13Source01.cpp on the Web site contains a program that measures performance differences between the solution of 13.8 and the solution of 13.9.

Note that a good math book can help you a long way in finding and optimizing mathematical functions.

Operating System–Based Optimizations

This section focuses on optimizing the interaction between parts of your program that execute simultaneously and/or interact with shared resources. Multitasking and callback functions are used for these purposes. There are different ways and program states in which to use these, as well as some traps and difficulties to look out for when using them. This section gives explanations and field examples.

Multitasking

When used correctly, multitasking can greatly enhance program performance. However, it should not be used indiscriminately because it does bring with it some overhead and extra things to look out for during design and implementation. This section explains what multitasking is exactly, how to handle the problems it can bring along with it, and what kind of hidden overhead to watch out for.

What Is Multitasking?

Basically, single processor systems can perform only one task at a time. A processor takes an instruction from memory and executes it. After completion, the processor can take the next instruction from memory and execute it. A collection of instructions that is executed in this sequential way is called a task. You could compare a processor performing a task to a person reading instructions from a manual. Generally, a person will read instructions from a manual one at a time and follow them carefully. Only when an instruction could be followed successfully is the next instruction dealt with. However, if you had five people working for you, you could give them five manuals and have them execute five different tasks for you simultaneously. This is true also for multiprocessor systems; each processor can perform a task independently from the other processors.

No doubt you know already that it is possible for single processor systems to have multitasking operating systems. In fact, any operating system that allows you to run more than one program at a time is in effect a multitasking OS. Think of starting up a calculator program while you are already using a word processor and perhaps a paint program. So how is this possible? Let's return to the example of the person—let's call him Bob—reading a manual. What if you gave Bob five manuals and a stopwatch, and told him to switch manuals every ten minutes? This way he would seem to perform five different tasks. When you look at a single task however, it advances for only ten minutes after which it halts for another forty minutes. In fact, it probably halts for more than forty minutes because Bob needs time to put down one manual and pick up another (maybe he even needs some time to find his place in the manual he just picked up or to determine the order in which he deals with the manuals). This is also what happens when a multitasking OS with a single processor runs more than one task; the processor still performs only one task at a time; however, it switches between tasks at certain moments. This behavior is called task switching. Task switching brings some overhead with it, which means that the total amount of time spent on pure task execution decreases when the number of task switches increases. In the sections that follow you will see what kind of overhead is incurred.

Tasks can take different shapes. The next three sections discuss the shapes called Process, Thread, and Fiber.

What Is a Process?

Although not all literature and all systems define the word *process* in exactly the same way, there are some general things that can be said about processes. Most often the word process is used to indicate a *program*, or at least *program characteristics*. When a processor switches from one process to the next, it needs a lot of information to be able to continue with the next process at exactly the same place/context where it left off last time. This is the only way process execution can continue as if it was never interrupted by a task switch. A process is therefore defined by the information that is needed during a task switch. Think of:

- The values of the CPU registers

  These contain the context created by executed processor instructions.

- A stack

  This contains the context created by function calls, variable definitions, and so on (refer to Chapter 8, "Functions," for more details on registers in function calls).

- Address space

  This memory is sometimes called the *apartment* or *working set*. It is that part of system memory (the range of memory addresses) that is available to the process.

- Meta data

  Think of security privileges, current working directory, process name, process priority, and so on.

This is a lot of information and consequently process switching is the most expensive kind of task switch there is, as far overhead is concerned. The reason for this is robustness of the OS. By using virtual memory management (refer to Chapter 9, "Efficient Memory Management," for more details on memory management) to give each process its own private piece of memory, it is possible to create the illusion that each process has the system all to itself. This means that when a process goes into some kind of faulty state, it can mess up its own memory and resources but not that of another process. This holds true as long as the virtual memory management system does not get messed up and no resources are locked by the misbehaving process. The two sections that follow show some lighter ways to switch between different tasks.

Listing 13.10 shows how new processes can be created under Windows. In the section "Task Switching" you will see what kinds of strategies an OS can use to determine when and how to switch between tasks.

LISTING 13.10 Creating a New Process Under Windows

```
#include <windows.h>

void main(void)
{
    STARTUPINFO st;
    PROCESS_INFORMATION pr;

    memset(&st, 0, sizeof(st));
    st.cb = sizeof(st);

    CreateProcess(NULL, "c:\\windows\\calc.exe ",
                  NULL, NULL, 1, 0, NULL, NULL, &st,  &pr);
}
```

Note that starting a process under Windows is actually nothing more than telling the OS to start up a specific executable. Certain parameters can be set for this executable, such as working directory, command line arguments, and so on. Consult your compiler documentation for more details on process execution. Listing 13.11 shows how a new process can be created under UNIX.

LISTING 13.11 Creating a New Process Under UNIX

```
#include <stdio.h>
#include <sys/unistd.h>

void a( void *dummy )
{
    for(;;)
      printf("a");
}

void b( void *dummy )
{
    for(;;)
        printf("b");
}

void main()
```

LISTING 13.11   Continued

```
{
    if (fork() == 0)
        a();
    b();
}
```

Note that under UNIX it is possible to start a new process with a function from the original address space.

A new address space is created in which this function is executed.

The next section discusses a less overhead-intense way of creating a new task.

What Is a Thread?

Most often the word *thread* is used to indicate a path of execution within a process. As you have already seen, different processes can be run simultaneously by switching between them. The same trick can be performed within a process; that is, different parts of a process can be run simultaneously by switching between tasks within the process. These kinds of tasks are called threads. As a thread *lives* within a certain process, it needs less defining information:

- The values of the CPU registers
- A stack
- Thread priority (Often specified in relation to the priority of the process in which the thread lives.)

All threads of a process inherit the remaining defining information from the process:

- Address space
- Meta data

There are three conclusions to be drawn from the preceding two bulleted lists:

1. Task switching between two threads in the same process does not introduce much overhead.
2. All threads in the same process share the same address space and can therefore use the same global data (variables, file handlers, and so on) They can of course also mess up each other's memory. For more information see the section titled "Problems with Multitasking."
3. Task switching between threads of different processes introduces the same overhead as any other task switch between processes.

Note that each active process has at least one thread of execution. This thread is called the *main* thread.

Listing 13.12 shows how threads can be used under Windows.

LISTING 13.12   Creating Multiple Threads in Windows

```
#include <windows.h>
#include <process.h>
#include <fstream.h>

struct StartInput
{
        char    name[8];
        int     number;
        int     length;
};

void StartThread(void* startInput)
{
        StartInput *in = (StartInput*) startInput;

        int k = in->number;
        int j = in->length + k;

        for(; k < j; k++)
        {
            cout << k << in->name << endl;
        }
        _endthread();
}


void main(void)
{
        StartInput startInputA, startInputB;

        strcpy(startInputA.name,"ThreadA");
        strcpy(startInputB.name,"ThreadB");
        startInputA.number = 0;
        startInputB.number = 5;
        startInputA.length = 10;
        startInputB.length = 15;
        _beginthread(StartThread, 0, (void*) &startInputA);
        _beginthread(StartThread, 0, (void*) &startInputB);

        Sleep(6000);
}
```

Listing 13.12 shows one way of creating two new threads from within a Windows process. By passing a pointer to a function in the call `beginthread`, a new thread is created and scheduled for task switching by the OS. Its execution starts with the first instruction of the function that was passed—in this case the function `StartThread`. As the format used for passing arguments to a new thread is fixed (`void*`) a casting trick must be performed in order to pass more than 4 bytes of information. In Listing 13.11 a pointer to a structure is passed. Because the receiving function `StartThread` knows exactly what kind of structure to expect, it can retrieve all the structure fields without a problem.

There are three more interesting points to note about Listing 13.12. First, the two created threads receive pointers to two different structures, `startInputA` and `startInputB`. In a sequential program you would probably have passed `startInputA` first to one function, changed some of its fields, and then passed it to another function. However, because two threads will run simultaneously and because the threads share the same address space, changing any field in `startInputA` would change the values used in both threads! Second, the function `StartThread` is used as a starting address for tasks (threads). The reason this is possible is that threads have their own private stack. This means each thread will have a private copy of `k` and `j`. Third, the main thread is put to sleep after starting the two new threads. The reason for this is that all threads of a process terminate when the process itself (the main thread) terminates. The `Sleep` function is used as a trick to keep the main thread alive long enough for the two new threads to do their jobs. Strictly speaking the `endthread` call in the function `StartThread` is not really necessary, as threads end automatically when they run out of instructions. `Sleep` is an ideal way to suspend a thread, because a sleeping thread is not scheduled until its *nap time* is over. Note that using `Sleep` is therefore an infinitely better construction than using a long running loop. Not only does `Sleep` guarantee more precisely when the thread will continue executing, but a loop is also very processor intense. This means that a loop slows down all other tasks on the system.

Do not forget to set the compiler code generation settings to `multithreaded` when writing multithreaded programs under Windows. In the file 13Source02.cpp on the Web site, you can find what the same program would look like under UNIX. Compile it with:

```
g++ 13Source02.cpp -o example -lpthread
```

It is also possible to perform your own task scheduling within a thread. The next section tells more about this.

What Is a Fiber?

It is, of course, always possible to implement your own paths of execution through a process and take care of task switching within your own code. The tasks created this way are often called *fibers*—because they are a subset of a thread. Exactly which information is accessible within a fiber and which information is needed upon a task switch is dependent on how you implement a fiber; however, it will be difficult to shield the rest of a process from damages the fiber might inadvertedly do. The fiber will almost always inherit the address space of the process (and therefore also that of any other threads within the process). Some OSes offer supporting calls to help you create your own fibers and switch between them. Check your OS and compiler documentation for more information.

Task Switching

Task switching is sometimes called *process scheduling* or *thread scheduling*. A multitasking OS must at the very least have a thread that takes care of scheduling the different tasks that need to run simultaneously. A task that is scheduled is said to have received a *time slice*, which means it can run for a certain period of time. This section presents different strategies that task schedulers can use for determining which task receives a time slice and how long this time slice will be.

Scheduling Processes and Threads

Tasks are usually scheduled according to their priority, which is an attribute that can be set for each task. However, the OS still has to decide how to define what a task actually is. For instance, the scheduler could see the system as running a collection of threads, and schedule these based solely on their priority. In this case no consideration is given to the fact that switching between threads in the same process costs less overhead than switching between threads of different processes. Another strategy would be to try and schedule a certain percentage or number of threads within the same process before scheduling a thread in another process.

Consult your OS and compiler documentation in order to determine how your system defines scheduling of tasks.

Cooperative Multitasking

An OS that uses cooperative multitasking assigns an equal amount of time to each task. The importance, or priority, of the task is not taken into consideration. Tasks that do not need a full time slice can decide to be *cooperative* and give up the remainder of their slice so another task can be scheduled earlier. A problem here can be that tasks with a very low priority take up a disproportionate amount of time.

Preemptive Multitasking

An OS that uses preemptive multitasking assigns time slices according to task importance or priority. This means that a task with a high priority will be scheduled more often (and perhaps even with a larger time slice) than a task with a low priority. A danger here is that setting the priority of a task too high can mean that other tasks have little or no opportunity to do any processing. This includes a task that you might try to start in order to lower the priority of the task that is causing the problems.

Tasks can also be preempted when they block themselves for synchronization or enter an idle state, such as is done with the `Sleep` function.

Real-Time OS

For certain critical tasks (such as processes running in an embedded environment), a minimal response time must be guaranteed by the OS. This means that scheduling strategies must keep the incurred task-switching costs to a minimum and allow worst-case scenarios to be predicted. These kinds of requirements specify a real-time OS.

Problems with Multitasking

As you have seen in the section "What Is a Thread?" the address space of a process can be accessed by all the threads of that process. And, because threads can run simultaneously, they can also access the same memory addresses simultaneously—this is why in Listing 13.11 each starting thread is given its own data structure. This section highlights the kinds of problems that can occur because of this characteristic of multitasking, and how to prevent them from happening inside your code.

Memory Corruption

Because all the threads in a process have the same address space, a bug in one thread can corrupt the data and instructions of another thread. This makes debugging extra difficult.

Protecting Shared Resources

Every once in a while different threads have to access the same resources (memory, files, ports, libraries, and so on). This does not necessarily have to cause a problem. Think, for instance, of two threads used for Internet access—two file download threads perhaps—which share a single data structure with initialization data (IP address, port number, modem settings, and so on). When both threads only read from this data there is no need for extra security. However, if one of the threads changes the data (writes to it) then something special must be done. The reason for this is that the programmer of a thread can never anticipate when a task switch will occur, and therefore cannot guarantee that it will never occur during the write action. A thread may want to change the IP address in a shared structure from 127.1.1.0 to 212.33.33.00. If the OS switches from this writing task to a task that reads from this structure during the middle of the write action, the reading thread will read a corrupt IP-Address: 212.33.1.0. This is why programmers need a way to lock a certain resource for a specific thread. There are different kinds of locks available on most OSes, but they all work according to the same basic principles:

- A lock can be claimed and released.

- The claim and release functions of locks are atomic. This means a task switch cannot occur during the execution of these functions.

- When thread A tries to claim a lock that is already claimed by thread B, thread A is put on hold until thread B releases the lock. When thread B releases the lock, thread A becomes the owner of the lock and continues its execution. From that moment on, other threads will be blocked when trying to claim the lock. These other threads in turn stay blocked until thread A releases the lock.

- Most locks are associated in some way with a list of threads. This means if several threads try to claim the same lock, the first will own it and the remaining threads have to wait in line for their turn.

- The programmer makes the association between a lock and a resource.

The last bulleted item in the preceding list is a very important one. It means that it is perfectly possible to program a thread to use a resource without claiming the associated lock first. This often causes problems when different programmers work on the same multithreaded code; a programmer making changes to an existing thread may not be aware of the fact that certain resources are associated with locks and add code that uses the resources without locking them first.

Listing 13.13 shows a Windows program with two worker threads. One thread writes to a structure at given times and the other thread reads from it. The structure is protected by a lock that is imaginatively called lock. The functions EnterCriticalSection and LeaveCriticalSection are used, respectively, to claim and release this lock. The definition of the lock and the claim and release calls is of course OS specific. The set of instructions placed between the claim and release of a lock is called a critical section, which is where these OS calls get their names.

LISTING 13.13   Protecting a Shared Resource in a Windows Program

```
#include <windows.h>
#include <process.h>
#include <fstream.h>


struct
{
    int     number;
} SharedData;


CRITICAL_SECTION Lock;

void ReadThread(void* dummy)
{
    int prevnr = -1;
    int nr     = 0;
```

LISTING 13.13   Continued

```
    // Get initial number and print it.
    EnterCriticalSection(&Lock);
        nr = SharedData.number;
    LeaveCriticalSection(&Lock);

    prevnr = nr;

    cout << nr << endl;

    for(;;)
    {
        EnterCriticalSection(&Lock);
            nr = SharedData.number;
        LeaveCriticalSection(&Lock);

        // Print only changed numbers.
        if (nr != prevnr)
            cout << nr << endl;

        Sleep(100);
    }
}


void WriteThread(void* dummy)
{
    int nr      = 100;

    for(;;)
    {
        EnterCriticalSection(&Lock);
            SharedData.number = nr++;
        LeaveCriticalSection(&Lock);

        Sleep(5);
    }
}


void main(void)
```

LISTING 13.13 Continued

```
{

    InitializeCriticalSection(&Lock);

    SharedData.number = 0;

    _beginthread(WriteThread, 0, NULL);
    _beginthread(ReadThread,  0, NULL);

    Sleep(20000);

}
```

In Listing 13.13 you can clearly see that the association between the lock and the resource is one introduced by the programmer. By simply removing a pair of EnterCriticalSection and LeaveCriticalSection calls you can program the threads to access the SharedData structure without protection. Note also that if you want the program in Listing 13.13 to output to screen really nicely, you have to make sure that no task switch can occur during the execution of the cout function. The way to do this is to create a second lock and place EnterCriticalSection and LeaveCriticalSection calls around each cout function call. For proof that the ReadThread and the WriteThread actually wait for each other you can add another call to the function Sleep() within one of the critical sections. You will then notice that this causes both threads to halt, the first because it is sleeping and the second because it is waiting for the sleeping thread to release the lock. This is also a useful technique to use when testing for possible deadlocks. Functions that are normally so fast that a deadlock almost never occurs can be artificially slowed down.

In Listing 13.13 only one thread could access the shared resource at a time. Sometimes, however, optimizations in locking strategy can be made by looking carefully at when a shared resource really needs to be locked. Consider the following example. A process contains three threads that use the same data structure. One thread only reads from this structure—let's call this the read thread—the two other threads need to read from and write to this structure—let's call these read/write threads. Instead of each thread locking the resource when it accesses it, you can make a distinction between read access and write access. There is no reason why the read thread cannot access the data structure while one of the read/write threads is also only reading it. However, as soon as a read/write thread wants to write to the data structure, locking must be done to make sure the read thread is not reading the data at the same time. Listing 13.14 shows, in pseudocode, how this can implemented.

LISTING 13.14   Optimized Locking Strategy: Simultaneous Reading from Different Threads

```
ReadThread()
{
    EnterCriticalSection(&readlock);

        // No other ReadThread can access the data
        //   during this critical section. One other
        //   ReadWriteThread can access the data but
        //   only for reading.

        // Do as much reading here as you want.

    LeaveCriticalSection(&readlock);

    // Now another ReadThread or ReadWriteThread can lock the
    //   data, do not perform any reading or writing here.
}


ReadWriteThread()
{
    EnterCriticalSection(&writelock);

        // No other ReadWriteThread will access the data
        //   for reading or writing during this critical section.

        // Do as much reading here as you want because only
        //   this thread and one ReadThread can access the data.

        EnterCriticalSection(&readlock);

            // No other thread  (Read nor ReadWrite) will access
            //   the data during this critical section.

            // Here you can change the data (write to the data)

        LeaveCriticalSection(&readlock);

        // Back to previous critical section; readlock has been
        //   released so only perform read actions here.

    LeaveCriticalSection(&writelock);

    // Now another ReadThread and ReadWriteThread can lock the data.
    //   do not perform any reading or writing here.
}
```

Several threads can use the ReadThread and ReadWriteThread functions. A thread that wants to read as well as write the data structure has to claim the writelock just before accessing the data for reading. This way it is sure that no other read/write thread is changing the data. However, it allows another reading thread to continue unbothered. When a read/write thread wants to change the data, it has to claim both the writelock and readlock (in that order!) to ensure that no other thread has access to the data. These kinds of optimizations can improve program performance by eliminating as much idle waiting time incurred by locks as possible. However, the use of the locks can become quite complex and needs to be documented well, especially in light of future changes that may be made to the program. Functions that contain sufficient locks, so they can be called by different threads without causing problems with shared resources, are called *re-entrant* functions. As was stated before, there are many different kinds of locks. Some use counters with which the programmer can specify how many threads can claim a lock. The characteristics of the different kinds of locks that are available to you on a certain OS-plus-compiler combination should be taken into account when devising an optimized locking strategy. Consult your OS and compiler documentation for more information.

Deadlocks

Using locks enables programmers to create threads that do not corrupt shared resources. However, these locks have the effect that they halt (or block) certain threads at certain times, and halted threads cannot release locks that they have claimed. When a locking strategy is not carefully designed from the start, this can cause a situation to occur in which two or more threads wait for each other to release a lock. This is called a deadlock. The pseudocode in Listing 13.15 demonstrates a potential deadlock.

LISTING 13.15 Potential Deadlock Situation

```
CRITICAL_SECTION resourceA, resourceB;

void ThreadA()
{
    EnterCriticalSection(&resourceA);

        // Do something with resourceA

        EnterCriticalSection(&resourceB);

            // Do something with resourceB (and A)

        LeaveCriticalSection(&resourceB);
```

LISTING 13.15 Continued

```
    LeaveCriticalSection(&resourceA);
}


void ThreadB(void* dummy)
{
    EnterCriticalSection(&resourceB);

        // Do something with resourceB

        EnterCriticalSection(&resourceA);

            // Do something with resourceA (and B)

        LeaveCriticalSection(&resourceA);

    LeaveCriticalSection(&resourceB);
}
```

A deadlock occurs in Listing 13.15 when the following happens:

1. `ThreadA` claims `resourceA`
2. A task switch occurs which makes `ThreadB` active
3. `ThreadB` claims `resourceB`

No matter what happens after this, `ThreadA` and `ThreadB` will ultimately become deadlocked. This is because `ThreadB` will try to claim `resourceA` before it releases `resourceB` and `ThreadA` will not even consider releasing `resourceA` before it is able to claim `resourceB`. `ThreadA` will block on the call `EnterCriticalSection(&resourceB)` and `ThreadB` will block on the call `EnterCriticalSection(&resourceA)`

Listing 13.15 also demonstrates why deadlocks are often so hard to find. Potential deadlocks may never actually occur or they may occur only sporadically. The fewer instructions placed between the claiming of resources (steps 1 and 3 in the preceding list), the less likely it becomes that a task switch will occur exactly at that point. This is also why debugging deadlocks is so difficult; as you have seen in Chapter 4, "Tools and Languages," the timing of a debug executable is very different from that of a release executable.

Another good way to introduce a deadlock is to claim a lock and never release it. This can happen when functions become more complicated and/or claims and releases are harder to match.

```
void functionQ()
{
    EnterCriticalSection(&lock)
    if (conditionA)
        if (conditionB)
            return;
    LeaveCriticalSection(&lock)
```

When both condition A and B are true, functionQ is terminated (return). However, the lock is never released. When a lock is left open like this, another thread trying to claim the lock will block. However, the thread that has the lock will, in all likelihood, not block when it calls the functionQ next time, because on most OSes a thread can not block on a lock that it has already claimed.

The correct way to write an exit like this would be:

```
void functionQ2()
{
    EnterCriticalSection(&lock)
    if (conditionA)
        if (conditionB)
        {LeaveCriticalSection(&lock); return;}
    LeaveCriticalSection(&lock)
```

Preventing Multitasking Problems

Here are some programming practices that can help you minimize multitasking problems.

- Place claims and releases of locks as tightly around the usage of shared data as possible. In practice, critical sections should contain only instructions that directly or indirectly make use of the shared resource (see Listing 13.13).

- Check all exit points of functions that claim locks.

- Style your code in such a way that it is easy to see which claims go with which releases. See Listing 13.13, where extra indentation is used for the instructions of the critical sections.

- Write clearly in the design, and in comments in the code, which locks should be associated with which resources and how the locks should be used (counting locks, read locks, and write locks separated and so on; see Listing 13.14).

When to Use Multitasking

As you have seen in the sections "What Is a Process?" and "What Is a Thread?" using multitasking brings with it a certain amount of overhead. This means that for most purely sequential programs, using multithreading will decrease performance. This section shows when multitasking can be used to boost program performance.

Different Program States

Using different threads to represent different program states is a good way to use multitasking to boost program performance and keep the software relatively simple. Think, for instance, of a TCP/IP program that communicates over the Internet. The main thread can be used to process user input and give user feedback, a second thread can take care of sending data, and a third thread can take care of receiving data. Because the threads basically run simultaneously, the programmer does not have to incorporate complex and time-consuming polling routines throughout the code to check if the program state should be changed. Refer to Chapter 1 for more details on polling.

Working During Idle and Waiting Times

When a programmer expects that a program has to wait when trying to claim a certain resource (hard disc, external disc, network, printer, and so on), he can decide to place interaction with the resource in a separate thread so the main thread can continue working. The new thread will not take up a lot of scheduling time because it will not be scheduled while it is waiting for the resource to become available. Listing 13.16 shows a function in pseudocode called WriteBackup, which can be used in a separate thread to interact with a device for output.

LISTING 13.16   Using Threads for Slow Device Interaction

```
struct BackupInfo
{
    DEVICE              dev;
    CRITICAL_SECTION    *dataLock;
    unsigned char       *data;
    int                 datalen;
};

void WriteBackup(void* input)
{
    BackupInfo  *info = (BackupInfo*) input;


    // Wait until device can be claimed.
    Claim(info->dev);

        // Lock data for output.
        EnterCriticalSection(info->dataLock);

            // Write data to device.
```

LISTING 13.16   Continued

```
            WriteData(info->dev, info->data, info->datalen);

        // Release data.
        LeaveCriticalSection(info->dataLock);

    // Release device.
    Release(info->dev);
}
```

Callback Functions

Callback functions can be used perfectly in combination with multithreaded programming as a way of increasing overall program performance. Callback functions were introduced in Chapter 1 as a way for tasks to signal that they have completed a certain job. Listing 13.16 can easily be adapted to make use of a callback function to signal that the backup was successfully written. There are more applications for callback functions. Listing 13.17 shows how a timer function can be started in a separate thread. This timer receives information on how many times per second it should call a certain callback function, and how many times this callback function should be called in total.

LISTING 13.17   Using a Timer Callback

```
#include <windows.h>
#include <process.h>
#include <fstream.h>

void PrintStatus(int in)
{
    cout << in << endl;
}

struct TimerData
{
    void    (*CallBack)(int in);
    int     delay, nrAlarms, data;
};

void Timer(void *input)
{
    TimerData *info = (TimerData*) input;

    for (int i = 0; i < info->nrAlarms; i++)
    {
        Sleep(info->delay);
```

LISTING 13.17   Continued

```
            info->CallBack(info->data);
    }
}

void main(void)
{
    TimerData    timedat;

    timedat.CallBack    = PrintStatus;
    timedat.data        = 5;
    timedat.delay       = 1000;
    timedat.nrAlarms    = 20;

    _beginthread(Timer, 0, &timedat);

    // Do something useful.

    Sleep(6000);
}
```

Such a timer can be used to print status information periodically or to update data (sprite position on screen and so on) while the main thread continues with the work at hand. Note that the timer in Listing 13.17 can be activated with different callback functions in order to do different kinds of things. Timers are sometimes used in watchdog threads. A watchdog periodically checks the status of a certain resource (a task, a device, a piece of memory and so on). When this resource is found to be in a faulty state (printer out of paper or tasks set in a deadlock) it can perform a predefined action such as warn the user or reboot the system.

Summary

Often arithmetic functionality can be broken down into several smaller, simpler steps that are ideal candidates for optimization. These smaller steps are generally used repeatedly on large amounts of data, and most contain looped or recursive functionality, which is why high levels of gain can be had. Several optimization techniques can often be introduced in arithmetic functionality:

- Rewriting recursive routines into iterative routines
- Loop unrolling
- Using data-specific knowledge (using bit arithmetic operations and so on)

- Using lists of predetermined answers or intermediate results
- Using optimized mathematical equations

Multitasking is either performing different tasks on different processors simultaneously (multi-processor system) or switching between tasks on a single processor (single processor system). Multitasking can be used to enhance the performance of a program running on a single processor system by, for instance, moving different program states or slow device interaction into a separate task. This way, waiting times do not slow down the main program and complex-polling strategies can be simplified. Tasks come in different shapes, each shape with its own characteristics:

- Process
- Thread
- Fiber

While multitasking software can be the answer to many problems, there are things to look out for, such as task switching overhead, possibility of deadlocks, shared memory corruption, and so on.

13

OPTIMIZING YOUR
CODE FURTHER

Tips and Pitfalls

PART

III

This third part gives programming tips and shows sneaky problems and traps you can encounter when using C/C++. Furthermore, it shows how you can set up and maintain you code in a way that keeps it as portable as possible.

Part III consists of the following chapters:

Tips

IN THIS CHAPTER

Besides programming techniques, mathematics, and so on, it is also the small useful tips that can often help a programmer out. Here you will find small samples that can easily be put to use. Some tips make the programmer's job easier; others specifically help determine system and development environment dependencies. The second half of this chapter focuses on keeping sources compatible and portable for future use in different projects and on different systems. This allows you to write your sources in such a way that reusing them in different environments becomes easier, often without the need of added development time.

Tricks

Little-known facts that can make the job of a programmer easier are the focus of these sections. Some of these help determine system and development environment characteristics, and are reused in the second half of the chapter, in which compatibility and portability of sources is discussed.

Recognizing Code: C or C++

When mixing C and C++, you may at some point want to determine at runtime what kind of compiler was used. This is because C and C++ compilers generate subtly different code (think of calling conventions for function, sizes of variable types, and so on). Listing 14.1 shows how you can determine at runtime whether a source was compiled with a C compiler or a C++ compiler. It does this by looking at the size of a constant character. In C++ the size of a constant character ('A') equals that of the type char, which is something you would expect. In C, however, the size of a constant character equals that of the type int.

LISTING 14.1   Determining C or C++ Compilation at Runtime

```
inline int cplusplus()
{
    return(sizeof(char) == sizeof('A'));
}

if (cplusplus)
    printf("Compiled with a C++ compiler");
else
    printf("Compiled with a C compiler");
```

Determining the kind of compiler can, of course, also be done at compile time, which is preferable in most cases as this only costs compile time (no function needs to be executed at runtime to make this assessment). Listing 14.2 shows how you can determine at compile time whether a C or C++ compiler is used.

LISTING 14.2 Determining C or C++ Compilation at Compile Time

```c
#ifdef __cplusplus
    printf("Compiled with a C++ compiler");
#else
    printf("Compiled with a C compiler");
#endif
```

The reason this works is that C++ compilers define the __cplusplus definition automatically. For more differences between C and C++ refer to the section "Compatibility" later in this chapter.

Endianness

As explained in Chapter 10, "Blocks of Data," in the section on Radix sort, endianness is the byte order used by a system (storing the hexadecimal long word 0xAABBCCDD in memory in the byte order 0xAABBCCDD or 0xDDCCBBAA). Knowing the byte order of a system becomes important, for instance, when sources will be used on different platforms (development platform is perhaps different from target platform; refer to Chapter 1, "Optimizing: What Is It All About?"), or when they contain code that needs to communicate over networks and so on. Listing 14.3 shows how you can test the endianness of a platform by simply storing the value 1 (0x000001) in a long word and checking in which byte the bit is set.

LISTING 14.3 Determining Endianness of a System

```c
bool little_endian()
{
    unsigned int ii = 0x01;
    if (*(unsigned char *)&ii == 0x01)
        return(true);
        else
            return(false);
}

void cpu_info()
{
    if (little_endian())
        printf("LITTLE Endian, ");
    else
        printf("BIG Endian, ");

    printf("%d bit architecture\n", sizeof(int)*8);
}
```

14

TIPS

Variable Number of Arguments

Although part of the standard library, the use of a variable number of arguments in user-defined functions is not very well known. By placing ... as the last argument in a function definition, you can signal the compiler that you intend to use a variable number of arguments. This means that you can repeat the *one before last* argument as often as you want. For instance, a function defined as:

```
int UseMe(int a, ...);
```

can be called as:

```
int result = UseMe(1);
```

but also as:

```
int result = UseMe(1,2,3,4,5,6,7,8,15);
```

What is done during the call to such a function is that a terminated array of arguments is placed onto the function stack. Within the function, the arguments can be read from the stack one by one until the terminator is encountered. Table 14.1 shows the statements that can be used with variable argument lists.

TABLE 14.1 Statements Used with Variable Argument Lists

va_list	A typedef used for creating an index in the argument list.
va_start	A macro that initializes the index with the first argument in the list.
va_arg	A macro that retrieves the next argument from the list.
va_end	A macro to reset the index of the list.

Refer to your compiler and language documentation for more details on variable argument list statement definition. Listing 14.4 shows an implementation of a function that uses a variable number of arguments to receive a list of filenames that it should open. Note that this function receives two normal arguments also.

LISTING 14.4 Implementing Functions with a Variable Number of Arguments

```
#include <stdarg.h>
#include <stdio.h>


int OpenFileArray(FILE ***array, char * MODE, char *filename, ...)
{
    char    *pName    = NULL;
```

LISTING 14.4 Continued

```
int     nrFiles     = 0;
int     arrayIndex  = 0;


// Determine the number of files in the list.

if (filename == NULL)
    return 0;

va_list listIndex;
va_start(listIndex, filename);
do
{
    nrFiles++;
    pName = va_arg(listIndex, char*);
}
while (pName != NULL);


// Reserve memory for the file handles plus an array terminator.

*array = new FILE*[nrFiles+1];


// Open the files.

pName = filename;
va_start(listIndex, filename);
do
{
    if(!((*array)[arrayIndex++] = fopen(pName, MODE)))
    {
        // Not all files could be opened.
        (*array)[arrayIndex-1] = NULL;
        return 0;
    }
    pName = va_arg(listIndex, char*);
}
while (pName != NULL);

(*array)[arrayIndex] = NULL;

// All files opened.

return 1;
}
```

The first argument of the function OpenFileArray in Listing 14.4 is a pointer to an array of FILE pointers. As such, it returns an array filled with the pointers to the files it has opened. The second argument is a string that defines the mode that opens the files. This is the same argument that fopen expects as a second argument. Listing 14.5 shows how you could use the OpenFileArray function.

LISTING 14.5   Calling Functions with a Variable Number of Arguments

```
void main(void)
{
    FILE ** array;

    OpenFileArray(&array, "r", "name1.txt", "name2.txt", "name3.txt");


    // Close the files.

    int i = 0;
    while (array[i] != NULL)
    {
        fclose(array[i++]);
    }
    delete [] array;
}
```

Avoiding Unnecessary Checks

In order to make optimizations, it is often necessary to perform checks to determine which path of execution is most optimal in a given situation. These checks in themselves are extra overhead and you always have to think carefully about whether added overhead will be outweighed by the optimization you are trying to make. Sometimes, however, the overhead can be optimized out of existence almost entirely. Listing 14.6 shows a piece of pseudocode that contains two functions that calculate something with floating point values. One of the functions is optimized to work with a floating point processor, and the other is optimized to work without a floating point processor. Whenever a floating point calculation is needed, a check is done to determine whether a floating point processor is present in the system and the most optimal calculation function is called accordingly.

LISTING 14.6   Unnecessary Checks

```
void CalcWithoutFP(void *data)
{
    // calculation.
```

LISTING 14.6   Continued

```
}

void FPCalc(void *data)
{
    // alternative calculation.
}

void Calc(void *data)
{
    if (FLOATINGPOINTPROCESSOR)
        FPCalc(data);
    else
        CalcWithoutFP(data);
}
```

When many floating point calculations are made (perhaps you need millions per second), it is a shame that this check is performed as an extra overhead for each calculation. Who knows how time-consuming the check FLOATINGPOINTPROCESSOR actually is? That is why it helps performance when this check only needs to be executed once. Listing 14.7 shows how thiso can be achieved.

LISTING 14.7   Avoiding Unnecessary Checks

```
// Define a pointer to Calc.
void (*Calc)(void*);

// Set the value of the pointer.
void init(void)
{
    if (FLOATINGPOINTPROCESSOR)
        Calc = &FPCalc;
    else
        Calc = &CalcWithoutFP;
}
```

14

Tips

An init() function needs to be called once, before the first calculation. After that a pointer is initialized to point to the most optimal calculation function. Anywhere in the program, a floating point calculation can be performed by simply calling:

```
Calc(data);
```

This kind of optimization should only be used for decisions with a certain dynamic nature, where the information on which the decision is based becomes available during program start-up. If the presence of a floating point processor could somehow be determined at compile time, a better solution would be to use precompiler directives as shown in Listing 14.2.

Avoiding Unnecessary Bugs

A typo often made by even the most experienced programmers is placing an `if (a = 1)` statement where an `if (a == 1)` is meant. Instead of checking whether the value of variable a equals 1, the first statement will *assign* the value 1 to a, and the `if` will always be true. These kinds of bugs can be very hard to find but are easily avoided by simply adopting a different coding style. When you train yourself to turn around the elements of which the expressions are made up, the compiler will 'warn' you when you make this kind of typo.

```
if (1 == a)
if (NULL == fp)
. . .
```

By placing the constant first, the compiler will complain about you trying to assign a value to a constant as soon as you forget the second =.

Avoiding Unnecessarily Large Data Structures

Because of the way compilers align data types in structures, the size of a structure is determined partly by the order in which the fields are defined (for more detail on alignment see Chapter 6, "The Standard C/C++ Variables"). The following two structures demonstrate this:

```
typedef unsigned char byte;

struct large
{
    byte    v1;     // 20 byte structure.
    int     v2;
    byte    v3;
    int     v4;
    byte    v5;
};
```

The structure `large` contains three bytes and two integers. Its size, however, is 20 bytes! This is because the integers are allocated at four byte boundaries. By combining the byte variables in groups of four, you can reclaim this wasted alignment space.

```
struct small
{
    byte    v1;     // 12 byte structure.
    byte    v3;
    byte    v5;
    int     v4;
    int     v2;
};
```

Structure small can hold exactly the same information as large, but it is only 12 bytes in size. This is because fields v1, v3, and v5 share the same longword. This kind of optimization can save a lot of runtime memory when a structure is used for a large number of data elements.

Using ANSI Predefined Macros

ANSI C specifies six macros which ANSI-compliant compilers must support. As was explained in Chapter 4, "Tools and Languages," macros are expanded at compile time, which means that they can provide compile information during runtime. Table 14.2 shows which macros are predefined by ANSI-C.

TABLE 14.2 ANSI-C Predefined Macros

__DATE__	Expanded to contain the date on which the source file was compiled.
__TIME__	Expanded to contain the time at which the source file was compiled.
__TIMESTAMP__	Expanded to contain the date and time at which the source file was compiled.
__FILE__	Expanded to contain the name of the source file which is compiled.
__LINE__	Expanded to contain the line number at which the macro is set (integer).
__STDC__	Expanded to contain the value 1 when the compiler complies fully with the ANSI-C standard (integer)

Note that the ANSI predefined macros use a double underscore! All macros are expanded to character arrays except __LINE__ and __STDC__, which are integer values. Listing 14.8 shows how the macros __DATE__ and __TIME__ can be used to do a kind of versioning of a C++ class.

LISTING 14.8 Using ANSI Macros __DATE__ and __TIME__

```
// In the class header file.
#include <ostream.h>

char anyCompilationDate[] = __DATE__;
char anyCompilationTime[] = __TIME__;

class Any
{
public:
    void SourceInfo(void)
    {
        cout << "Compiled at: ";
        cout << anyCompilationDate << " " << anyCompilationTime << endl;
    }
};
```

In Listing 14.8, two character arrays are defined along with the class definition in the header file. When the class is compiled, these character arrays receive the date and time of compilation. By calling the SourceInfo() function of the class, other parts of the program can ask the class when it was compiled.

```
// In any source file.
void funct()
{
    Any aclass;

    aclass.SourceInfo();
}
```

Because the source files of a project can be compiled at different times (think of recompiling a project in which not all files were changed) different files will often have a different compilation date and time.

Listing 14.9 shows how you can use the __FILE__ and __LINE__ macros to facilitate debugging and logging. The function LogError() receives a string and an integer and logs these. By calling this function with the __FILE__ and __LINE__ macros as arguments, LogError() will log exactly in which source file and at which line the logging function was called.

LISTING 14.9   Using ANSI Macros __FILE__ and __LINE__

```
// Definition of the Error log function.
#include <ostream.h>

void LogError(char * fname, int lnr)
{
    cout << "Error in file: " << fname;
    cout << " on line number: " << lnr << endl;
}

~
// Each file will pass its own name and line number.
void somefunct(void)
{
    if (error) LogError(__FILE__, __LINE__);
}
```

Static Information Generated by the Compiler

For the use of static values it can sometimes be helpful to let the compiler generate them instead of calculating them yourself. This can save time because you do not have to recalculate static values when they need to be updated (when their base or meaning changes, for instance). Listing 14.10 shows how the compiler can be abused to generate bit count information such as was needed in Chapter 13, "Optimizing Your Code Further."

LISTING 14.10   Static Value Generation by the Compiler

```
template<int Num>
class BitCount
{
    public: enum { bits = ((Num & 0x80) >> 7) +
                          ((Num & 0x40) >> 6) +
                          ((Num & 0x20) >> 5) +
                          ((Num & 0x10) >> 4) +
                          ((Num & 0x08) >> 3) +
                          ((Num & 0x04) >> 2) +
                          ((Num & 0x02) >> 1) +
                          ((Num & 0x01))
            };
};


int main(int argc, char* argv[])
{
    int i = BitCount<255>::bits;

    return i;
}
```

Stack Versus Heap

When a certain amount of memory is needed in a function or a class, it pays to think carefully about whether this should be stack or heap memory—for more details on stacks and the heap refer to Chapters 8, "Functions," and 9, "Efficient Memory Management." Even when the amount of memory is static (when the number of bytes needed is known at compile time) it is a good idea to allocate in on the heap. Listing 14.11 shows two classes: the StackSpace class, which allocates a chunk of stack memory, and the HeapSpace class, which allocates a chunk of heap memory.

LISTING 14.11   Use of Stack Member Variables and Heap Member Variables

```
#include <stdio.h>

struct WData
```

14

TIPS

LISTING 14.11   Continued

```
{
    double a;
    float  b;
};

class StackSpace
{
    WData   vectors[1000];
};

class HeapSpace
{
public:
    HeapSpace() {vectors = new WData[1000];}
    ~HeapSpace(){delete [] vectors;}
private:
    WData   *vectors;
};

void f(void)
{
    int a;
    StackSpace sd;
    int b;
    HeapSpace  hd;

// variables on stack:
// a  = -4
// sd = -16004
// b  = -16008
// hd = -16012
}
```

Upon creation in function f(), both StackSpace and HeapSpace immediately allocate memory for a thousand instances of the WData structure. StackSpace does this by claiming stack memory as the WData array is part of the class and the class is created locally. HeapSpace does this by claiming memory from the heap by calling new. When you examine the placement of variables on the stack by function f(), for instance, by looking at the generated assembly (refer to Chapter 4), you will see that 4 bytes of stack space are reserved for variable a, 1600 bytes for variable sd, 4 bytes for variable b, and 4 bytes for variable hd. This has a number of consequences; using stack space will be faster than using heap space, but when significant amounts of memory are used—through recursive calls for instance—using stack space can become problematic. This means that the design should specify what kind of usage is expected and what response times should be. From this, the most favorable implementation can be determined.

Preparing for the Future

Over time, sources tend to be used for different purposes than those for which they were initially created. Although the original life cycle, or project scope, of sources can usually be determined quite easily, it often happens that sources are reused in different (or follow-up) projects. This means that issues can arise in different areas when sources are at some point compiled with a different compiler (compatibility) and perhaps even for a different target system (portability). This section provides tips that help you write sources that do not suffer from many of the problems encountered during reuse. Most of these tips concern standard coding practices and therefore do not take up any *extra* development time. This is good because in many projects you do not have the luxury to spend time on compatibility and portability issues when you have no idea whether they will ever be needed.

Compatibility

Compatibility and portability are closely related issues, but there are distinct differences between the two.

The compatibility of sources expresses how well they can be used in different development environments on the same system. Think of switching compilers, using C sources within a C++ project, compiling sources from a network drive instead of locally, and so on. The portability of sources expresses how well the sources can be used on different (target) systems. Compatibility is, in a way, a subset of portability because using sources on a different system will also entail using a different compiler. This section discusses compatibility; the next section discusses portability.

Using Vendor Specifics

In order to write sources with a high level of compatibility, it is always wise to use statements and functions as defined in the standards (ANSI) for the language you are using. However, it is not always apparent when you are using compiler (or vendor) specifics. The following example demonstrates the use of vendor-specific libraries and types.

```
// Compatible code.
char a[] = "Print me if you dare.";
short b = 5;

// Vendor specific code.
CString a = "Print me if you dare.";
__int16 b = 5;
```

14

Character arrays and shorts are defined in the language. However, the CString class is part of Microsoft's MFC classes and __int16 is a Microsoft-specific type so these can only be used when compiling with a Microsoft compiler. Another kind of vendor specific is the use of compiler settings and options.

```
#pragma pack(push, 1)
struct tightstruct {char a; int b;};
#pragma pack(pop)
```

As compiler directives are defined for a specific compiler, chances are that using a different compiler will cause some kind of syntax error on these statements. Another more tricky part of vendor specifics is the way they interpret standards. Sadly, sometimes standards specify what statements should look like and how they should behave, but not how they are implemented. Other times, standards are used before they are fully worked out. This means that different compilers will generate different executables even when using the same source as input and generating code for the same system. The following example demonstrates the expected compiler implementation.

```
struct Access {int a; char b;};

Access data;
char *p = (char*)(&data) + 4;
*p = 'B';
```

This code works correctly only when the fields of the structure are kept in the same order in the generated executable as they were defined in the source file. Only in that case can the memory for field b be found at an offset of 4 bytes from the start address of the structure. A compiler that moves fields around, perhaps for optimization purposes, does not guarantee that this kind of access is possible. Another such example is how comment lines are interpreted.

```
// start of a long comment line \
which is divided \
\
over several lines...
```

Each line in the preceding example is officially a comment line; however, not all compilers will recognize them as such. The last line, especially, can be problematic. The same kind of problems can occur when you try to nest comments. The following are valid comment lines:

```
/* a comment /* li
ne
*/

// another /* comment..*/ line

/* and yet // another nested/*
comment */
```

The thing to remember here is that /* */ blocks may not be nested; however, /* and // simply do not mean anything when used inside a /* */ comment block.

To make sure you are not using vendor specifics, consult documentation based on the standards or consult the compiler documentation. The compiler documentation should specify whether a certain call or type is standard or specific. Sometimes, of course, it is necessary to use vendor specifics to solve a certain problem. In that case you can keep a certain level of compatibility by investing some development time. Think of moving all specifics to separate source, or header, files. That way the compiler-dependent files can simply be replaced when changing development environment. Another option is to use the precompiler to switch between sources and parts of sources. The following example uses functions to create threads on different systems, as explained in Chapter 13, to demonstrate this:

```
#include <stdio.h>
#ifdef _MSC_VER
    #include <process.h>
    _beginthread(StartThreadA, 0, (void*) &startInputA);
#else
    #include <pthread.h>
    pthread_t  thread1;
    pthread_create(&thread1, NULL, StartThread, (void*) &startInputA);
#endif
```

Compatibility Between C and C++

As C is a syntactical subset of C++, you would perhaps not expect any difficulties when compiling "old" C sources with a C++ compiler. Sadly, there are some subtle differences that can cause compatibility problems. C++ for instance is stricter concerning default parameters. The statement extern int fn() in C will define an external function which returns an integer and has zero or more arguments. In C++ extern int fn() equals extern int fn(void). C in turn does not understand the use of // as remark indicators. When parts of your code have to be compiled by a C compiler, because they will be part of an embedded system, for instance, it is better not to use these indicators because not all C compilers are lenient enough to allow this.

As you saw in Chapter 4 in the section on mixing C and C++, including C header files in C++ is done by placing extern "C" {} around the includes in order to have the compiler switch to C mode. When a file should include a C header *and* should still compile with a C++ compiler as well as a C compiler, use the following construction.

Place the following construction in the C header file:

14

Tips

Cheader.h:
```
#ifdef __cplusplus
extern "C" {
#endif

// definitions
void CFunction(char*);

#ifdef __cplusplus
}
#endif
```

Then include this file, normally in either a C source or a C++ source:

Cfile.c:
```
#include "Cheader.h"
...
```

Cppfile.cpp:
```
#include "Cheader.h"
...
```

Portability

When you port sources to a different system, you can run into all the problems identified in the previous section "Compatibility." This is because a different system will have a different development environment. However, with porting come extra problems that are system related. This section points out the areas in which systems can prove to be incompatible.

File System Characteristics

Problems with portability can be caused by something as simple as file system characteristics. For instance, some file systems are case sensitive (*Process.h* is a different file from *process.h*) while others are not (*Process.h* and *process.h* are two names for the same file). When a software project is moved from a non–case-sensitive file system to a case-sensitive file system, chances are that it will not even compile or preprocess without added development effort. Entries in the make file, resource files, and even include statements are now for the first time checked against case errors. And this is true also for the use of special characters in filenames (spaces, *, _, /, and so on) and the allowed filename lengths.

A similar kind of problem can occur when moving a project from a file system that uses symbolic links (UNIX) to one that does not. Symbolic links can be used to refer to a file from several different directories. This means the file is only physically present in one directory. However, via links placed in other directories, it seems to be located there also. When such a directory structure is copied to a file system that does not support these kinds of links, a file that is linked to it is simply copied to each place where a link resides. This means problems arise when this file is updated. Unless the developer making the updates is very aware of what he is doing and changes all the instances of the file, a synchronization problem will occur. Not all instances of the file contain the same information.

These kinds of problems can occur when porting a project (or a set of source files) to a different system, or when you decide to move a project from a local hard disk to a network drive. This is because the network drive you move the project to may use a different file system than your local drive. The easiest way to avoid running into file system problems is to use filenames in your projects which are all in uppercase (or all in lowercase), without any characters outside the alphanumeric range, and which are not too long (eight-character names and three-character extensions.)

Operating System Characteristics

Apart from OS-specific libraries and commands, it is also necessary to take into account operating system behavior, such as the way tasks are switched or how locks perform queuing (refer to Chapter 13 for more details). Because of these kinds of differences the dynamic behavior of multitasking programs can change. A well set up multitasking program should not have too many problems with this; however, it pays to think about how much your program depends on how the OS behaves in certain situations. For instance, you may expect your task to be preempted automatically when waiting for interaction with a slow device or even a screen. This may not be true for the system you are porting to.

Another thing that often differs between operating systems is the way in which they implement text files. First, there is the matter of line termination. Some operating systems expect only a CR (byte value 0x0d) to indicate where one line ends and another begins. Other operating systems expect a CR and LF (byte values 0x0d and 0x0a) or only an LF. Secondly, some operating systems use identification characters at the beginning or end of a file (think of Unicode files starting with a special value). This means that no matter how portable you keep your source files, it is possible that a compiler will not even be able to read them. Also, you have to think very carefully when using text files as data storage or configuration files. Moving a project, along with the configuration files used by the original executable, to a new file system or operating system can mean that a newly compiled executable is still able to read the original configuration files, but only as long as they are not opened and edited by hand. When the original text files are opened and edited on the new operating system, new line terminators will be added.

Include Paths

Another thing that can differ per system is whether or not the \ character is accepted in include path names. Some OSes accept the following include style:

14

TIPS

```
#include "\libraries\include\hi.h"
```

while others demand the following include style:

```
#include "/libraries/include/hi.h"
```

In order to keep your sources portable you should always use the second notation because this is accepted by all compilers.

Hardware Characteristics

When C/C++ sources or projects are ported to systems that use other hardware, issues can arise that are related to hardware characteristics. Think of endianness; an example of this can be found in Chapter 10 in the section on Radix sort. The implementation of Radix sort will compile on any system but it only executes correctly when the algorithm takes the system's endianness into account. Another thing that can differ between types of hardware is the memory size associated with certain variable types. Think of the number of bytes allocated for an `int` or `long`. Examples of this can be found in Chapter 6.

Pitfalls

IN THIS CHAPTER

Pitfalls in software development come about because developers expect a certain behavior from, for instance, the compiler, the operating system, or the hardware. Because of differences between compilers, different versions of programming languages, interpretation of standards, and typos that may coincidentally compile, these expectations are not always valid. This explains why bugs resulting from falling for pitfalls are so very hard to find. When examining the code during a bug search, developers are likely to overlook the pitfall time and again. This chapter deals with common and not-so-common pitfalls of programming in C/C++.

Algorithmic Pitfalls

The first group of pitfalls you find here are those hidden in algorithmic choices. These are the kinds of pitfalls you have run into or read about just to find out they exist.

Arrays and Inheritance

Arrays of objects—structures, classes, and base types—are a popular storage structure (refer to Chapter 11, "Storage Structures"). However, when using arrays in combination with inheritance there is something to watch out for, as shown in Listing 15.1.

Listing 15.1   Incorrect Use of Object Arrays

```
#include <iostream.h>

class AverageJoe
{
   public:
        long socialSecurityNumber;
};

class JetSet : public AverageJoe
{
   public:
        long VIP;
};


void SetSocialSecurity(AverageJoe* person, long id, long number)
{
     person[id].socialSecurityNumber = number;
}

void main ()
{
     JetSet vips[50];
```

LISTING 15.1 Continued

```
for(int i = 0; i < 50; i++)
        vips[i].VIP = 1;

    SetSocialSecurity(vips, 1, 0);

    if (1 == vips[0].VIP)
        cout << "VIP!!" << endl;
    else
        cout << "Ordinairy Joe!! " << endl;
}
```

The SetSocialSecurity() function in Listing 15.1 is set up to be able to change the social security numbers in arrays of JetSeters as well as arrays of AverageJoes; this is why it takes a pointer to the base class, AverageJoe. Listing 15.1 compiles just fine, but when SetSocialSecurity() is called upon to change the social security number of the second VIP in the vips array, something unexpected happens. Instead of the social security number of vip[1] changing, the VIP status of vip[0] changes.

```
// The statement:
SetSocialSecurity(vips, 1, 0);

// Expected result:
vips[1].socialSecurityNumber == 0

// Actual result:
vips[0].VIP == 0
```

The reason for this becomes apparent when you add the following line to the SetSocialSecurity() function:

```
// Array element size = 4.
int i = int(&person[1]) - int(&person[0]);
```

And this line to the main() function:

```
// Array element size = 8.
i = int(&vips[1]) - int(&vips[0]);
```

The size of an AverageJoe is 4 bytes (it has one member: a long word). The size of a JetSeter is 8 bytes (it has two members: the long word that is part of the base class and its own long word). This means that the AverageJoe pointer used in SetSocialSecurity() thinks it is iterating over AverageJoe elements and its pointer increases in groups of 4 bytes instead of 8 bytes. person[1] therefore points to the address of the VIP field of the first VIP. The bug in Listing 15.1 can be circumvented by declaring person as a JetSet pointer in SetSocialSecurity(), but then the function can only be used on arrays of JetSeters. If you really need to change `JetSeters` and `AverageJoes` with a single function, you should make this function part of the base class:

```
// New definition of SetSocialSecurity:
void AverageJoe::Set SetSocialSecurity(long number)
{
    socialSecurityNumber = number;
}
```

```
// Call to SetSocialSecurity from main:
vips[1].SetSocialSecurity(0);
```

Do not forget to add the definition of `SetSocialSecurity()` to the definition of the base class.

Wrap Around of Loop Counters

A danger with counters is that they wrap around when they contain their maximum value and something is added to them (refer to Chapter 6, "The Standard C/C++ Variables," for more details on ranges of types). Adding 1 to a byte that already has the value 255 will cause it to contain the value 0.

```
// A == 0.
unsigned char a = 255;
a++;
```

This means you have to think carefully about the variable type you choose for your counters. If, for instance, you want to count the number of IP packets your program receives and you use a short for this, be sure to realize that this counter will reset itself when packet 65536 arrives. When, at a given point, this counter contains the value 5, the number of packets received can be 5, 65541, 131076, and so on. Even sneakier is the following example of a loop that never ends:

```
unsigned char i;
for(i = 0; i < 256; i++)
{
    cout << "test";
}
```

Because this loop needs to iterate over 256 elements, an unsigned char was chosen; however, counter i can contain 256 different values (0-255), although its maximum value is of course 255. This means the counter will wrap around before ever reaching the stop clause i >= 256.

Even more deceptive is the following pitfall:

```
void Cnt(int *a)
{
    char i;
    for(i = 126; i < 200; i++)
    {
        *a += i;
    }
}
```

Two things go wrong in the function `Cnt()`: First, at some point in the loop the value of `*a` will decrease instead of increase. Second, the loop is never-ending. This time the pitfall is caused by the range of the signed variable `i`. Variable `i` starts out with the value 126, after the first iteration its value is increased to 127, and after the second iteration its value is suddenly -128. From this point on, the value of `i` increases again, passing 0 and continuing to 127, then it becomes -128 once more. For more details on signed and unsigned ranges of variables, refer to Chapter 6.

Scope of Loop Counters

In C++ it is no longer necessary to define variables globally or at the very beginning of functions, as is the case in C. Sadly, because of changes in the C++ standard, there is a pitfall associated with this, in particular with defining variables in the headings of `for` loops. Listing 15.2 shows this pitfall.

LISTING 15.2   Scoping Pitfall

```
#include <ostream.h>

#define dataLen 254
#define TERM    13

// Initial Values.
char dataString[dataLen] = {0,2,3,4,13,8,8,8,8};

void main(void)
{
    // find first terminator.
    for(int i = 0; i < dataLen; i++)
    {
        if (TERM == dataString[i])
            break;
    }
    cout << "Terminator at: " << i << endl;
}
```

15

On some C++ compilers Listing 15.2 will compile and run just fine. These are the compilers that see the scope of variable `i` as the body of the function in which it is declared—in this case main(). Consequently, variable i also has a value outside the for loop and can therefore be used to print the position at which the loop was terminated. The construct shown in Listing 15.3 is obviously illegal with these compilers.

LISTING 15.3   Illegal in Some C++ Compilers

```
for(int i = 0; i < dataLen/2; i++)
{
    /*process first half.*/
}
for(int i = dataLen/2; i < dataLen; i++)
{
    /*process second half.*/
}
```

This is because variable i is defined twice.

In the latest version of the C++ standard, the scope of a variable defined in a for heading is limited to the body of that for loop. This means that the following statement in Listing 15.2 will not compile when using a compiler that follows the new standard:

```
cout << "Terminator at: " << i << endl;
```

The compiler will complain that variable i is undeclared. The scope of i with these compilers looks like this:

```
// i undefined
for(int i = 0; i < dataLen; i++)
{
    // i defined.
}
// i undefined.
```

Listing 15.3, however, is a legal construction with these compilers. In order to write portable/compatible code, it is better to define variables that are used for loop iteration—and variables that need to retain their value outside the loop—as follows:

```
int i;
for(i = 0; i < dataLen; i++)
```

Variables for which the scope is the loop body only can of course still be declared inside the loop.

```
for()
{
    int r, g;
```

Expression Evaluation and Operator Overloading

Although perhaps not expected, using operator overloading changes the way expressions are evaluated. Listing 15.4 shows how expressions are evaluated normally.

Listing 15.4   Normal Expression Evaluation

```
#include <ostream.h>

class A
{
public:
    int isvalid() { cout << "Check" << endl; return 0; }
};

void main ()
{
    A    Object1, Object2, Object3, Object4;

    if (Object1.isvalid() && Object2.isvalid() &&
        Object3.isvalid() && Object4.isvalid())
    {cout << "Conditions are TRUE" << endl;}
    else
    {cout << "Conditions are FALSE" << endl;}
}
```

In the expression `Object1.isvalid() && Object2.isvalid() && Object3.isvalid() && Object4.isvalid()`, a call is made to each object's `isvalid()` method from left to right as long as the call to the preceding object's `isvalid()` method returned a value greater than zero. The result of Listing 15.4 is thus:

```
Check
Conditions are FALSE
```

This is because the call to `Object1.isvalid()` returns false (0) and therefore there is no need to evaluate the rest of the expression—the result will be false (refer to Chapter 7, "Basic Programming Statements," for more details on expression evaluation). When operator overloading is used, this is no longer the method of evaluation, as Listing 15.5 shows.

15

LISTING 15.5   Overloaded Expression Evaluation

```cpp
#include <ostream.h>

class A
{
public:
    friend int operator&& (const A& left, const A& right)
    {cout << "Check" << endl; return(0);}

    friend int operator&& (const int left, const A& right)
    {cout << "Check" << endl; return(0);}
};

void main ()
{
    A   Object1, Object2, Object3, Object4;

    if (Object1 && Object2 && Object3 && Object4)
    {cout << "Conditions are TRUE" << endl;}
    else
    {cout << "Conditions are FALSE" << endl;}
}
```

The result of Listing 15.5 is:

```
Check
Check
Check
Conditions are FALSE
```

This means that each part of the expression if (Object1 && Object2 && Object3 && Object4) is evaluated. This is important to keep in mind because sometimes you do not want part of an expression evaluated if the preceding part was not true.

Memory Copy of Objects

Using a memory copy method to copy an object can be a very fast way of cloning objects. The standard function memcpy() can be used for this purpose, for instance. There are some pitfalls to watch out for, however. This kind of copy action is known as a shallow copy, which means it does a straightforward copy of all the fields of an object, regardless of its type. Problems arise when one or several of these fields happen to be pointers. A copied object contains the same values as the original, which means that any pointers it contains will point to the exact same addresses as the corresponding pointers in the original object. Listing 15.6 shows how easily this can cause problems.

LISTING 15.6   Erroneous Shallow Copy

```cpp
#include <string.h>
#include <memory.h>

class Object
{
public:
    ~Object(){delete [] data;}
    int  id;
    char name[200];
    char *data;
};

Object* CloneObject(Object *in)
{
    Object *p = new Object;

    memcpy(p, in, sizeof(Object));
    return p;
}

void main(void)
{
    char * DataBlock = new char[230];

    Object *object1 = new Object;
    object1->id   = 1;
    object1->data = DataBlock;
    strcpy(object1->name,"NumberOne");

    Object *object2 = CloneObject(object1);
    delete object1;

    // Big Problem:
    delete object2;
}
```

In Listing 15.6, object2 is a clone of object1; because the cloning was done through a shallow memory copy, both object1 and object2 have a data pointer that points to DataBlock. Objects have their own destructor which releases the memory pointed to by the data pointer. This means that when object1 is deleted, the memory of DataBlock is released. When object2 is deleted, its destructor will try to release the memory of DataBlock a second time. This, of course, causes strange behavior if not a crash. The use of a shallow copy in this context is obviously flawed, but when using complex and/or third party structures it may not be this obvious. Think of structures that contain a pointer to themselves, and so on.

15

Typos that Compile

It is also possible to get unexpected behavior by making a typo that is not picked up by the compiler. This can happen when a typo causes a statement to look like a different, but equally valid, statement.

Difference Between Mathematical Statements and C/C++ Statements

Some mathematical expressions conform to the C/C++ syntax, but have a different meaning in C/C++ than they do in mathematics. This section shows pitfalls related to misconception of notation.

X Between Y and Z

Consider the mathematical expression $7 < x < 16$, denoting that the value of x resides between 7 and 16. When this expression is used in C/C++, it does not behave as expected. Listing 15.7 demonstrates:

LISTING 15.7   Incorrect Use of a Mathematical Expression

```
int x = 32;
if (7 < x < 16)
{
    printf("x has a two nibble value.");
}
```

Instead of printing x has a two nibble value when the value of x resides between 7 and 16, the piece of code in Listing 15.7 first evaluates $7 < x$, to which the answer is either true (1) or false (0). Then this 0 or 1 answer is compared to 16, inevitably resulting in true (1).

Power of X

In some programming languages (Pascal, for instance) the ^ character is used to denote the power of a variable. In C/C++ this character is used to denote a bitwise exclusive or (*xor*), which is why some programmers will fall for the following pitfall:

```
// a becomes 2.
int a = 0, x = 0;
a = x^2;
```

Instead of a receiving the value of x to the power of 2 (which is 0), it receives the value 2. This is because xor-ing 0 with 2 makes 2. Use the pow() function in C/C++ to get a power of a number.

In order to make large numbers easier to read, it is customary to space digits in groups of three with a comma or period separating the groups. For instance, ten thousand is written as 10.000 or 10,000 depending on which country you live in. This, however, is not done in C/C++. Listing 15.8 demonstrates how this can lead to a pitfall.

LISTING 15.8   Incorrect Use of Digit Grouping

```
double x;
for (x=0; x < MAXRANGE; x += 1,500)
    printf("X= %f\n", x);
```

Instead of x increasing by fifteen hundred on each iteration, it is increased merely by one. This means that the number of effective iterations is MAXRANGE instead of MAXRANGE/1,500. The compiler sees the numbers after the comma as a new statement. This may seem strange, but the following three (meaningless) statements compile also.

```
5;4;
500;
```

Inadvertently Creating Labels

Sometimes typos cause the compiler to interpret a statement differently than expected. Listing 15.9 shows how a simple typo can cause the wrong method to be called.

LISTING 15.9   Typo Causing the Wrong Method to be Called

```
#include <ostream.h>

class base
{
public: void Info() {cout << "BaseInfo." << endl;}
};

class derived: public base
{
public:
    void Info() {cout << "DerivedInfo." << endl;}
    void GiveInfo(int a)
    {
        if (a)
            base:Info();
        else
            Info();
    }
```

15

LISTING 15.9   Continued

```
};

void main(void)
{
    derived der;

    der.GiveInfo(0);
    der.GiveInfo(2);
}
```

It looks like the author of Listing 15.9 is trying to invoke two different versions of the Info() method by calling the method GiveInfo() with two different values (first 0 and then 2). The method GiveInfo() decides to call the Info() method of the base class or the Info()method of the derived class, based on the value of its input parameter a. Sadly, the output of this program is:

```
DerivedInfo.
DerivedInfo.
```

Why? Because the author made a typo and instead of calling the base class method Info() by typing base::Info(), he made a label called base and called the local Info() method by typing base:Info()(note the missing second colon!). Because the object der is of class derived, the Info() method of derived is called in both cases. A good way to avoid these kinds of typos is to set the compiler warning level so that it warns against the definition of unused labels.

Inadvertently Creating Comments

Listing 15.10 shows another example of how a new statement can be created via a typo. This time a calculation is transformed into something new.

LISTING 15.10   Typo Causing the Wrong Calculation to Be Performed

```
#include <string.h>

char data[200] = "How many tabs can fit in this line?";

void GetTabInfo(int *tabsize)
{
    int tabsline = 0;

    tabsline = strlen(data)/*tabsize;
    int linediff = strlen(data) /* subtract diff*/ - (*tabsize*tabsline);
}
```

In Listing 15.10, the author is trying to determine how many tabs would fit in a given line by dividing the number of characters in that line by the size of a tab (`tabsline = strlen(data)/*tabsize;`). However, by omitting a space between the division operator `/` and the scope operator `*`, the author has inadvertently created the start of a multiline comment `/*`. This comment ends with the next occurrence of `*/`, and so the statement actually seen by the compiler is not:

```
tabsline = strlen(data)/*tabsize;
```

but:

```
tabsline = strlen(data)-(*tabsize*tabsline);
```

A good way to avoid these kinds of typos is to use source editors that change the colors of comment lines.

Inadvertently Causing Loop Problems

Other annoying typos, which can have disastrous effects and can be difficult to spot, are placing a semicolon directly after a loop definition and omitting the `{}` characters around a loop body.

```
// Loop without statements.
for (i = 0; i < MAX; i++);
    cout << i++;
```

The preceding loop has no statements. Consequently the `cout << i++` statement is executed only once, changing `i` from `MAX` to `MAX+1`.

```
// Never ending loop.
while (i < MAX);
    cout << i++;
```

The preceding loop also has no statements. Consequently, the `cout << i++` statement is executed only once, when `i` happens to be smaller than `MAX`. In all other cases the `while` becomes a never-ending loop, locking the program (or thread) in which it is executing.

```
// Loop with a single statement.
for (i = 0; i < MAX; )
    cout << i;
    i++;
```

The preceding loop also has only one statement, this time because the `for` is not implemented with a compounded body, which is why the statement `i++` is not part of the `for` loop. Consequently, the preceding loop either does not execute or executes without end. These kinds of bugs often arise when a loop with only one statement is extended. This is why it is a good programming practice to give all loops a compounded body, even those with only a single

15

body statement. This way a developer can never make the mistake of adding body statements where there is no body to begin with.

```
// Single statement loop.
for (i = 0; i < MAX; i++)
{
    cout << i;
}
```

When this loop is expanded it can look like this:

```
// Expanded loop.
for (i = 0; i < MAX; i++)
{
    cout << i;
    cout << " of " << MAX << endl;
}
```

Mixing Statically Bound Methods with Dynamically Bound Methods

A simple oversight can turn a method that should be dynamically bound (refer to Chapter 8, "Functions," for more information on dynamically binding methods) into one that is statically bound, as Listing 15.11 shows.

LISTING 15.11   Inadvertently Statically Binding Methods

```
#include <ostream.h>

class A
{
    public:  void print() { cout << 'A' << endl; };
};

class B: public A
{
    public:  void print() { cout << 'B' << endl; };
};

void main ()
{
    // Create a single object
    B anObject;

    // Create two references to the object.
    A *ptr1 = &anObject;
```

LISTING 15.11   Continued

```
    B *ptr2 = &anObject;

    ptr1->print();
    ptr2->print();
}
```

The output of Listing 15.11 looks like this:

```
A
B
```

So why do the two pointers, which point to the same instance of B, call two different `print()` methods? It seems that the type of pointer itself determines which method is called—A* versus B*. The reason for this is that a pointer to an A object *knows* only of one kind of `print()` method, namely that of class A. To correctly redefine the `print()` method for class B, it should be made virtual. By changing the definition of class A to

```
class A
{
    public:  void virtual print() { cout << 'A' << endl; };
};
```

The output of Listing 15.11 becomes

```
B
B
```

Omitting the `virtual` keyword (when done unintentionally) can be a bug that is hard to find, because as you have seen, it occurs at runtime depending on how a class is accessed. The methods in Listing 15.11 are all statically bound, compared to the virtual solution in which the methods are dynamically bound.

Other Pitfalls

As you have seen so far, pitfalls can occur in the most unexpected places—for example, algorithms, translations from mathematical equations—and through common typos. What you have not yet seen are pitfalls generated by external influences to source files. This section looks at pitfalls that can occur because of the way in which character arrays are implemented by compilers, and the use of hardware addresses from source files.

Pitfalls with Character Arrays

This section presents pitfalls related to character arrays and the difference of interpretation of character arrays between C and C++. Consider the following statement:

```
// Does not compile in C++.
char text[3] = "fit";
```

This statement attempts to reserve three bytes of memory for an array called `text`, and fill it with the characters `f`, `i`, and `t`. When you run this statement through a C compiler it will compile just fine; however, it cannot be compiled with a C++ compiler. This is because the C++ compiler wants to add a terminating zero (`'\0'`) character at the end of the constant string, and for this it would need an array of four bytes. The proof of this is given by the following example:

```
// Array of 4 elements.
char text[] = "fit";
int sizetext = sizeof(text);
```

This time the compiler can decide how large the `text` array should be and this length is placed in the variable `sizetext`. It should not surprise you that the value of `sizetext` is four in this example. What is surprising is that `sizetext` is four also when a C compiler is used. So when given a chance it appends a terminator also. Sometimes, however, you want to specify exactly how much memory is needed for a character array, and whether or not a terminator is needed. Think of fixed length strings for a user interface or for configuration files. If you know beforehand that a string is always three characters in size, you probably do not need a fourth terminating character. In that case you could try the following:

```
// Alignment pitfall.
char threeC[3] = {'f','i','t'};
char fourC [4] = {'f','i','t','s'};
```

This compiles just fine in both C and C++; however, now you have to deal with an alignment pitfall (for more details on alignment refer to Chapter 6). Some compilers will align any array on a four-byte boundary or sometimes even an eight-byte boundary. This means that there will be a stuffing byte between arrays `threeC` and `fourC`, or, put differently, `&threeC[4] == &fourC[0]`. On compilers that align character arrays on a one-byte boundary, there is no stuffing byte, or, put differently, `&threeC[3] == &fourC[0]`. This may not be a problem until you try to copy data into the arrays with the `strcpy()` function.

```
// Possible copy error.
strcpy(threeC,"abc");
```

This statement copies the constant string `"abc"` into the array `threeC`, up to and including its zero terminator! This means that with four-byte alignment, the string `fourC` is not affected by the string copy (the extra zero terminator of `"abc"` is placed in the extra stuffing byte following `threeC`). But with one-byte alignment this copy changes the value of the first character of `fourC` into a zero. Even more deceptive, the following string copy causes a problem with both alignment strategies.

```
// definite copy error.
strcpy(fourC,"abcd");
```

This time there is no stuffing byte to contain the terminator and the memory following array fourC is corrupted. When you do not want to use terminators in (character) arrays, use a loop, memcpy(), or strncpy() instead of strcpy().

```
memcpy (fourC, "abcd", 4);
strncpy(fourC, "abcd", 4);
```

Using Hardware Addresses (Memory-Mapped IO)

When you make use of data that becomes available through specific hardware addresses—for instance, when accessing data in memory-mapped IO schemes—it is important to be sure exactly how this data access is treated in the executable code that is generated by your compiler. The use of normal variables for directly accessing specific hardware addresses can cause problems with efficiency of the code, and more importantly, the actual correctness of the code. This section explains how to access hardware addresses correctly and efficiently.

Correct Access to Hardware Addresses

Different compilers generate different executable code with different levels of optimizations. This is why you should use the volatile keyword with memory-mapped objects to indicate to the compiler that no optimization may be performed with those objects. Using volatile guarantees that the executable code will reload the value of the object each time it is used, allowing external changes to the value (system events/interrupts, OS states, other processes, and external devices) to be visible in your code. Often you will access specific hardware addresses through pointers. In these cases, it is important to note that the value on the address that is pointed to is volatile and not the address in the pointer itself. The difference is denoted by the place of the volatile keyword in the pointer declaration.

```
// Error, here pointer p is volatile (p)
char* volatile p = 0xC000050;
```

In the preceding example, the value of pointer p is denoted as volatile, meaning that internal as well as external influences may cause it to point to a different hardware address.

```
// Correct, value on address in p is volatile (*p)
volatile char *p = 0xC000050;
```

The preceding example specifies that the byte value on address 0xC000050 may be changed due to internal or external influences, and its usage should therefore not be optimized.

Another keyword that you might like to use in combination with volatile is const, to tell the compiler that the value of an object should *not* change. It stands to reason that you use const oppositely to volatile; this way you can tell the compiler that pointer p should always point

15

to address `0xC000050` (it is not allowed to change and point to any other address), but that the value in address `0xC000050` can change at any given time.

```
// Constant pointer to a volatile address value
volatile char const *p = 0xC000050;
```

Listing 15.12 shows different ways of accessing the same address through pointers.

LISTING 15.12   Using `volatile` and `const` Pointers

```
char hw1 = 'A';
char hw2 = 'A';

void main(void)
{
    char * p1 =&hw1;
    volatile char * p2 = &hw1;
    volatile char * const p3 = &hw1;

    // Legal actions:
    *p1 = 'b';  p1 = &hw2;
    *p2 = 'c';  p2 = &hw2;
    *p3 = 'd';

    // Illegal action:
    p3 = &hw2;
}
```

In Listing 15.12, pointer p1 may be subject to compiler optimization, so accessing address hw through p1 may not always work correctly. Accessing hw through pointer p2 is never optimized and is therefore safe, as long as you do not (accidentally) change the value of p2 itself. The safest way to access hw is through pointer p3, as it is never optimized and its address cannot change; the last statement p3 = &hw2; therefore does not even compile. Note that the value of p3 can, of course, be corrupted through non-const pointers to the address of p3 itself and through other memory corruption, such as writing past array bounds and so on.

Efficient Access to Hardware Addresses

Now that you have a correct way of accessing specific hardware addresses, the next step is to make sure that access is done efficiently. Often you will want to read a stream of bytes from a device. When this device has memory-mapped IO, information is retrieved by continuously reading from the mapped addresses. That is, when no DMA is available. Each read action signals the underlying device to place the next value on the address. Reading a number of bytes from such a device can be done as follows:

```
unsigned char buffer[1024];
for (int i = 0; i < buflen; i++)
    buffer[i] = *HARDWAREMAPPEDREGISTER;
```

HARDWAREMAPPEDREGISTER is a pointer to a specific hardware address on which a device places bytes of data. The buffer is used to store sequentially read bytes. Although this implementation seems pretty straightforward and looks lean because of the small number of statements it contains, it is far from efficient. This is because data is read from the hardware address and placed in *normal* memory. As you have seen in Chapter 5, "Measuring Time and Complexity," using memory can be slow because of caching and paging schemes. (Cache needs to be consistent with memory, resulting in cache updates if a write-through scheme is used. You can minimize these updates by using processor registers so that such an update is necessary only once per 4 bytes.) Listing 15.13 shows how this kind of memory access can be speeded up by using a register as a four-byte IO buffer.

LISTING 15.13   Efficient Hardware Address Access (Big-Endian)

```
unsigned char buffer[1024];
for (int i = 0; i < buflen; i+= 4)
{
    register long tmp;

    tmp = *HARDWAREMAPPEDREGISTER;
    tmp << 8;
    tmp |= *HARDWAREMAPPEDREGISTER;
    tmp << 8;
    tmp |= *HARDWAREMAPPEDREGISTER;
    tmp << 8;
    tmp |= *HARDWAREMAPPEDREGISTER;

    buffer[i] = tmp
}
```

Because of the small number of variables used within the loop in Listing 15.13, it is very likely that the compiler will assign tmp to a register. However, the register keyword is added to urge the compiler in the right direction. Now four consecutive read actions can be performed very fast. Each byte that is read is shifted upwards in the long word to make room for the next byte to be read. When the long word is full, it is finally placed into the buffer. With larger registers, IO can be speeded up further; however, make sure that you choose a type for variable tmp that can easily be mapped on a CPU register. If, for instance, you define a 64-bit tmp when the processor does not have any (or a sufficient number of) 64-bit registers, the compiler will choose a normal memory variable for tmp instead of a register. This means you just lose IO speed because of the extra statements added in Listing 15.13.

15

Note that the way in which data is placed in `tmp` and shifted upwards in the direction of the most significant byte, makes it ideal for big-endian implementations. If, however, you would like to receive the bytes of the device in a little-endian order, some changes need to be made as shown in Listing 15.14.

LISTING 15.14 Efficient Hardware Address Access (Little-Endian)

```
unsigned char buffer[1024];
for (int i = 0; i < buflen; i+= 4)
{
    register long tmp;

        tmp =  (*HARDWAREMAPPEDREGISTER);
        tmp |= (*HARDWAREMAPPEDREGISTER) << 8;
        tmp |= (*HARDWAREMAPPEDREGISTER) << 16;
        tmp |= (*HARDWAREMAPPEDREGISTER) << 24;

    buffer[i]  = tmp
}
```

INDEX

SYMBOLS

NUMBERS

A